HISTORIC CARRIAGE

DRAWINGS

(Series Editor: David Jenkinson)

VOLUME TWO:

LMS AND CONSTITUENTS

David Jenkinson

PENDRAGON

Pre-1933 carriages from LMS design Periods I and II (for further explanation see page 5) form the introduction to this survey. The first picture shows a 1930-built Period I 60ft corridor composite No.9383 (later No.3748), whose drawing appears on page 17 and the second view is an 'all steel' 57ft Period II corridor brake third from 1932, No.5190 (later No.5427), further details being found on pages 28/29. In their own way, both were highly influential on subsequent designs.

This book is dedicated with my sincere thanks to those many draughtspersons (past and present) whose work I have been delighted to incorporate in this book

Note: Unless stated otherwise, all drawings in this book are 4mm = 1ft scale and all pictures from official railway sources. Many of the latter are now at the National Railway Museum to which all requests for official pictures should be addressed.

© David Jenkinson and The Pendragon Partnership 1998

Published by the Pendragon Partnership, PO Box No.3, Easingwold, York, YO61 3YS

Designed by Barry C. Lane, Sutton-in-Craven

Text set in Times Roman by the author

Printed in England by the Amadeus Press Ltd, Huddersfield, West Yorkshire

British Cataloguing-in-Publication Data: a catalogue reference for this book is held by the British Library

ISBN No. 1 899816 06 2

Contents

Editor's General Introduction	4
The LMS and its Constituents	5
LMS Carriage Numbering and Liveries	6
LMS Insignia and Panel detail	8
LMS Standard Underframes and Bogies	10
LMS Standard Carriage Ends	11
LMS Standard Period I Corridor Brake Third	12
LMS Standard Period I Corridor Stock	14
LMS Standard Period I Corridor Stock (later style)	16
LMS Standard Period I Vestibule Stock	18
LMS Standard Period I/II Luxury Semi-Open First	20
LMS Standard Period II Corridor Brake Composite	22
LMS Standard Period II Corridor Stock	24
LMS Standard Period II Gangwayed Stock	26
LMS Standard Period I/II 'All Steel' Stock	28
LMS Standard Period III Corridor Stock - I	30
LMS Standard Period III Corridor Stock - II	32
LMS Standard Period III Corridor Stock - III	34
LMS Standard Period III Corridor Stock - IV	36
LMS Standard Period III Corridor Stock - V	37
LMS Standard Period III Vestibule Stock - I	38
LMS Standard Period III Vestibule Stock - II	40
LMS Standard Period III Articulated Stock	42
LMS Standard Period I First Class Sleeping Car	44
LMS Standard Period I Third Class Sleeping Car	46
LMS Standard Period II Composite Sleeping Car	48
LMS Standard Period III First Class Sleeping Car	50
LMS Standard Period III Third Class Sleeping Car	52
LMS Standard Period II Dining Cars	54
LMS Standard Period III Third Class Dining Car	58
LMS Standard Period I 57ft Non-Corridor Stock	60
LMS Standard Period I 54ft and 51ft Non-Corridor Stock	62
LMS Standard Non-Corridor Lavatory Stock	64
LMS Standard Period II/III 57ft Non-Corridor Stock	66
LMS Standard 50ft Full Brakes/50ft Underframe	68
LNWR 50ft Arc Roof Non-Corridor Stock	70
LNWR 50ft Cove Roof Non-Corridor Lavatory Stock	72
LNWR 50ft Arc Roof Corridor Stock	74
LNWR 57ft Cove Roof Corridor Stock	78
LNWR 57ft Elliptical Roof Corridor Stock	82
LNWR/WCJS Clerestory Sleeping & Dining Cars	86
LNWR Clerestory Composite Dining Car	88
WCJS Special 12-wheel '2pm' Corridor Stock	90
Midland Railway Six-wheel Stock	94
Midland Railway 48ft Lavatory Clerestory Stock	96
Midland Railway 48ft Low Roof Bain Suburban Stock	98
Midland/MSJS Bain Corridor Clerestory Stock	100
Midland Railway 59ft First Class Clerestory Dining Car	104
LYR Attock Stock	106
LYR Attock Stock Developments	108
LYR Arc Roof Open Stock	110
LYR Elliptical Roof General Service Stock	112
LYR Elliptical Roof Open Stock/Dining Car	114
North Staffordshire Railway Bogie Stock	116
Maryport & Carlisle/Furness Railway Stock	118
Furness Railway Bogie Stock	120
Caledonian Railway 'Grampian' Corridor Stock	122
Caledonian Railway 57ft Non-Corridor Stock	124
Caledonian Railway Corridor Stock	126
G&SWR 43ft General Service Non-Corridor Stock	128
G&SWR Gangwayed Stock	130
Highland Railway Bogie Non-Corridor Stock	132
Highland Railway Bogie Corridor Stock	134
Colour Panels, Bibliography	136

Editor's General Introduction

In Volume One of this series, I explained how all rights in the original LMS/LNER historic carriage drawings book of 1968-9 by myself and my good friend Nick Campling had reverted to us, thus allowing us to take a fresh and updated look at this most fascinating subject. There is thus no need to repeat that rationale here, save to make the point that it is our intention in this revised version to re-offer the bulk of the previous material for the benefit of a newer generation of enthusiasts, along with a few alterations and improvements compared with the original version. These take the form of extra prototype data (along with modest photographic coverage - absent in the first version) plus a few extra drawings. We have also reorganised the presentation to offer a 'wipe clean' cover with page layouts arranged so that they mostly open away from the reader and help the modeller on his workbench.

We were delighted at the positive response to the first revised version (dedicated to the LNER only) in 1997 but since there were a few comments and criticisms, most of them probably arising as a result of a misunderstanding of our aims, it now falls to me, both as series editor and individual compiler of this particular volume, to explain a little more fully just what we are trying to do in this series.

Firstly, I should state that it was not and will not be our intention to provide a total carriage history in either the technical or social sense. For many companies, this is already in print for those who would seek it and a short bibliography for the LMS (and its constituent companies) will be found elsewhere. Neither are we seeking to provide drawings which would allow a full size replica to be made......! Rather, our aim is to give accurate data at the sort of level which will allow a fair appreciation of the major characteristics of a large variety of historical carriages to be gained, plus offering sufficient information to allow modellers in the conventional scales (say from 2mm to 10mm = 1ft) to be able to re-create a close enough copy of the original to be able to satisfy most tastes. We are confident enough to think that readers who may wish to delve more deeply into the further minutiae of carriage construction will be able to do so without our help!

That said, it still seems worth re-iterating the caveats mentioned in the first volume regarding the subject in general. Firstly, although most drawings in this book have been prepared from original sources (ie works drawings and/or actual vehicles), it has to be stated that since carriage building (in the historic context) rarely followed the strict laws of the Medes and Persians(!), many variations could and did occur, more than a few of them unrecorded. Thus, as far as the LMS is concerned, though I can be quietly confident about the overall configuration of the many carriages featured, I would never claim (nor would those

who have helped me) that every single vehicle was an exact clone of its theoretically identical running mate.

As for choice and variety offered, I have to concede that this is a combination of my subjective preferences plus availabilty of suitable drawings and I will happily accept that others may have chosen differently from the huge variety available. What I have done in this case, bearing in mind the greater diversity of the LMS compared with the rest of the 'Big Four', is to add eight pages to the total content of the book and, in some cases, offer extra drawings (rather than photographs and data) on 'left hand' pages. Even so, there are still noteable gaps (the LMS was a very big railway!) and I can only hope that readers will understand.

In general, the structure of the book remains mostly unchanged from Volume One (ie drawings opposite data, all laid out in 'landscape' form to facilitate easier 'bench' use - above) and I can only hope that where I have departed from this general principle, the reasons will be clear. I have also added extra background detail and expanded the LMS livery section in the light of more recent research. This means that space does not allow a separate page for the pre-group livery summary of the original 1968/9 book, basic though it was. In its place, I have added appropriate, albeit brief, pre-group livery details on the text pages accompanying each of the LMS constituent companies.

Finally, unlike Volume One where most of the drawings were by the author himself, I am pleased to acknowledge the assistance of many other draughtspeople in this particular part of the series. I am but a self-trained draughtsman (with all the faults that this implies) and although the majority of drawings offered in this book originated on my own drawing board, I could not have put this compilation together without much outside help, both in terms of drawings themselves (all duly credited where not from my pen) but also in context of the prototype information accompanying them. Many of my contributors were or still are fellow members of the LMS Society and I record all their names with deepest gratitude: (the late) Gordon Heywood, (the late) Ralph E.Lacy, (the late) John B.Hinchliffe, Julie Hinchliffe, Barry C.Lane, Ken Morgan, Mike Peascod, (the late) Iain R.Smith, Peter Tatlow, Graham Warburton, Arthur Whitehead and Alistair Wright.

As for prototype information, and additional to most of the above folk, I owe further debt for the Scottish material to my good friend, the late Duncan Burton, along with Dr Niall Ferguson and Jim Smellie, all of whom are or were, yet again, fellow members of the LMS Society. My only hope is that this compilation does credit to all who have been involved and my very sincere thanks go to them all.

David Jenkinson
Series Editor

Raskelf, North Yorkshire
November 1998

The LMS and its Constituents

Before offering the drawings, livery and other data, a few words in explanation may help. The LMS pursued a ruthless policy of standardisation from an early stage, both before and after the famous William Stanier arrived on the scene in 1932. As far as new carriages were concerned, this first took the form of adopting superficial Midland lineaments and livery, but that was about all: new carriages may have given the impression of 'Greater Derby' (the old Midland HQ), but in terms of types and utilisation of coaching stock, it was the LNWR influence which prevailed, most noticeably in the long distance field. One has only to consider the fact that the LNWR owned more humble corridor third class carriages in 1923 than the whole of the Midland's gangwayed fleet added together to realise how vital was the LNWR input.

Thus, although LMS standard carriages may have looked 'Midland' in those early days, the LNWR *conceptual* influence was always profound, which may well explain why in terms of carriage policy and building, there never seems to have been the internal conflict which so affected the locomotive field. Most LMS standard carriage lengths were those of the LNWR (50ft, 57ft, 68ft), though it must also be stated that the Caledonian and Lancashire and Yorkshire companies had also adopted 56-57ft as a sort of quasi-standard for main line stock and even the MR had gone to that dimension for a few (but only a few!) of its final elliptical roof designs.

Whatever, LMS standard carriage design can readily be divided into the three design periods summarised below, the 'shorthand reference' being of my own devising back in the early 1960s but which has now become widely accepted and has been adopted in this book:

'Period I' (1923-c.1928-9): Wooden bodied carriages on steel underframes with full waist and eaves panelling and almost entirely undiluted Midland Railway cosmetic details - the then LMS carriage superintendent, R.W.Reid, was an ex-MR officer! However, Period I 68ft first class sleeping cars retained much external evidence of LNWR styling, probably stemming from reasons given above.

'Period II' (1929-1932): This short-lived period (supervised by E.J.H.Lemon) saw the suppression of the waist panel and its substitution by a new low-waisted style, along with the total elimination of side doors to compartments in side-corridor stock for new building (a process which actually started at the end of Period I) and the more general use of a new 60ft chassis for many designs. Many folk reckon this to have been the most handsome LMS carriage design period (an opinion shared by the author) and from c.1931, exterior wooden panelling gave way to flush steel outer panelling allied with traditional earlier detailing. These were the first new carriages to be distinctly 'LMS' in style rather than reflecting pre-group influence.

'Period III' (1932-1947 and early BR): These, the familiar 100% flush-sided 'Stanier' types, began to appear in 1932-3, soon after his arrival. For the most part (certainly in the main line field) they were superior to most other contemporary British stock (arm rests, courtesy lights and no draughty outside compartment doors were third class 'norms' on express trains during LMS days) and, with relatively little change, were still regarded as 'state of the art' in early BR times until BR designs took over.

About half of this book is given over to drawings of the more typical carriages which came from these three periods and this section of the book is little changed from the original 1968-9 survey, save for one or two additional types and, of course, their photographic coverage. But no matter how much new building took place (and it was formidable in quantity), there remained a need for older carriages too and I have tried to reflect this in terms of the pre-group selections offered. In fact, compared with the original edition, it is the pre-group section which has gained most from this revision, being proportionally larger than before.

I have tried to offer vehicles which lasted well into LMS days and which reflect the relative importance of its many constituents - hence the (relatively) large space given to the ex-LNWR corridor fleet (see above) and the inclusion of some noteworthy West Coast Joint Stock types, this latter operation also explaining why the Caledonian element in this book is relatively small. Sleeping cars on the CR were of WCJS origin and since the 'Caley' also sub-contracted its train catering to Pullman, it had no dining cars either.

The LYR carriage fleet was numerically large and long-lasting and since that company was also a pioneer of what is now the almost universal form of long distance carriage - the centre-aisle open type (an idea also investigated by the MR but first exploited to the full in LMS days - in the light of MR and LYR experience?), it merits proper coverage. As for the MR itself, I have deliberately excluded those carriages which displayed the external style copied by the LMS in the 1920s, in favour of equally long-lived types which had more specific 'Midland' characteristics, not forgetting several examples of the famous clerestory style, of course.

Smaller companies get their shout too, although there are not as many examples as I and others might have liked; so all I can suggest to those who might wish to know more of the areas not covered in such great depth is that they study as many of the printed sources as they can find and maybe join (or consult) the specialised 'line' societies devoted to many of the LMS consitituents. If my experience is any guide, they will find them all to be extremely helpful.

LMS Carriage Numbering and Liveries

LMS CARRIAGE NUMBERING

In 1923, Midland carriages mostly retained their old numbers, M&GSW stock being renumbered into the MR series. Other pre-group carriages were given consective blocks of new LMS numbers. New carriages were given numbers in the vacant spaces in the series, usually quite random. Some new carriages were given the LMS numbers of older carriages 'nominally' replaced, but if the latter were not scrapped, their original number was 'cyphered' by way of a '0' prefix to the original LMS number.

Things were becoming chaotic by 1932, so the LMS renumbered all stock generically by *carriage type*. This '1933 renumbering' allocated defined number blocks to each type of vehicle, starting with Dining Cars, Sleeping Cars and Saloons (1-999), general service gangwayed stock (1000-9999), followed by non-corridor stock, non-passenger coaching stock and articulated stock in that order (various five figure blocks). LMS standard types had the lowest numbers in each block (usually in ascending order of age), pre-group types were numbered *backwards by company* from the end of the block(s), ex-HR carriages carrying the highest numbers, the gap between standard and pre-group types being for new construction. If this exceeded the planned space, vacant blocks elsewhere in the system (of which there were many to chose from) were taken up.

Ex-M&NB stock was nominally independent to 1928 when divided between LMS and LNER. Carriages coming to the LMS were usually numbered in the ex-MR series until 1933. Finally, running number blocks quoted in this book are all taken from the 1933 series but sample pre-1933 numbers are also given, where known and applicable.

LMS CARRIAGE LIVERIES

*(Note: A comprehensive livery specification is offered for the LMS standard styles, supported by **sample colour panels on page 136**. However, not all details were universally adopted; exceptions could and did occur. Likewise, dates offered can only be approximate. Most carriages normally ran for six or seven years between full repaints and styles overlapped the periods quoted, full livery being not unknown even in the war years)*

LMS standard carriage livery: 1923-33

Sides/Ends: Crimson Lake (Midland Red) - NB **not** the same colour as Maroon...!

Roof: Lead grey between rainstrips, glossy black below (most new carriages). Many carriages, mostly **non**-Midland pre-group, all grey

Chassis: Bogies and underfame black, wooden wheel centres, if used, having a natural varnished finish. Unshaded sans-serif code markings (if applicable) on the outside faces of solebars, size/colour not formally specified but the latter usually white or creamy-yellow.

Lining: *(sides only)* Fully panelled style (even on steel panelling without raised beading) in black (1in) edged both sides with 3/8in gold/gilt (gangwayed stock) or primrose yellow (non-gangwayed stock). Outer edges of the gold/yellow line had a fine vermilion (1/16in) line, overall line width thus being 1/2in. *(NB: if raised beading was present, all lining was on the beading itself, the width of the central black band being adjusted accordingly).* On most carriages, a fine vermilion line (c.1/8in) ran the full length of the carriage at the extreme lower edge of side panelling and along the lower outside face of the gutter edge moulding.

Ends: Details usually picked out in black without lining (steps, pipes &c.). End beading (if any) usually black and unlined (as MR)

Insignia: Gold Leaf (gilt), blended red shading to left and below, shadow shaded black to right and below, types as follows, all heights quoted without shading:
'LMS' and definitive lettering ('SLEEPING CAR' &c.) in elongated serif style, 4in high
Running numbers (1923-29): Scroll pattern. c.3in high
Running numbers (1929-32): Elongated scroll pattern, 4in high
Running numbers (1933): Sans serif but no shading, 4in high
Class figures (doors): Scroll pattern, 8in high

*(Note: Rather smaller (c.3in) characters, LMS **and** definitive wording, were adopted if the waist panel could not contain the larger dimensions quoted. These smaller characters were most often, but not exclusively, found on ex-LNWR/WCJS carriages and, in the latter cases, regularly used even if there was no waist panel!)*

Layout: 1923-28: Insignia in waist panel, LMS in centre (or as near as possible - ie never on doors), running number applied twice, once towards each end but to no set 'rule' regarding distance from carriage end. Class figures on all outside doors except if regarded as for 1st or 3rd Class use (usually dining vehicles)
1929-33: As before but LMS now moved to left hand end in place of previous left hand running number, the number now appearing once only towards the right hand end. LMS standard carriages without waist panel (real or simulated) had insignia below waist lining

Emblem: This nominally 14in diameter device (actually 1/8in larger) had gold(gilt) letters/surrounds and was never applied to non-corridor stock or to gangwayed stock with a full set of compartment outer doors. It was set central end-to-end as nearly as possible (but never on doors) and midway between waist and solebar. Definitive words were in the waist panel, central above the emblem (Period I) and flanking it at the same level as the running number (Periods II & III)

LMS standard carriage livery: 1934-47

From 1934, several changes took place, save for insignia layout, most obvious being the considerable reduction in the exterior lining in the so-called 'Simple' livery. These changes were gradual and the earliest dates of change (where known) are given.

Colour: Changed from Crimson Lake to Maroon in 1946, but not all carriages were thus repainted - see note on '1946 Livery', below

Roof: From c.1933/4, all-over metallic silver grey was specified (universally applied to all new Period III stock) but many older coaches had a non-metallic all grey roof which became normal practice during and after the war

Ends: Changed from red to black during 1936

Lining: From late 1933/early 1934, simple lining was applied in chrome yellow for all save a few carriages (see *Special Note* below):
Two yellow lines, each 1/2in wide, running full length of carriage along the top edge of the eaves panel and above the windows (both lines interrupted by ventilators &c. if present). Fully panelled stock had these lines along top and bottom eaves panel beading but where no eaves panel appeared on a fully beaded carriage (eg much LNWR stock) the lower line was often, but not always(!), omitted
Double yellow lines (each 1/2in wide and separated by 1in black) along the waist line or upper waist panel beading where applicable

(Special Note: There is sound evidence, but unconfirmed by any official sources consulted by the author, that in deference to tradition, the older gold lining with its vermilion edging was retained on first class sleeping and dining cars - possibly all 12-wheelers - but arranged in the new simple style: overall gold/vermilion line width still 1/2in. The writer is happy to accept that this was so - see also 'Special Note' after Insignia details - below)

Insignia: The base colour changed from gold to chrome yellow c.1934/5, as did letters and surrounds of the circular LMS emblem. Shading remained as before as did the seriffed 'LMS' and definitive lettering, but further numeral changes appeared:
Running Numbers (1934/5-40): shaded sans-serif style, 4in high, shape as per the unshaded gold numbers of 1933 (above)
Running Numbers (1940 onwards): scroll pattern shaded numerals. much as 1923-29 (above) but now 4in high with flat-topped '3'.
Classification Figures: The 8in '3' on outside doors became flat-topped c.1940 and from c.1945-6, a serif style '1' (about 8in high) also began to appear on the windows of first class areas, unshaded and creamy-white in colour.

(Special Note: As with the lining (above), the gold leaf emblem and insignia are thought to have remained in use on 12-wheel dining/sleeping cars with simple livery)

1946 Livery Modifications

From 1946, the LMS officially specified maroon as the new carriage colour - a darker and more drab shade than the previous rich Crimson lake - with grey roofs. This was intended to go with some revision to lining (colour only) and insignia (style and colour) but it was never widely applied and no generalisations can be made. Lining of the simplified form (above) was now described as 'straw' (pale creamy-yellow, almost off-white) and a third version of the LMS emblem appeared with new pale coloured lettering and surrounds. It was also intended to use new sans-serif insignia throughout (straw with black edging but no other shading), running numbers to be 4½in and lettering 6in; but relatively few carriages were thus adorned and although many carriages were indeed given the new maroon shade (by no means all of them, however), the majority continued to get the older scroll/serif insignia.

Dining Cars (if repainted) were now re-branded 'RESTAURANT CAR', examples appearing in both the new insignia and the older style; it was all very messy when BR came on the scene. After 1947 and until the onset of new BR liveries, LMS carriages came out in final LMS style (usually maroon but without company markings) and with running numbers (often with 'M' prefix) almost always rendered in scroll/serif style (old transfer stock?). Modellers of this period are advised to use dated views, if they can find any.....

(Note: Unlike the previous volume, space is unavailable at this point for a review of pre-group liveries as they were in 1923. Instead, a brief resumé of relevant styles is given on the first narrative page of each of the pre-group sections of the book. These are necessarily offered in outline form only but will give some idea of the variety existing when the LMS took over)

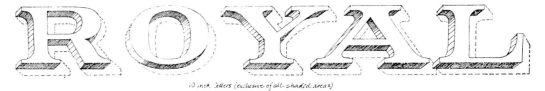

LMS Insignia and Panel detail

These drawings are mostly self-explanatory, but a word about insignia is called for, since few official sources have survived. The LMS was meticulous in these matters, so possibly the 'standard' drawings were lost. Whatever, 'ROYAL MAIL' lettering is included (though no TPOs feature in this work), for it was the same *shape/colour* as the 4in serif insignia and can thus be used to develop accurate versions of the latter. The panel drawings give *approximate* indication of insignia used with that style of carriage *when new*. Other details are as follows:

INSIGNIA

I   **Carriage Headboards**: 12ft 6in long, 6in deep, 5in lettering in black on a white ground - possibly cream after 1933 (unconfirmed). Letter style/width was adjusted to suit the train name or service. Boards were mounted on lower roof (Periods I, II and early III) or eaves panel (later Period III). Some Period III coaches had brackets in both locations.

II   **Destination Boards**: 2ft 4in long, usually fixed to brackets on eaves panel close to an entrance door:
         Upper: 1923-33, black letters on white ground
         Lower: 1933 and later, black letters on cream ground

III   **Principal 10in 'Royal Mail' Lettering**

PANELLING DETAIL

These 3/8in = 1ft scale drawings of no particular vehicles illustrate typical external details and dimensions of the three periods of LMS gangwayed stock, though there were minor fluctuations in vertical dimensions above and below the windows in the 'all steel' Period II stock (page 28) and in some Period III carriages. Period II steel panelled stock was as drawn but without raised beading, while non-corridor stock at all times had the high waist level established in Period I, along with virtually unchanged quarterlight and droplight dimensions.

LMS panel beading was normally 3/8in proud of main panels, window frame (bolection) mouldings of fixed windows in both Periods I and II adding a further 3/8in depth (wood-panelled stock) or projecting 3/8in from the main panel layer (steel clad stock). Fixed windows in the 'flush-sided' Period III stock were set immediately behind the outer panel sheeting, normally c.1/8in thick. Droplight door frames at all times (almost always wood, regardless of period), together with other droplights during Period I, had glazing c.3/8in 'behind' the framing, the latter being typically set about one inch (or a little more) behind the main panel layer. 'Frameless' droplights (mostly Period II but some Period I - see individual drawings for further details), were also c.1in behind the main panel layer.

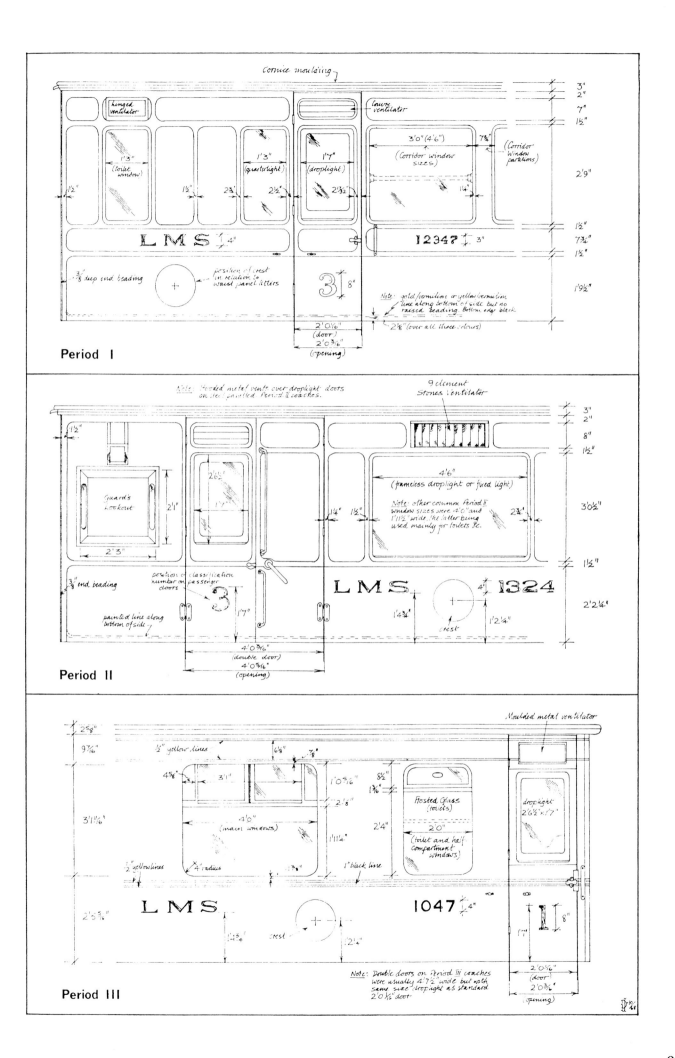

Period I

Period II

Period III

9

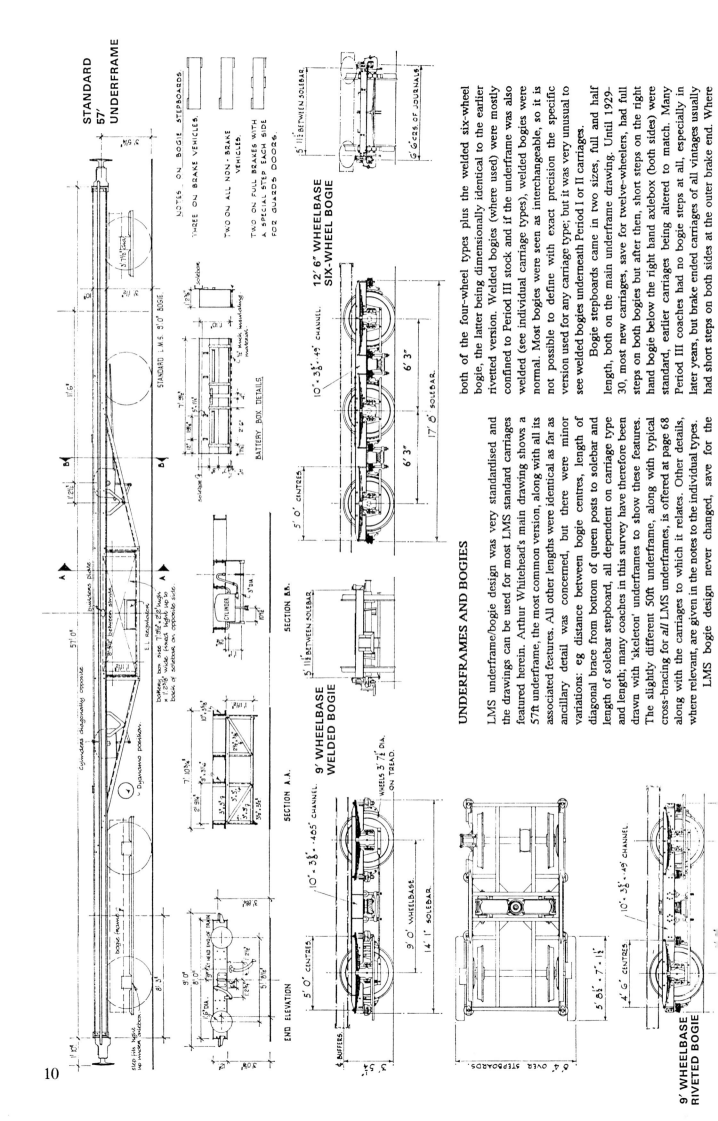

UNDERFRAMES AND BOGIES

LMS underframe/bogie design was very standardised and the drawings can be used for most LMS standard carriages featured herein. Arthur Whitehead's main drawing shows a 57ft underframe, the most common version, along with all its associated features. All other lengths were identical as far as ancillary detail was concerned, but there were minor variations: eg distance between bogie centres, length of diagonal brace from bottom of queen posts to solebar and length of solebar stepboard, all dependent on carriage type and length; many coaches in this survey have therefore been drawn with 'skeleton' underframes to show these features. The slightly different 50ft underframe, along with typical cross-bracing for all LMS underframes, is offered at page 68 along with the carriages to which it relates. Other details, where relevant, are given in the notes to the individual types.

LMS bogie design never changed, save for the

both of the four-wheel types plus the welded six-wheel bogie, the latter being dimensionally identical to the earlier riveted version. Welded bogies (where used) were mostly confined to Period III stock and if the underframe was also welded (see individual carriage types), welded bogies were normal. Most bogies were seen as interchangeable, so it is not possible to define with exact precision the specific version used for any carriage type; but it was very unusual to see welded bogies underneath Period I or II carriages.

Bogie stepboards came in two sizes, full and half length, both on the main underframe drawing. Until 1929-30, most new carriages, save for twelve-wheelers, had full steps on both bogies but after then, short steps on the right hand bogie below the right hand axlebox (both sides) were standard, earlier carriages being altered to match. Many Period III coaches had no bogie steps at all, especially in later years, but brake ended carriages of all vintages usually had short steps on both sides at the outer brake end. Where

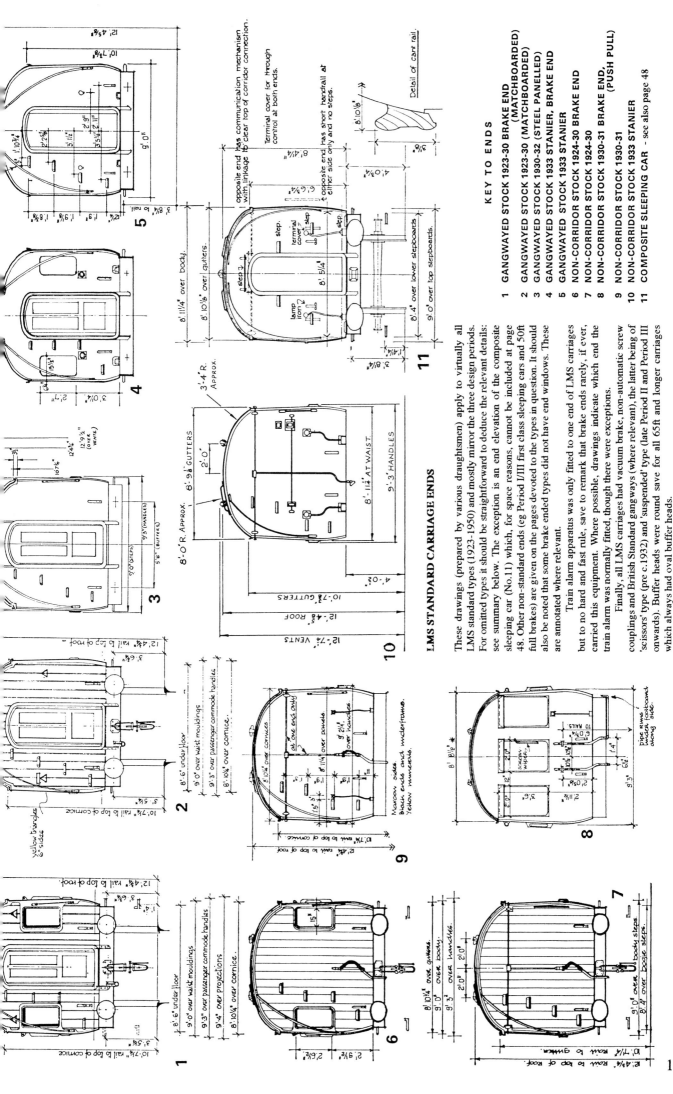

KEY TO ENDS

1 GANGWAYED STOCK 1923-30 BRAKE END (MATCHBOARDED)
2 GANGWAYED STOCK 1923-30 (MATCHBOARDED)
3 GANGWAYED STOCK 1930-32 (STEEL PANELLED)
4 GANGWAYED STOCK 1933 STANIER, BRAKE END
5 GANGWAYED STOCK 1933 STANIER
6 NON-CORRIDOR STOCK 1924-30 BRAKE END
7 NON-CORRIDOR STOCK 1924-30
8 NON-CORRIDOR STOCK 1930-31 BRAKE END, (PUSH PULL)
9 NON-CORRIDOR STOCK 1930-31
10 NON-CORRIDOR STOCK 1933 STANIER
11 COMPOSITE SLEEPING CAR - see also page 48

LMS STANDARD CARRIAGE ENDS

These drawings (prepared by various draughtsmen) apply to virtually all LMS standard types (1923-1950) and mostly mirror the three design periods. For omitted types it should be straightforward to deduce the relevant details: see summary below. The exception is an end elevation of the composite sleeping car (No.11) which, for space reasons, cannot be included at page 48. Other non-standard ends (eg Period I/III first class sleeping cars and 50ft full brakes) are given on the pages devoted to the types in question. It should also be noted that some brake ended types did not have end windows. These are annotated where relevant.

Train alarm apparatus was only fitted to one end of LMS carriages but to no hard and fast rule, save to remark that brake ends rarely, if ever, carried this equipment. Where possible, drawings indicate which end the train alarm was normally fitted, though there were exceptions.

Finally, all LMS carriages had vacuum brake, non-automatic screw couplings and British Standard gangways (where relevant), the latter being of 'scissors' type (pre c.1932) and 'suspended' type (late Period II and Period III onwards). Buffer heads were round save for all 65ft and longer carriages which always had oval buffer heads.

LMS Standard Period I Corridor Brake Third

This is the basic Period I corridor coach drawing. Prepared by the late John Hinchliffe and representing the most common (five compartment) Period I Third Brake to LMS Diagram 1696, it shows the standard features of all corridor types in the days before the abolition of separate outside compartment doors. The type had standard matchboard ends (one normal with train alarm, one brake), 'torpedo' pattern roof ventilators, cell box on the compartment side, full length bogie stepboards when new (later altered: page 10) and full livery when new. The type became extinct at the end of 1962.

PROTOTYPE DETAILS

Lot No.	Quantity	Date	Works	Running Numbers
125	40	1926	Derby	5222-5261
148	60	1926	Derby	5262-5321
412	25	1930	Derby	5322-5346

Sample pre-1933 numbers: 15363-7; 16492-3; 201; 7772

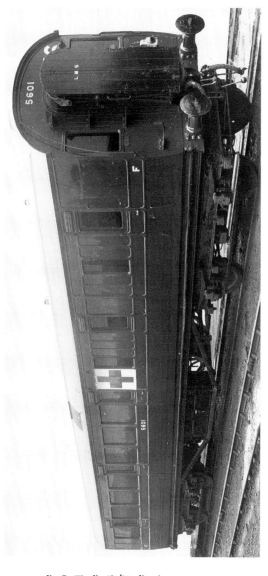

A wartime corridor side view of No.5601 (Ambulance series renumbering, original LMS number not known), but otherwise little changed from its normal external condition, along with a compartment side view of No.16199 (later LMS No.5281) ex-works when built in 1926. Note the change from full to short bogie stepboards

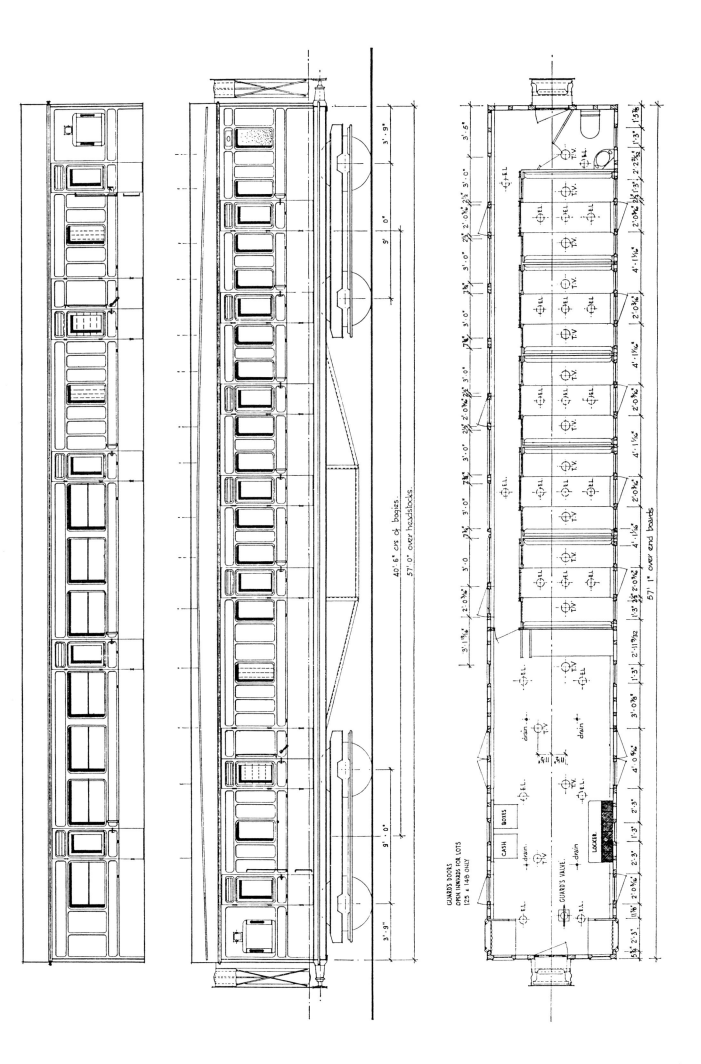

GUARD'S DOORS
OPEN INWARDS FOR LOTS
125 & 148 ONLY

40'. 6" crs of bogies.

57'.0" over headstocks.

57' 1" over end boards

LMS Standard Period I Corridor Stock

These carriages were contemporary with the third brake shown on the previous page and shared similar detail treatment - additional data marked on the drawings themselves. All three had a standard corridor side elevation whose external doors therefore bore no relation to the interior arrangement of the carriage. All three varieties had full livery when new and became extinct during the early 1960s (Firsts - 1961; Composites - 1962; Thirds - 1964)

PROTOTYPE DETAILS

Lot No.	Quantity	Date	Works	Running Numbers
FIRST: LMS D1747				
246	10	1926	Wolverton	1003-1012
COMPOSITE: LMS D1694				
30	41	1924	Wolverton	3505-3545
72	15	1925	Wolverton	3546-3560
120	25	1925	Wolverton	3561-3585
157	35	1925	Derby	3586-3620
207*	35	1926	Wolverton	3621-3655
319*	50	1927-9	Wolverton	3656-3705
THIRD: LMS D1695				
9	18	1924	Derby	1262-1279
71	17	1924	Derby	1280-1296
95	45	1925	Derby	1297-1341
147	40	1926	Derby	1342-1381
158	40	1926	Derby	1382-1421
388*	75	1928	Derby	1422-1496

* These lots had hinged vents over toilet windows, possibly also Lots 147,157,158 (unconfirmed)

Sample pre-1933 numbers:
First: 15301; 15460; 15504-5. **Composite:** 8751-5; 9308-10; 9235-42; 18997-9
Third: 25; 71; 972; 1702; 14250-89

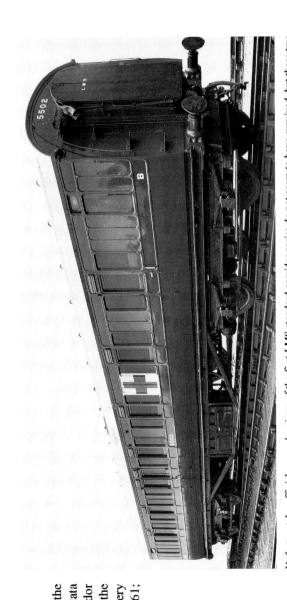

Unfortunately, official ex-works views of the first LMS standard corridor series do not seem to have survived, but these two wartime ambulance conversions give a clear indication of their nature. No.5502 shows a compartment side view of a D1694 composite, little changed in external detail, while No.5414 (also ex-composite) shows the corridor side which was common to all three types, save that the full thirds and firsts had a 3ft window where the double panel (carrying the red cross) is located. It has not been possible to find the original LMS numbers of either of these examples.

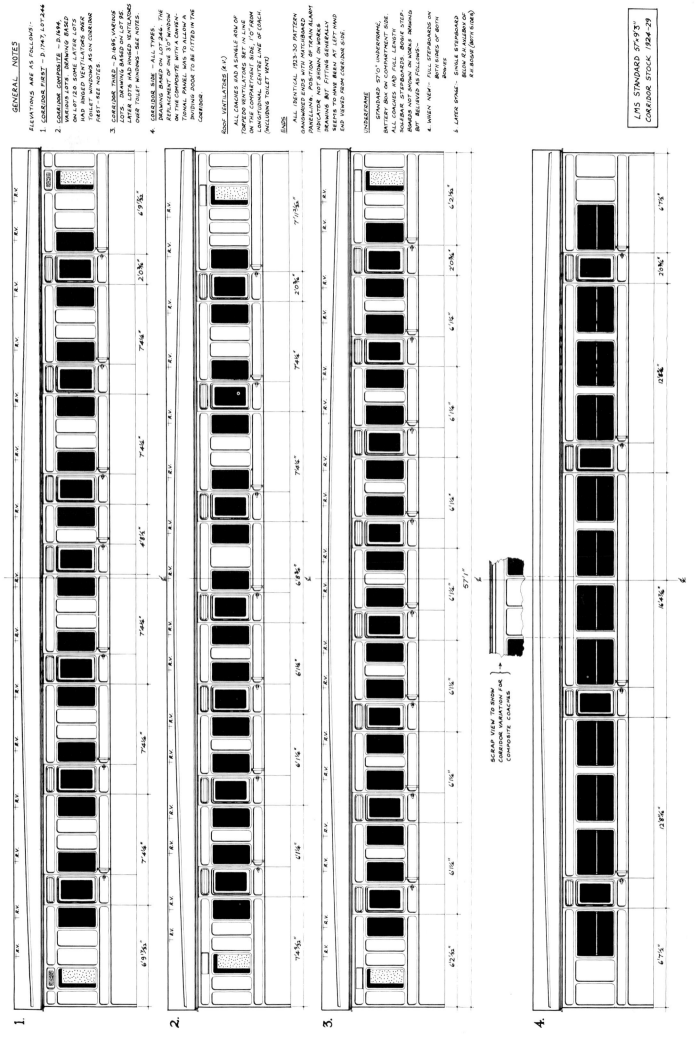

LMS Standard Period I Corridor Stock (later style)

The first significant change in LMS side corridor stock came with the introduction of end entrance lobbies and the abolition of individual outside compartment doors. Apart from convertible third class sleeping cars (page 46), this was confined to firsts and composites during Period I and the two varieties shown are typical. The twin window feature on the compartment side mirrored contemporary open stock (see next page) save for the use of a frameless droplight as the left hand element of the pair. The composites also saw the use of large 4ft 6in windows on the corridor side (a style first seen on the 1928 period I Luxury stock - page 20) along with a new 60ft length which then remained standard for LMS corridor composites. Both types had full livery when new and became extinct in late 1963.

PROTOTYPE DETAILS

Lot No.	Quantity	Date	Works	Running Numbers
BRAKE FIRST: LMS D1654				
326	25	1927	Derby	5011-5035
COMPOSITE: LMS D1716				
450	50	1930	Wolverton	3731-3780

Sample pre–1933 numbers:
Brake First: 18503-7; 18559-64
Composite: 2602-6; 9396-9; 9404-14; 15461

Close-up detail of the corridor side brake end of D1654 No.18564 (later No.5035) and a full compartment side view of brake first No.18503 (later No.5015) when new in 1927. The date of the close-up view cannot be established but was clearly after the change from full to short bogie stepboards, probably c.1929-30. A view of the composite to D1716 will be found amongst the introductory pictures on page 2

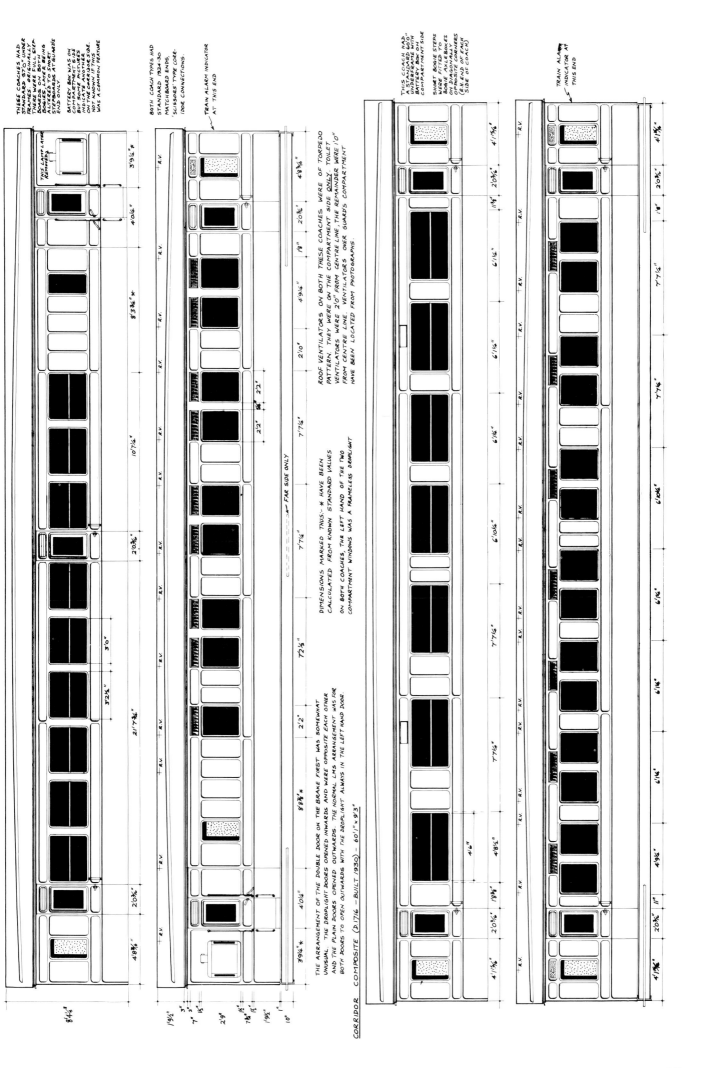

THESE COACHES HAD STANDARD 57'0" UNDER FRAMES, ORIGINALLY THESE WERE FULLY STEP-BOARDED ON BOTH BOGIES, LATER BEING ALTERED TO SHORT STEPBOARDS AT GUARDS END ONLY.

BATTERY BOX WAS ON COMPARTMENT SIDE BUT SOME PICTURES INDICATE ANOTHER ON THE CORRIDOR SIDE. NOT KNOWN IF THIS WAS A COMMON FEATURE

THIS LAMP LATER REMOVED

BOTH COACH TYPES HAD STANDARD 1924-30 MATCHBOARD ENDS. 'SCISSORS' TYPE CORR- IDOR CONNECTIONS.

TRAIN ALARM INDICATOR AT THIS END

← FAR SIDE ONLY

ROOF VENTILATORS ON BOTH THESE COACHES WERE OF TORPEDO PATTERN. THEY WERE ON THE COMPARTMENT SIDE ONLY. TOILET VENTILATORS WERE 20" FROM CENTRE LINE, THE REMAINDER WERE 1'0" FROM CENTRE LINE. VENTILATORS OVER GUARDS COMPARTMENT HAVE BEEN LOCATED FROM PHOTOGRAPHS.

DIMENSIONS MARKED THUS:- ✱ HAVE BEEN CALCULATED FROM KNOWN STANDARD VALUES ON BOTH COACHES, THE LEFT HAND OF THE TWO COMPARTMENT WINDOWS WAS A FRAMELESS DROPLIGHT

THE ARRANGEMENT OF THE DOUBLE DOOR ON THE BRAKE FIRST WAS SOMEWHAT UNUSUAL. THE DROPLIGHT DOORS OPENED INWARDS AND WERE OPPOSITE EACH OTHER AND THE PLAIN DOORS OPENED OUTWARDS. THE NORMAL LMS ARRANGEMENT WAS FOR BOTH DOORS TO OPEN OUTWARDS WITH THE DROPLIGHT ALWAYS IN THE LEFT HAND DOOR.

CORRIDOR COMPOSITE (D1716 — BUILT 1930) — 60'1" x 9'3"

THIS COACH HAD A STANDARD 60'0" UNDERFRAME WITH BATTERY BOX ON COMPARTMENT SIDE

SHORT BOGIE STEPS WERE FITTED TO BOGIE AXLEBOXES ON DIAGONALLY OPPOSITE CORNERS (R.H. END OF EACH SIDE OF COACH)

TRAIN ALARM INDICATOR AT THIS END

17

LMS Standard Period I Vestibule Stock

Perhaps the most characteristic new *type* of LMS gangwayed carriage after 1922 was the open third - 'vestibule third' as the LMS preferred to call it. Centre-aisle open carriages were no new idea but the LMS was the first to build them in quantity. These drawings show the two fully panelled Period I versions, by far the most common being that with two windows per bay. Derived from the final Midland open designs, this styling was used on a number of different diagrams, differing only in seating and minor external detail - see summary below and notes on the drawing. There was also a rather less numerous brake-ended version which is covered on page 28, alongside contemporary 'all steel' types.

The single window variant was introduced in 1929, shortly after the luxury stock (see next page), the only real change being the new 'picture' windows which then carried on into Period II. Regarded as 'neutral' dining types, they had no class figures on the doors. With the advent of Period II and III types, these D1706 carriages were usually regarded as third class and numbered into the third class series in 1933.

All types had matchboard ends, full livery and (save D1706) full length bogie stepboards when new, altered to the usual shorter version (see page 10) at a later stage. All varieties became extinct in the early 1960s viz: D1353 - 1962; D1692 - 1963; D1699 - 1961; D1706 - 1962.

The original Vestibule Third design: LMS No.4649 (later No.7784) to Lot 1, showing the original Midland style recessed handles and hooded metal door vents - see also Note 5 regarding door ventilator differences on drawings opposite

'Classless' 42 seat vestibule dining carriage to D1706 No.14414 (later No.7677), with full length windows and short bogie stepboards.

Close-up view of the 'twin window', livery and bodyside detail of No.4649 (above)

Sample pre-1933 numbers:
D1353: 4630-54; 3317-9.
D1692: 16311/31/42-3; 14185-9; 15160-9; 18030-8
D1699: 7753-6; 7809-11.
D1706: 14215-23; 14444-51

PROTOTYPE DETAILS

Lot No.	Quantity	Date	Works	Running Numbers
LMS D1353 (recessed handles) *				
1	25	1924	Derby	7765-7789
16	6	1924	Derby	7790-7795
94	30	1924	Derby	7796-7825
LMS D1692 (56 seat standard type)				
154	50	1925	Derby	7826-7875
302	100	1927	Derby	8076-8175 #
343	80	1927-8	Derby	8176-8255
355	100	1928	Derby	8256-8355
375	100	1928	Derby	8356-8455
431	125	1929	Derby	8456-8580
LMS D1699 (42 seat dining cars) §				
156	35	1925	Derby	7630-7664
LMS D1706 (42 seat classless dining cars - large windows) §				
411	25	1929	Derby	7665-7689

* 56 seat version and externally identical to another 30 built in 1923 but to a MR diagram. These were 42 seaters and numbered 7600-7629 in 1933

The number series 7876-8075 was filled by 200 substantially similar 'all steel' carriages built by outside contractors - see also page 28

§ In 1933, the LMS numbered the 42 seat vestibules ahead of the 56 seat types, hence the lower 76xx number series for these diagrams

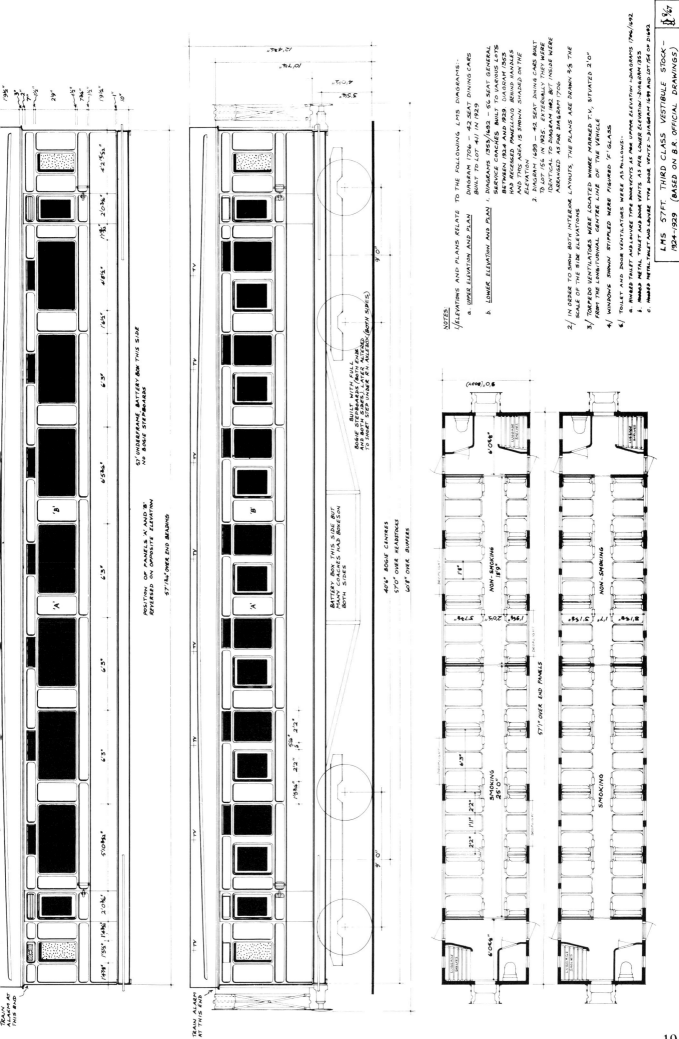

LMS Standard Period I/II Luxury Semi-Open First

The Period I examples of this type, drawn by the late John Hinchliffe, along with the open 'classless' diners (last page), corridor composites (page 16) and third class sleeping cars (page 46) were the first LMS gangwayed designs to incorporate large 'picture' windows. The semi-open style ('corridor-vestibule' in LMS parlance) was for the most prestigious trains and had the unusual arrangement of only four seats per compartment. The low waisted versions were, along with the brake composites (next page), the first Period II designs to appear. The plan is common to both types but the droplights in the dining end of the Period II version were reduced to three only - see notes on the drawing. They lasted until 1957 (Period I type) and 1960 respectively and were some of the first LMS designs to have short bogie stepboards from new.

PROTOTYPE DETAILS

Lot No.	Quantity	Date	Works	Running Numbers
LMS D1707 (Period I)				
379	5	1928	Derby	1023-1027
LMS D1719 (Period II)				
488	10	1929	Derby	1028-1036
626	1	1932	Derby	1037 *

* Built as a replacement for old No.15318 of Lot 488, destroyed in the Leighton Buzzard accident of 1931. It had steel side and end panelling whose details were identical to those given for the corridor composite and open third on page 26.

Sample pre-1933 numbers:
D1707: 15412; 15604; 15933   D1719: 2741; 10291; 15510; 15565; 15318 (Lot 626)

Period I semi-open first No.15412 (later No.1023) from the corridor side at the compartment end, together with the Period II equivalent No.15540 (later No.1035) from the opposite side. Note the change in both style and placement of insignia between the two versions - see also livery notes on pages 6/7

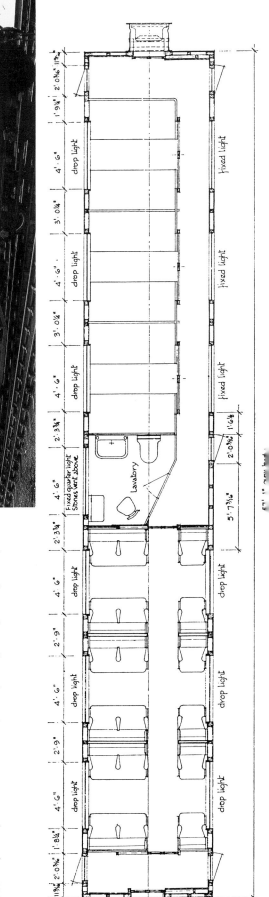

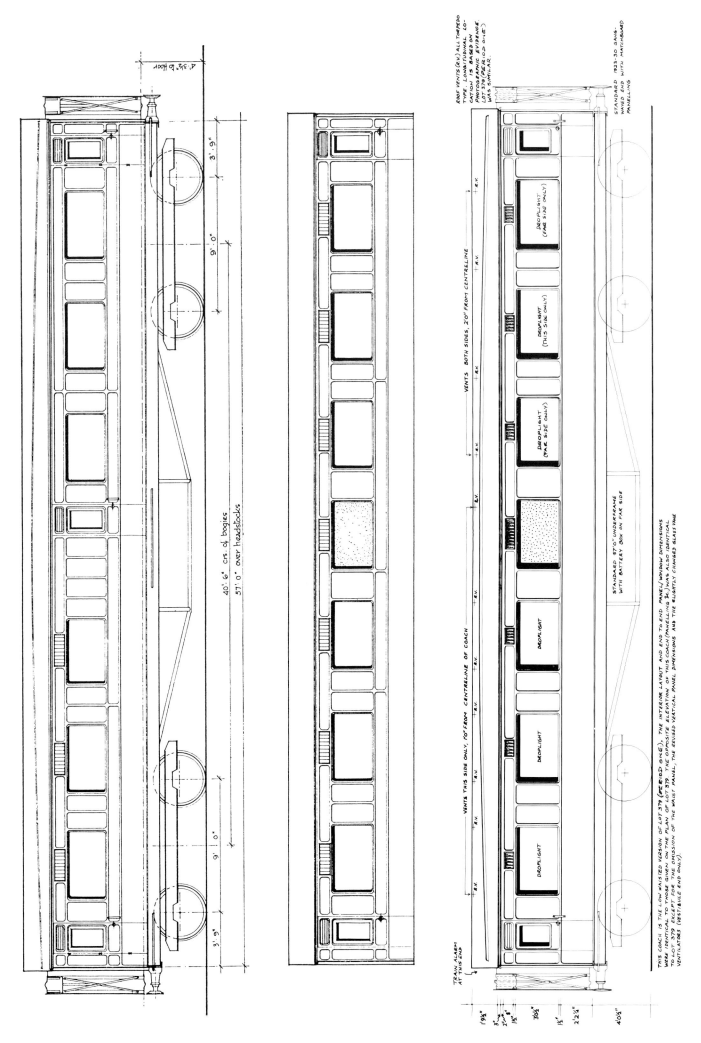

ROOF VENTS (R.V.) ALL TORPEDO TYPE. LONGITUDINAL LOCATION IS BASED ON PHOTOGRAPHIC EVIDENCE. LOT 379 (PERIOD ONE) WAS SIMILAR.

STANDARD 1923-30 GANG-WAYED END WITH MATCHBOARD PANELLING

4'-3½" TO ROOF

3'-9"

9'-0"

40'-6" crs. of bogies

57'-0" over headstocks

9'-0"

3'-9"

TRAIN ALARM AT THIS END

VENTS THIS SIDE ONLY, 10" FROM CENTRELINE OF COACH

VENTS BOTH SIDES, 20" FROM CENTRELINE

R.V.

R.V.

R.V.

R.V.

R.V.

R.V.

R.V.

R.V.

R.V.

R.V.

R.V.

R.V.

DROPLIGHT (FAR SIDE ONLY)

DROPLIGHT (THIS SIDE ONLY)

DROPLIGHT (FAR SIDE ONLY)

DROPLIGHT

DROPLIGHT

DROPLIGHT

STANDARD 57'-0" UNDERFRAME WITH BATTERY BOX ON FAR SIDE

19¾"

3"
2½"

30½"

1½"

40½"

2'-2¼"

THIS COACH IS THE LOW WAISTED VERSION OF LOT 379 (PERIOD ONE). THE INTERIOR LAYOUT AND END TO END PANEL/WINDOW DIMENSIONS WERE IDENTICAL TO THOSE GIVEN ON THE PLAN OF LOT 379. THE OPPOSITE ELEVATION OF THIS COACH (PANELLING &c.) WAS ALSO IDENTICAL TO LOT 379 EXCEPT FOR THE OMISSION OF THE WAIST PANEL, THE REVISED VERTICAL PANEL DIMENSIONS AND THE SLIGHTLY CHANGED GLASS VANE VENTILATORS (VESTIBULE END ONLY).

21

LMS Standard Period II Corridor Brake Composite

This fully detailed drawing by Julie Hinchliffe of the brake composites built to LMS Diagram 1720 represents the basic Period II fully panelled type. Unlike some Period II fully panelled stock, this design had steel panelled ends, transitional from the older matchboard type. The D1720 brake composites were not withdrawn in their original condition, being rebuilt to D1720A c.1939 with Period III side panelling, but retaining the original ends and roof. Pictures of this converted form are offered, together with further caption information and they lasted as such until mid-1964, always with short bogie stepboards.

PROTOTYPE DETAILS

Lot No.	Quantity	Date	Works	Running Numbers
490	25	1930	Wolverton	6734-6758
550	25	1930	Wolverton	6759-6783

Sample pre-1933 numbers: 9481/3-4/6/8; 11156-64

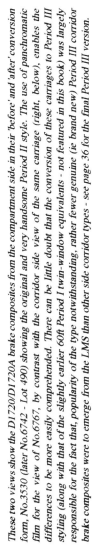

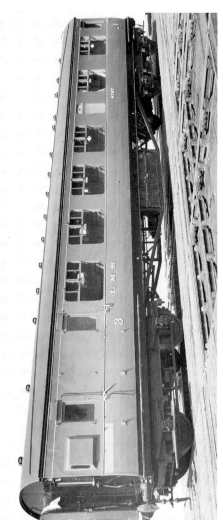

These two views show the D1720/D1720A brake composites from the compartment side in their 'before' and 'after' conversion form, No.3530 (later No.6742 - Lot 490) showing the original and very handsome Period II style. The use of panchromatic film for the view of No.6767, by contrast with the corridor side view of the same carriage (right, below), enables the differences to be more easily comprehended. There can be little doubt that the conversion of these carriages to Period III styling (along with that of the slightly earlier 60ft Period I twin-window equivalents - not featured in this book) was largely responsible for the fact that, popularity of the type notwithstanding, rather fewer genuine (ie brand new) Period III corridor brake composites were to emerge from the LMS than other side corridor types - see page 36 for the final Period III version.

This view shows the corridor side of No.6767 after rebuilding with Stanier pattern side panelling. The conversion was to D1720A and cannot be precisely dated save for the fact that the use of shorter length twin centre sliding elements to the window-top ventilators (a feature not normally seen on Period III stock until after the war) places it c.1939-40. It was built as No.11156 to Lot 550 in 1930 and renumbered c.1933-4, several years before conversion to the form shown here. It should be noted that after conversion, the large windows were reduced in width to the standard Period III 4ft dimension compared with the earlier 4ft 6in width, but the retention of original roof and ends is very apparent.

22

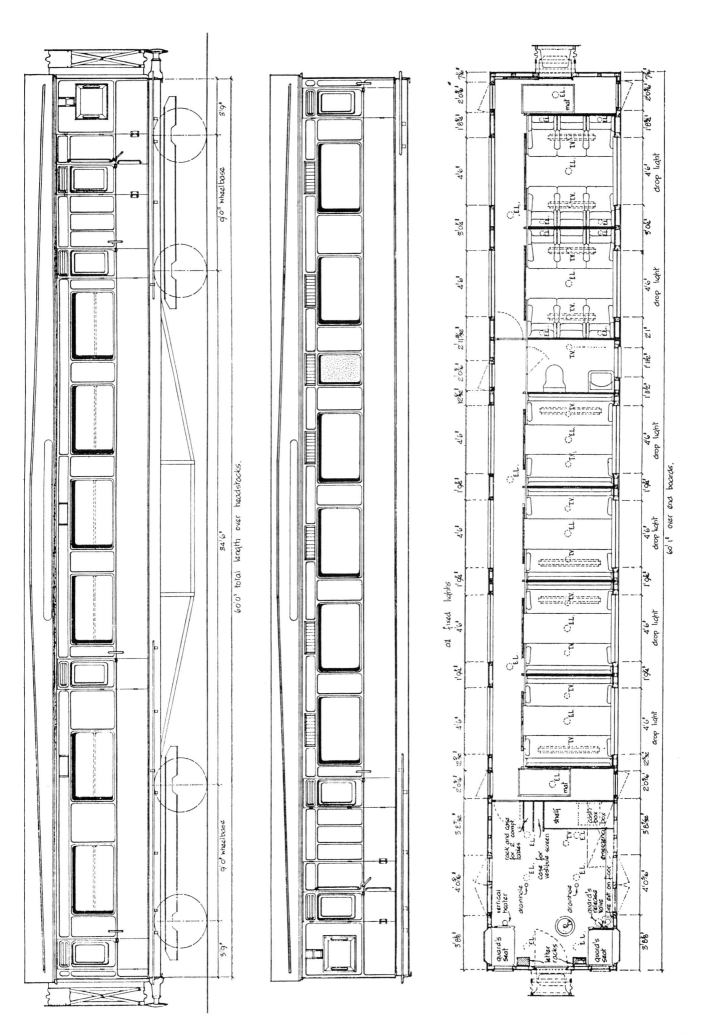

LMS Standard Period II Corridor Stock

Arthur Whitehead's drawings opposite offer two further fully panelled Period II types, 60ft corridor thirds to D1782 and 57ft 'luxury' brake firsts to D1717 with only four seats per compartment. Apart from the convertible sleeping cars (page 46), D1782 was the only LMS corridor third to have a 60ft underframe and was also the first 'daytime use only' corridor third to dispense with outside compartment doors. Brake firsts had matchboard ends (one normal, one brake), thirds had steel panelled ends and both had short bogie steps. On both types, compartments had frameless droplights, but all other side windows (eg toilets, brake van/brake end, corridor side &c) were fixed lights with bolection mouldings. Both types lasted until 1962.

PROTOTYPE DETAILS

Lot No.	Quantity	Date	Works	Running Numbers
THIRD CLASS LMS D1782				
551	10	1930	Derby	1497-1506
BRAKE FIRST LMS D1717				
477	6	1929	Derby	5005-5009
625	1	1932	Derby	5010 *

* This was a replacement for old 15458 of Lot 477 destroyed in the Leighton Buzzard accident in 1931. It had steel panelling and no raised beading, details as shown for the 57ft open third and 60ft corridor composite on page 27

Sample pre-1933 numbers:
Third Class: 3026-3035
Brake First: 15470; 15533; 15458 (Lot 625)

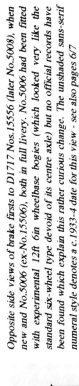

Opposite side views of brake firsts to D1717 Nos.15556 (later No.15008), when new and No.5006 (ex-No.15506), both in full livery. No.5006 had been fitted with experimental 12ft 6in wheelbase bogies (which looked very like the standard six-wheel type devoid of its centre axle) but no official records have been found which explain this rather curious change. The unshaded sans-serif numeral style denotes a c.1933-4 date for this view - see also pages 6/7

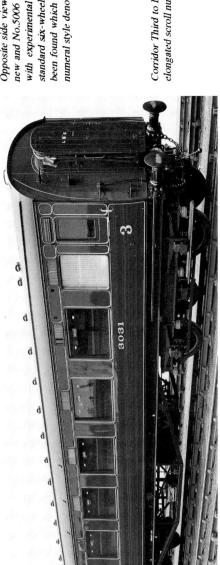

Corridor Third to D1782 No.3031 (later No.1502) when new in 1930. Note the elongated scroll numerals (page 6) and lack of LMS emblem

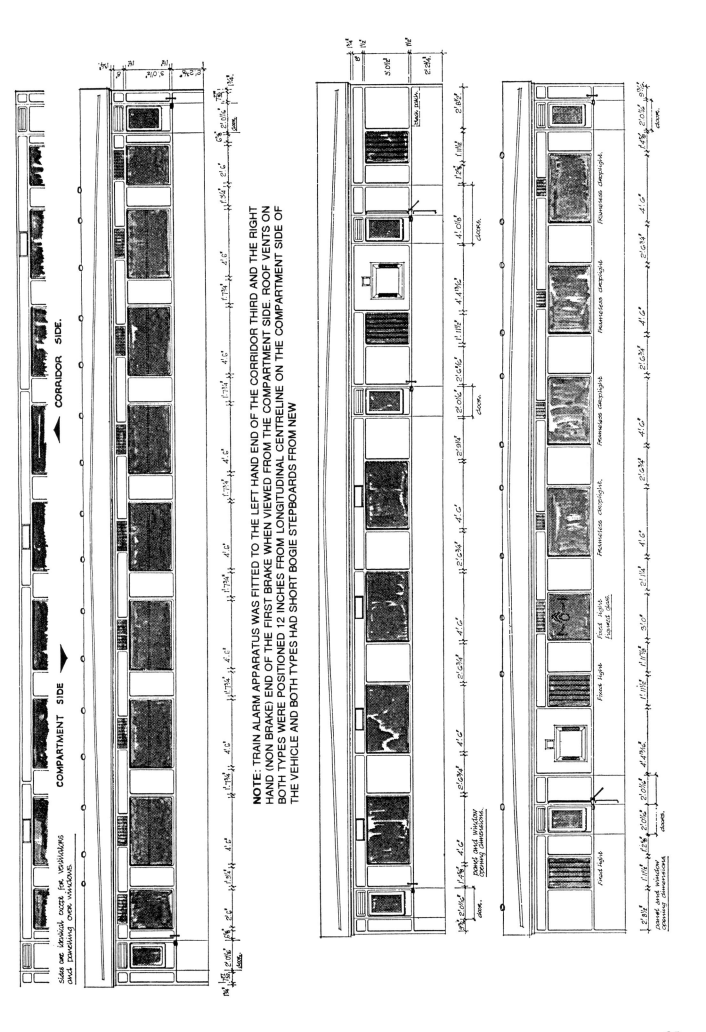

CORRIDOR SIDE.

COMPARTMENT SIDE

Sides are identical except for ventilators and panelling over windows.

NOTE: TRAIN ALARM APPARATUS WAS FITTED TO THE LEFT HAND END OF THE CORRIDOR THIRD AND THE RIGHT HAND (NON BRAKE) END OF THE FIRST BRAKE WHEN VIEWED FROM THE COMPARTMENT SIDE. ROOF VENTS ON BOTH TYPES WERE POSITIONED 12 INCHES FROM LONGITUDINAL CENTRELINE ON THE COMPARTMENT SIDE OF THE VEHICLE AND BOTH TYPES HAD SHORT BOGIE STEPBOARDS FROM NEW

LMS Standard Period II Gangwayed Stock

These three drawings show the transition from fully beaded to steel panelling during Period II. The upper elevation represents the 60ft fully panelled open type, built to several different diagrams (see summary). Next is the steel panelled 57ft third class general service version whose main windows were 6in narrower and the length reduction wholly in the toilet/luggage shelf areas. Within the passenger saloons, the interior plans of both types were as given for the Period I versions on page 19. The final drawing shows the 60ft steel panelled corridor composite which succeeded the 60ft steel panelled corridor composite shown on page 16. In this design, the main first class windows were 6in wider than the third class.

All three types had short bogie stepboards from new and lasted into the mid-1960s, withdrawal as follows: D1721/1726 - 1963; D1795 - 1964; D1807 - 1966; D1791 - 1964

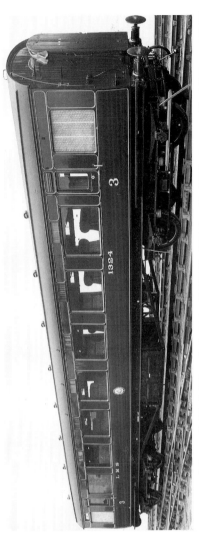

60ft, 42 seat fully panelled Period II vestibule third to D1721 No.1324 (later No.7711) when new. The full firsts to D1722 (later to be downgraded as LMS 9030-95 - see table), the 42 seat non-dining third class version to D1795 and the 56 seat third class version to D1738 (again see table) were all externally identical.......

56 seat, 57ft steel-panelled Period II vestibule third No.8867 (originally No.12031) to D1807. This was one of Lot 654 with the later pattern suspended type gangways and revised window ventilators compared with the drawing opposite.

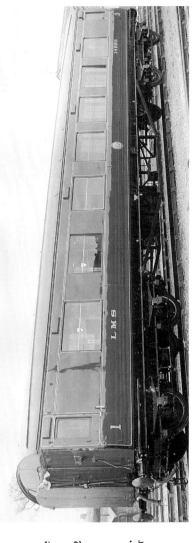

60ft Period II steel-panelled corridor composite No.14993 (later No.3810), taken from the corridor side when new in 1931

PROTOTYPE DETAILS

Lot No.	Quantity	Date	Works	Running Numbers
60ft VESTIBULE THIRD (42 SEAT DINING) LMS D1721				
491	25	1930	Derby	7690-7714
519	25	1930	Derby	9030-9054 §
60ft VESTIBULE THIRD (56 SEAT VERSION) LMS D1738				
522	25	1930	Derby	8880-8904
60ft VESTIBULE THIRD (42 SEAT NON-DINING - sic!) LMS D1795				
522	50	1930	Derby	7715-7763
628	1	1932	Derby	7764 *
57ft VESTIBULE THIRD (56 SEAT) LMS D1807				
575	140	1931	Derby	8581-8720
597	60	1931	Derby	8721-8780
648	50	1932	Wolverton	8781-8830 #
654	49 +	1932	Derby	8831-8879 #
60ft CORRIDOR COMPOSITE LMS D1791				
531	48	1931	Wolverton	3781-3828

§ Originally first class (7465-89 in 1933). Numbers quoted were allocated after they were downgraded on the advent of the 65ft Period III open firsts (page 40)

* This was a **steel panelled** (ie non-beaded) replacement for old 14733 of Lot 522 destroyed in the Leighton Buzzard accident in 1931, and took the old number until 1933

+ 50 originally built - one early (accident?) withdrawal pre-1933

Compared with version drawn, these lots had hooded metal ventilators over fixed lights, six-element Stones ventilators over droplights and 'suspended' type gangways, the latter being the first instance of such use on the LMS

Sample pre-1933 numbers:

Lot 491: 1262-3; 1274-5; 1313-5; 1323-5. Lot 519: 604; 6113-5; 6127-9; 6415
Lot 522(56 seat): 1811-2; 1836-8; 5905-6. Lot 522(42 seat): 6072-9; 13891-2; 14734-6
Lots 575/597: 136; 850; 7620; 11800; 13904-5; 15244-5; 15346-7; 15571-2
Lots 648/654: 286; 6349; 10275-8; 13667-8

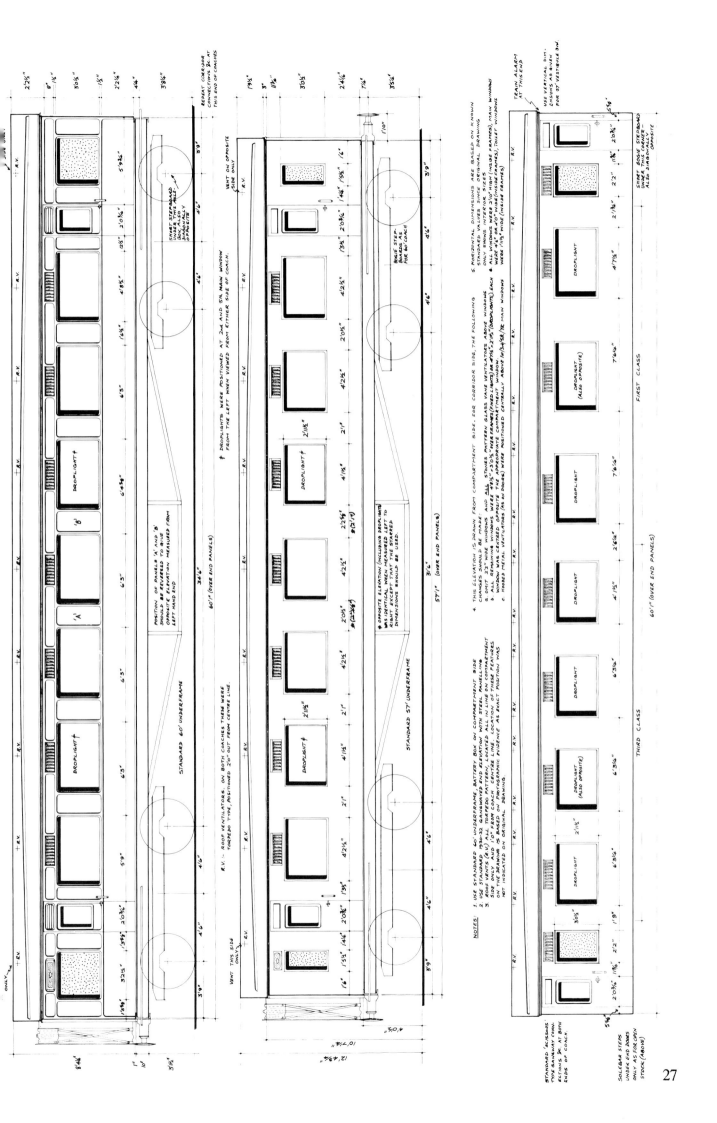

NOTES:

1. USE STANDARD 60' UNDERFRAME BATTERY BOX ON COMPARTMENT SIDE
2. USE STANDARD 1930-32 GANGWAYED END ELEVATION WITH STEEL PANELLING
3. ROOF VENTS (R.V.) ALL TORPEDO PATTERN, LOCATED ALL IN LINE ON COMPARTMENT SIDE ONLY AND 1'0" FROM COACH CENTRE LINE. LOCATION OF THESE FEATURES ON THE DRAWING IS BASED ON PHOTOGRAPHIC EVIDENCE AS EXACT POSITION WAS NOT INDICATED ON ORIGINAL DRAWING.

4. THIS ELEVATION IS DRAWN FROM COMPARTMENT SIDE. FOR CORRIDOR SIDE, THE FOLLOWING CHANGES SHOULD BE MADE:
   a. OMIT 3½" WIDE WINDOWS AND ALL STONES PATTERN GLASS VANE VENTILATORS ABOVE WINDOWS
   b. ALL REMAINING WINDOWS WERE 4'1½" × 3'0½" WIDE FRAMES (FIXED LIGHTS) OR 4'7½" × 2'1½" (DROPLIGHTS) EACH WINDOW WAS CENTRED OPPOSITE THE APPROPRIATE COMPARTMENT WINDOW.
   c. HOODED METAL VENTILATORS (AS IN DOORS) WERE POSITIONED CENTRALLY ABOVE 1'6"/½/5/8" (½/5/8) MAIN WINDOWS

5. HORIZONTAL DIMENSIONS ARE BASED ON KNOWN STANDARD VALUES SINCE ORIGINAL DRAWING ONLY SHOWS INTERIOR SIZES.
   ALL WINDOWS WERE 4¼" HIGH (INSIDE FRAMES), MAIN WINDOWS WERE 4'1½" WIDE OR 3'0½" WIDE (INSIDE FRAMES), TOILET WINDOWS WERE 1'1½" WIDE (INSIDE FRAMES)

R.V.:- ROOF VENTILATORS ON BOTH COACHES THESE WERE TORPEDO TYPE, POSITIONED 2'0" OUT FROM CENTRE LINE.

✝ DROPLIGHTS WERE POSITIONED AT 2nd AND 5th MAIN WINDOW FROM THE LEFT WHEN VIEWED FROM EITHER SIDE OF COACH.

POSITION OF PANELS 'A' AND 'B' SHOULD BE REVERSED TO GIVE OPPOSITE ELEVATION MEASURED FROM LEFT HAND END

✳ OPPOSITE ELEVATION (INCLUDING DROPLIGHTS) IS IDENTICAL WHEN MEASURED LEFT TO RIGHT EXCEPT THAT THE STARRED DIMENSIONS SHOULD BE USED.

THIRD CLASS

FIRST CLASS

27

LMS Standard Period I/II 'All Steel' Stock

From 1925, the LMS introduced some integral 'all steel' carriages (ie without conventionally separate chassis) built by outside contractors. No official LMS drawings have been located but they were of technical interest at the time and contemporary drawings of some of the types have survived to form the basis of this resumé. Most appeared during Period I but later, a few Period II designs were made this way, this time with body shells only from 'the trade', which the LMS then fitted out.

Drawings are offered of the Period I open third brakes from Leeds Forge, some details of the Period I full thirds from Metropolitan C&W and the Period II corridor third brakes from Metro-Cammell. The open brake third drawing can be used in conjunction with the fully panelled types on page 19 to evolve the fully beaded version to D1693, details of which are therefore given, along with a picture. There were subtle variations between each manufacturer but for completeness, details are offered for the whole 'all steel' range for the diagrams concerned.

Last survival dates: D1746 - 1962; D1693 - 1964; Lots 183/184 - 1962; Lot 185 - 1964; D1730 - 1964.

'All steel' vestibule third brake to D1746, No.7670 (later No.9816) from the Leeds Forge Co, together with full third to D1745 No.6260 (later No.8071) from Met.C&W, both taken when new in 1926 with elaborate 'full' livery

The first traditionally panelled open third brake to D1693 No.638 (later No.9835) together with an early all steel' corridor brake third to D1730 from Metro-Cammell No.6018 (later No.5352), both of them taken when new in 1927 and 1930 respectively. The later Lot 578 version of the latter type is given on introductory page 2

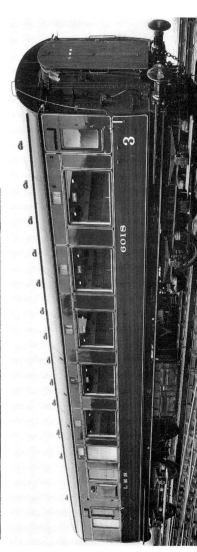

PROTOTYPE DETAILS

Lot No.	Quantity	Date	Works	Running Numbers
57ft 'ALL STEEL' VESTIBULE THIRD BRAKE LMS D1746				
181	20	1926	Leeds Forge	9800-9819
182	15	1926	Bham C&W	9820-9834
57ft VESTIBULE THIRD BRAKE (TRADITIONAL CONSTRUCTION) LMS D1693				
303	35	1927	Wolverton	9835-9869
328	20	1928	Wolverton	9870-9889
57ft 'ALL STEEL' VESTIBULE THIRD LMS D1745				
183	50	1925/6	Bham C&W	7876-7925
184	50	1925/6	Camm-Laird	7926-7975
185	100	1926	Met C&W	7976-8075
57ft 'ALL STEEL' CORRIDOR THIRD BRAKE LMS D1730 #				
507	5	1930	Met-Camm	5347-5351
508	5	1930	Met-Camm	5352-5356
542	40	1930/1	Met-Camm	5357-5396
578	50	1931/2	Met-Camm	5397-5446 *

\# Somewhat unusually, there were no brake end windows on these carriages. Lots 507/578 were fitted out at Wolverton, the remainder at Derby

* Lot 578 had longer Stones ventilators over the compartment windows than the version drawn

Sample pre-1933 numbers:

Lot 181: 7633-5; 7639-43; 7112-5; 7648-9
D1693: 638; 2094; 7731; 10876; 14270; 18731-2; 18848-50; 19028
Lot 183: 5291-5; 5980-5. **Lot 184:** 6000-17. **Lot 185:** 5281-9; 5680-9; 6030-9

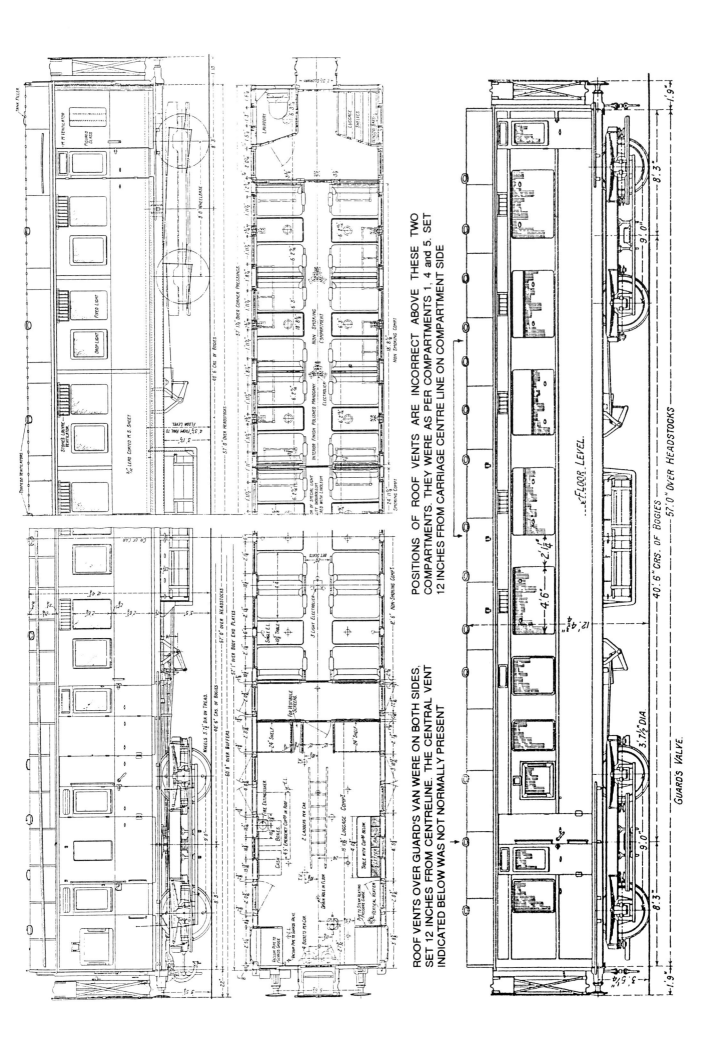

POSITIONS OF ROOF VENTS ARE INCORRECT ABOVE THESE TWO COMPARTMENTS. THEY WERE AS PER COMPARTMENTS 1, 4 and 5. SET 12 INCHES FROM CARRIAGE CENTRE LINE ON COMPARTMENT SIDE

ROOF VENTS OVER GUARD'S VAN WERE ON BOTH SIDES, SET 12 INCHES FROM CENTRELINE. THE CENTRAL VENT INDICATED BELOW WAS NOT NORMALLY PRESENT

LMS Standard Period III Corridor Stock - I

The two types shown here (both drawn by Arthur Whitehead) were the first Period III corridor thirds/brake thirds to be built in quantity. Both had standard ends/underframe detail and were finished in simple livery from new, save for 5517-41 (brake third) and 1537-1605 (full third), both of which emerged in fully lined livery just before the change. The corridor side of the full third was identical to that drawn save for the omission of windows opposite the toilets.

The matching Period III corridor composites to LMS Diagrams 1925/1969, which differed only in minor aspects of their internal toilet layout, can readily be derived from these drawings by increasing the corridor third to 60ft. This allows three first class compartments (each one foot longer than the thirds) to be included at the *right hand end* when viewed from the compartment side. Details of all three types are given below, but because so many lot numbers were involved, only the year of building is quoted. The full thirds became extinct at the end of 1965, the remainder during 1966

Period III Corridor Third No.2137 to D1899 in simple livery: view taken from corridor side

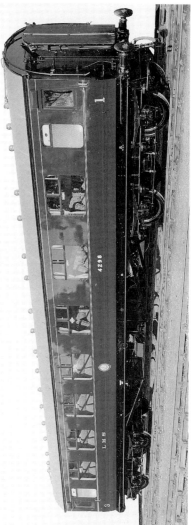

Period III 60ft Corridor Composite No.4298 in simple livery - note the black painted ends

PROTOTYPE DETAILS

Quantity	Date	Works	Running Numbers
57ft CORRIDOR THIRD BRAKE LMS D1905			
102	1933	Derby	5517-5566 *
		Wolverton	5567-5616
		Derby	5617-5618
25	1934	Wolverton	5619-5643
125	1935	Wolverton	5644-5768
163	1936	Derby	5769-5843 §
		Wolverton	5869-5956
57ft CORRIDOR THIRD LMS D1899			
35	1933	Derby	1537-1571
289	1934	Derby	1572-1740
		Wolverton	1741-1860
65	1935	Derby	1861-1925
75	1936	Derby	1926-2000
40	1937	Wolverton	2001-2040
89	1938	Wolverton	2041-2129
18	1937	Wolverton	2130-2147
60ft CORRIDOR COMPOSITE LMS D1925/1969			
180	1935/6	Derby	3934-3953
		Wolverton	3954-4113
70	1937	Wolverton	4114-4182 #
33	1938/9	Wolverton	4183-4215
84	1939	Wolverton	4216-4299
30	1939/40	Wolverton	4300-4329

* 5517-24: Lookout/top commode handle removed for 'Sunny South Express'

§ 5792/812/4: Modernised 1937 for 'Coronation Scot' - blue/silver livery

Period III Corridor Third Brake to D1905 No.5518 in fully lined livery - note the lack of LMS emblem

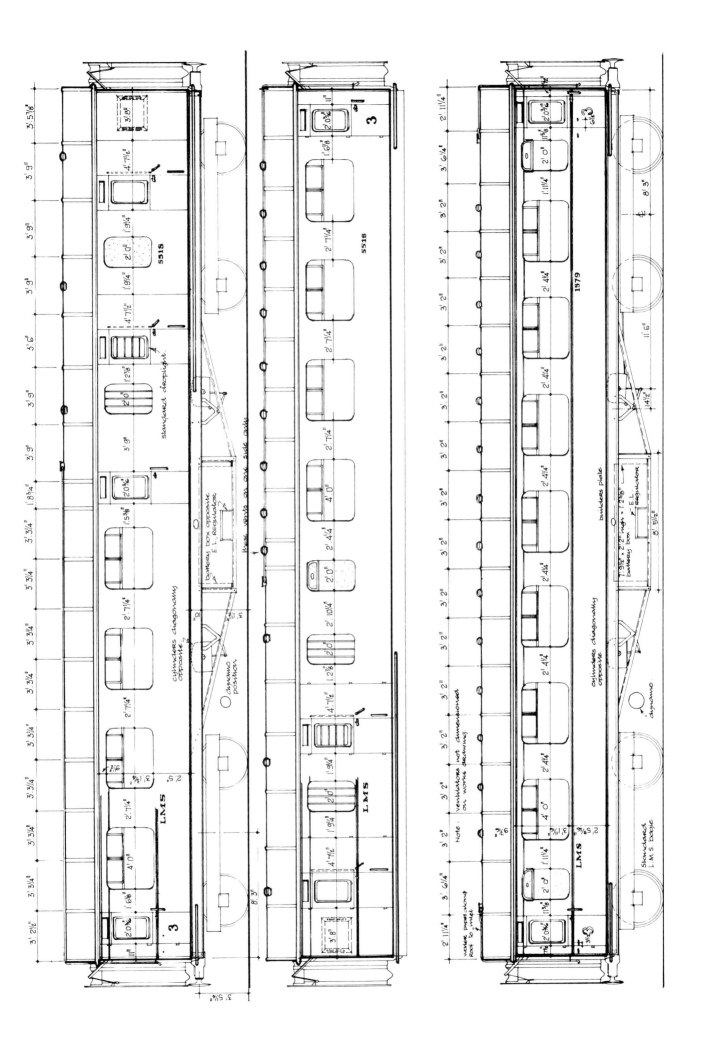

31

LMS Standard Period III Corridor Stock - II

This page shows the matching pre-war first and brake first types to the thirds/composites on the previous page. Both were relatively few in number and several diagrams were issued to denote minor variations in seating &c., including two specific diagrams for the more luxurious 'Coronation Scot' variants. Apart from these six blue/silver carriages, all came out in simple livery and there were no external dimensional differences between any of the two basic types. Apart from D1920 (1963) and the 'Coronation Scot' stock (1964), all survived until 1965.

PROTOTYPE DETAILS

Diagram	Quantity	Date	Works	Running Numbers
57ft CORRIDOR FIRST				
1920	1	1934	Derby	1038 *
1909	12	1934	Derby	1039-1050 §
1930	11	1936	Wolverton	1051-1061 #
	7	1937	Wolverton	1062-1068 #
	12	1938	Wolverton	1072-1083 #
1960	3	1937	Wolverton	1069-1071 +
57ft CORRIDOR BRAKE FIRST				
1910	1	1934	Derby	5051 *
	8	1938	Wolverton	5055-5062 #
1961	3	1937	Wolverton	5052-5054 +

*   Prototype carriages, three per side seating

§   Luxury batch, two per side seating

Main batches, three per side seating - 'luxury' finish

+   'Coronation Scot' stock, two per side seating, 'air conditioned' (sic!), luxury finish and blue/silver livery

The first two views on this page show Period III luxury 'two per side full first No.1047 and three per side brake first No.5062, both taken from the compartment side in LMS simple livery. Note the lack of LMS emblem on the full first - a not uncommon omission throughout the post-1929 period on several carriages with end doors only, but to no set pattern as far as can be judged and surprising in view of the luxury nature of this particular example! Note also the change from red to black ends between the building of the two types

The final view shows the very last of the full firsts as No.M1071M (one of the three built for the 1937 'Coronation Scot' sets) in BR red/cream colours c.1956/7, at or about the time of change to all maroon BR carriage livery. The view is taken from the corridor side: note the retained ventilation duct along the roof and the six equal sized windows, the nearest one being opposite the half compartment. (Author's Collection - 1)

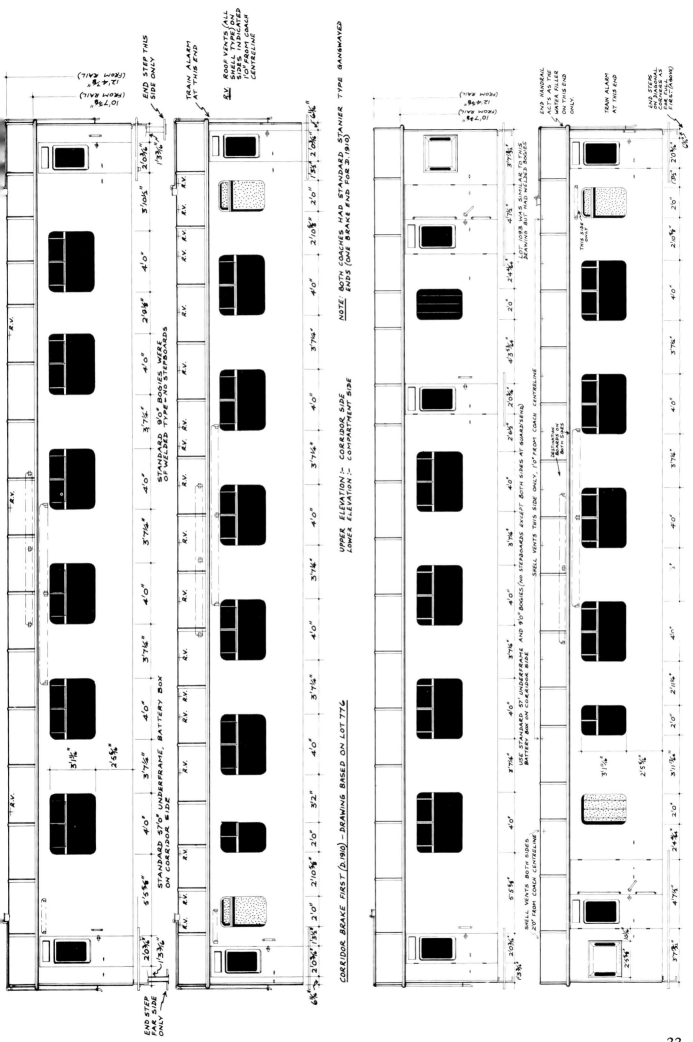

CORRIDOR BRAKE FIRST (D.1910) - DRAWING BASED ON LOT 776

UPPER ELEVATION :- CORRIDOR SIDE
LOWER ELEVATION :- COMPARTMENT SIDE

NOTE: BOTH COACHES HAD STANDARD STANIER TYPE GANGWAYED
ENDS (ONE BRAKE END FOR D.1910)

LMS Standard Period III Corridor Stock - III

These drawings show the later varieties of Period III third/brake third which followed the types described on page 30. The main difference was the move of the toilet compartment to the end of the carriage (brake third) and the two extra doors on the corridor side (full third). The brake third appeared in 1937 but the full third did not emerge until 1946. All types carried simple livery from new save for the 1948 batches (no LMS markings) and 12950-13084 (believed all to have had BR crimson/cream livery when built). Both types lasted until 1968

PROTOTYPE DETAILS

Quantity	Date	Works	Running Numbers
57ft CORRIDOR THIRD BRAKE LMS D1968			
64	1937	Derby	5957-6020
90	1938	Derby	26100-26189 *
130	1939	Derby	26191-26264
		Wolverton	26265-26320
50	1945	Derby	26321-26370
175	1946	Derby	26371-26545
57ft CORRIDOR THIRD LMS D2119			
50	1946	Derby	2151-2200
150	1947	Derby	2201-2350
116	1945-7	Met-Camm	2351-2466
50	1948	Derby	2467-2516
200	1948	Met-Camm	12750-12949 *
135	1949-50	Bham C&W	12950-13084

* Five figure number sequences opened up to cope with overflow building - see page 6. They were chosen from appropriate parts of the unused non-corridor blocks but for some reason, 26190 was never allocated in the brake third series

Compartment side view of one of the first examples of the new Period III brake thirds to D1968. No.6006 - compare with p.30 to note the different toilet position and altered van' doors. The concealment of the upper edge of the solebar consequent upon the welded construction is very clear and may also have been related to the contemporary work being carried out on articulated stock - see page 42. This body-side modification was not universal on subsequent Period III types and most reverted to traditional side panelling - see next view. An example of this important type is preserved in the NRM collection.

This view shows the first post-war Period III corridor third No.2151 to the new D2119. From this side it looked little different from the pre-war variety but had two extra corridor side doors - see drawing - which are believed (but not confirmed) to have been introduced for additional safety reasons. Note the flat-topped '3' on the doors and the new style running numbers at the far end. By this time, the livery ought to have been maroon (see page 7) but is thought more likely to have been the traditional crimson lake.

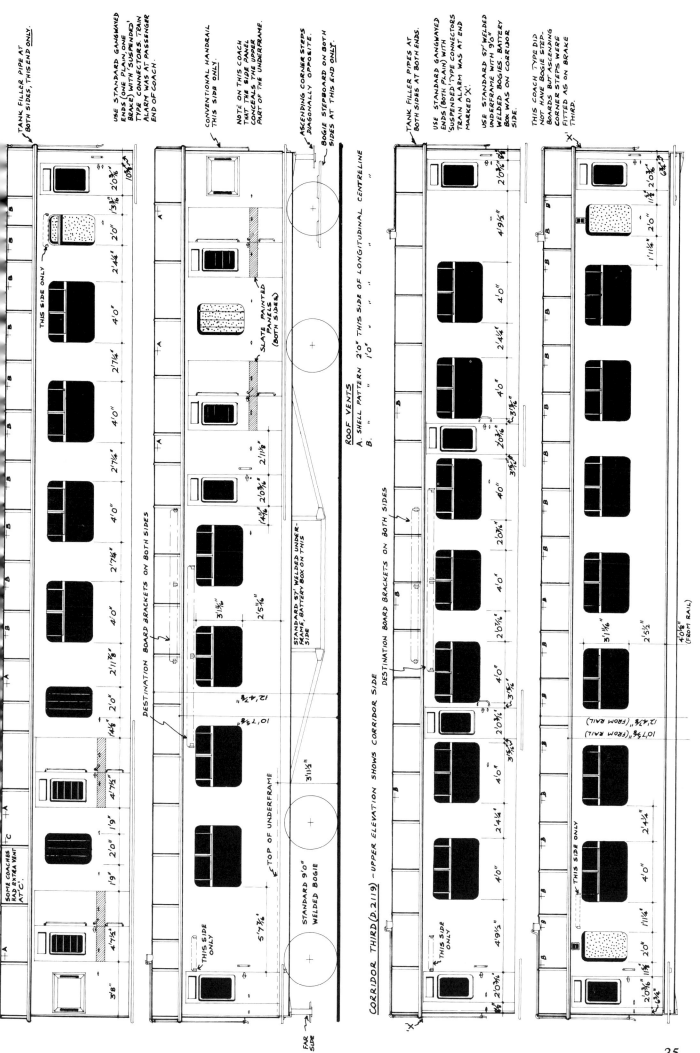

CORRIDOR THIRD (D.2119) — UPPER ELEVATION SHOWS CORRIDOR SIDE

ROOF VENTS
A. SHELL PATTERN   2'0" THIS SIDE OF LONGITUDINAL CENTRELINE
B.   "   "   1'0"   "   "   "   "   "

TANK FILLER PIPE AT BOTH SIDES, THIS END ONLY.

USE STANDARD GANGWAYED ENDS (ONE PLAIN, ONE BRAKE) WITH 'SUSPENDED' TYPE CONNECTORS. TRAIN ALARM WAS AT PASSENGER END OF COACH.

CONVENTIONAL HANDRAIL THIS SIDE ONLY.

NOTE ON THIS COACH THAT THE SIDE PANEL CONCEALS THE UPPER PART OF THE UNDERFRAME.

ASCENDING CORNER STEPS DIAGONALLY OPPOSITE.

BOGIE STEPBOARD ON BOTH SIDES AT THIS END ONLY.

TANK FILLER PIPES AT BOTH SIDES AT BOTH ENDS.

USE STANDARD GANGWAYED ENDS (BOTH PLAIN) WITH 'SUSPENDED' TYPE CONNECTORS TRAIN ALARM WAS AT END MARKED 'X'.

USE STANDARD 57' WELDED UNDERFRAME WITH 9'0" WELDED BOGIES. BATTERY BOX WAS ON CORRIDOR SIDE.

THIS COACH TYPE DID NOT HAVE BOGIE STEP-BOARDS BUT ASCENDING CORNER STEPS WERE FITTED AS ON BRAKE THIRD.

THIS SIDE ONLY

SOME COACHES HAD EXTRA VENT AT 'C'.

DESTINATION BOARD BRACKETS ON BOTH SIDES

STANDARD 57' WELDED UNDERFRAME, BATTERY BOX ON THIS SIDE

TOP OF UNDERFRAME

STANDARD 9'0" WELDED BOGIE

FAR SIDE

THIS SIDE ONLY

SLATE PAINTED PANELS (BOTH SIDES)

DESTINATION BOARD BRACKETS ON BOTH SIDES

THIS SIDE ONLY

X

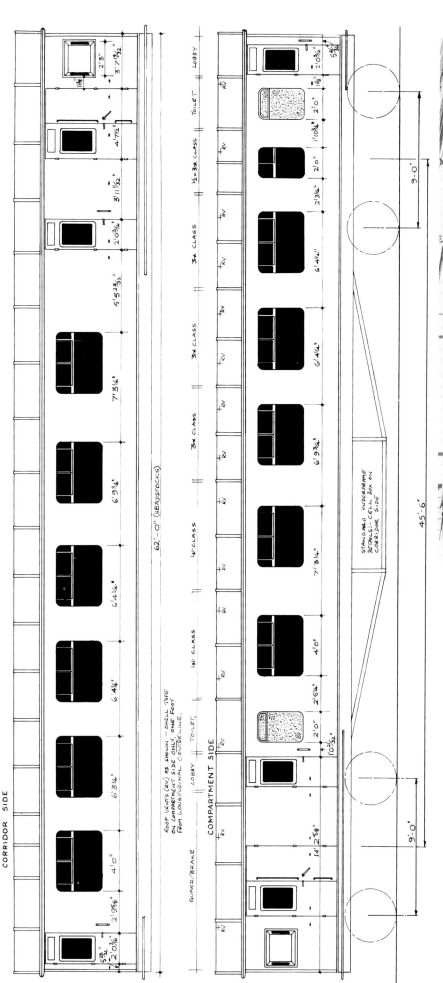

CORRIDOR SIDE

62'-0" (HEADSTOCKS)

ROOF VENTS (RV) AS SHOWN — SHELL TYPE ON COMPARTMENT SIDE ONLY, ONE FOOT FROM LONGITUDINAL CENTRELINE.

COMPARTMENT SIDE

GUARD/BRAKE   LOBBY   TOILET   1ST CLASS   1ST CLASS   3RD CLASS   3RD CLASS   3RD CLASS   ½ x 3RD CLASS   TOILET   LOBBY

STANDARD UNDERFRAME DETAILS:— CELL BOX ON CORRIDOR SIDE

9'-0"

45'-6"

9'-0"

LMS Standard Period III Corridor Stock - IV

Apart from a few 60ft examples between 1932 and 1934 (22 carriages to a layout never repeated in quantity), the popular corridor brake composite type was noticeable by its relative absence during Period III. By 1935, however, the first of a modest series to a new and unique 62ft length had appeared and forms the subject of the drawing on this page. Two diagrams were involved (D1932/2010), differing only in minor internal changes not affecting the external form, and examples were built until 1938, eventually becoming the most common Period III version of this type. They were rather extravagant of space and thereafter, the LMS contented itself with rebuilding older brake composites (see page 22) and no further new examples of any kind appeared after the war. The types shown here lasted until 1965.

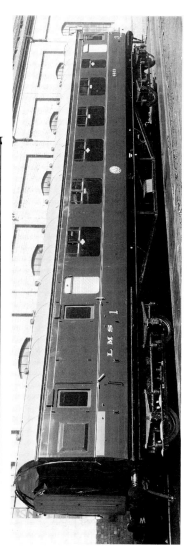

LMS No.6823 to D1932 from the compartment side, brand new ex-Wolverton, 1935

PROTOTYPE DETAILS:

Quantity	Date	Works	Running Numbers
51	1935-6	Wolverton	6806-6856
20	1938	Wolverton	6857-6876 *

LMS Standard Period III Corridor Stock - V

After 1947, BR continued pre-1948 company designs for a short period and this page shows two LMS pattern Period III full firsts built from 1948 to 1950. They were identical save for the circular end windows of the D2162 version: the so-called 'Porthole' style which, for the record, never appeared on *LMS-built* general service stock, though common in the BR continuation of several types not offered in this review.

The main changes were to six full compartments, rather than five plus coupé, two extra doors on the corridor side, elimination of hooded vents over the door droplights (a change later applied to much pre-1948 Period III stock) and the new shorter sliding elements at the tops of the main windows. The two variants came out in LMS simple livery (with no company markings - see picture of No.M1098, appended) and BR crimson/cream respectively, both types becoming extinct in 1965.

PROTOTYPE DETAILS

Diag./Lot	Quantity	Date	Works	Running Numbers
2121/1439	30	1948	Wolverton	1084-1113
2162/1585	15	1950	Wolverton	1114-1128

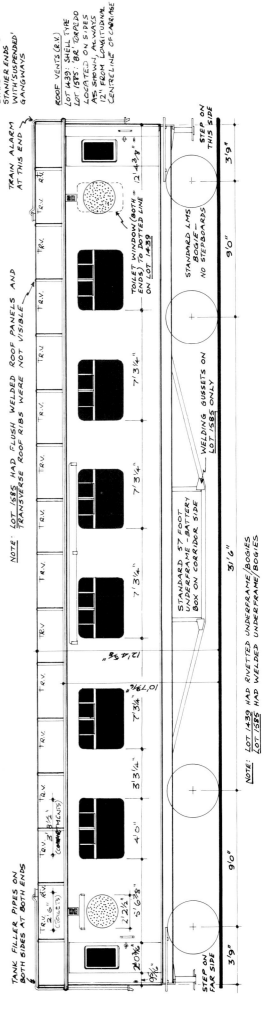

CORRIDOR FIRST (LOTS 1439, 1585) - LOWER ELEVATION SHOWS COMPARTMENT SIDE

NOTE: LOT 1585 HAD FLUSH WELDED ROOF PANELS AND TRANSVERSE ROOF RIBS WERE NOT VISIBLE

NOTE: LOT 1439 HAD RIVETTED UNDERFRAME/BOGIES
LOT 1585 HAD WELDED UNDERFRAME/BOGIES

STANDARD LMS STANIER ENDS WITH 'SUSPENDED' GANGWAYS

ROOF VENTS (R.V.)
LOT 1439: SHELL TYPE
LOT 1585: BR TORPEDO
LOCATED ON SIDES AS SHOWN, ALWAYS 12" FROM LONGITUDINAL CENTRELINE OF CARRIAGE

TRAIN ALARM AT THIS END

OMIT THIS WINDOW (BOTH ENDS) ON LOT 1439

TOILET WINDOW (BOTH ENDS) TO DOTTED LINE ON LOT 1439

STANDARD 57 FOOT UNDERFRAME - BATTERY BOX ON CORRIDOR SIDE

WELDING GUSSETS ON LOT 1585 ONLY

STANDARD LMS BOGIE - NO STEPBOARDS

TANK FILLER PIPES ON BOTH SIDES AT BOTH ENDS

STEP ON FAR SIDE

STEP ON THIS SIDE

LMS Standard Period III Vestibule Stock - I

During the Stanier period, the building of open stock continued to be common, though rather less than during 1923-32. Arthur Whitehead's two drawings on this page show early Period III open designs, one being the Period III version of the ubiquitous 56 seat open third, the other (D1903) being a new type altogether. Although classified 'general service', these new open composites were 36 seaters (seats arranged in 2 + 1 configuration) and generally used for dining. The single seats were on the far side of the carriage (as drawn) and a particularly common 'pairing' was with the 68ft third class kitchen dining cars featured on page 58

PROTOTYPE DETAILS

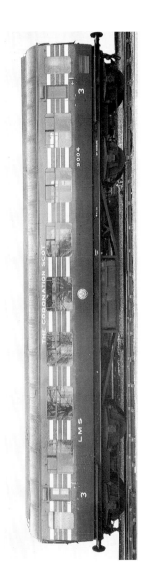

These two views show the full third to D1904 (No.8929) in the original fully lined livery given to Lot 736 (see table), together with the 'Coronation Scot' variant with roof top air duct and special blue/silver livery (No.9004). The remainder of lots 804/5 were given simple livery with red ends.

Lot No.	Quantity	Date	Works	Running Numbers
VESTIBULE THIRD LMS D1904				
736	25	1933	Derby	8905-8929
804	50	1934	Met-Camm	8930-8979 *
805	50	1934	B'ham C&W	8980-9029 *
VESTIBULE COMPOSITE LMS D1903 #				
735	10	1934	Derby	9730-9739
853	10	1934	Derby	9740-9749
1049	4	1938	Wolverton	9750-9753
1101	5	1939	Wolverton	9754-9758

* Nine subsequently converted with 42 seats, luxury finish and blue/silver livery for the 1937 'Coronation Scot' sets viz: 8930/50/61/93/6/9003-4/6/29

\# The full livery shown on the drawing was only given to No.9729, externally identical to the version drawn but to a different diagram

The 36 seat Period III vestibule composites, though relatively few in number by LMS standards, were of considerable significance in LMS days, being almost always regarded as dining carriages - hence the 2+1 seating - and rarely seen in general service. Beginning in 1933 with a shallow window ventilator version with full livery (D1862: LMS 9720-8), easily derived from the drawing offered here by using the vertical window dimensions given for the 1933 vintage sleeping cars featured on page 52, they were followed in 1934 by experimental 'one-off' No.9729 to D1984, generally regarded as having been diverted from the original order for ten D1862 carriages but which, apart from its original full livery (see table), set the external style for the rest of the series. The picture here shows one of the final batches to D1903, No.9751 (as per the drawing) in the standard mid to late-1930s condition: ie simple livery with black ends.

38

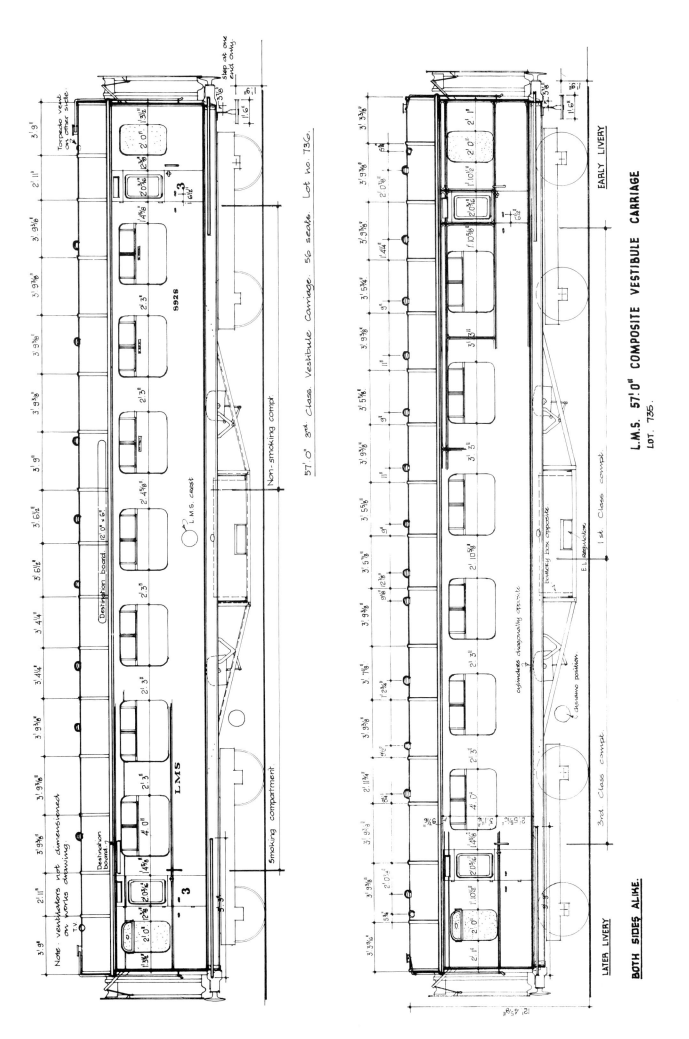

57'.0" 3rd. Class Vestibule Carriage. 56 seats. Lot No. 736.

L.M.S. **57'. 0"** COMPOSITE VESTIBULE CARRIAGE
Lot. 735.

BOTH SIDES ALIKE.

LATER LIVERY

EARLY LIVERY

Note: ventilators not dimensioned on works drawing.

LMS Standard Period III Vestibule Stock - II

The two designs on this page were both first class open carriages, the 65ft version being classified 'dining', though not branded as such. It was one of but three LMS types to have a 65ft underframe, the other two being sleeping cars of which one variety is offered at page 52. There was no difference in the seating layout or passenger space within either of the two versions and many of the 60ft carriages were used for dining should need arise. Lot 734 of the 65ft version had full livery from new and it was the introduction of this type which caused the downgrading of the first class Period II open carriages on page 26. Both types became extinct in 1965.

PROTOTYPE DETAILS

Lot No.	Quantity	Date	Works	Running Numbers
VESTIBULE FIRST LMS D1902 (65ft)				
734	25	1934	Wolverton	7490-7514 *
1187	10	1939	Wolverton	7566-7575
VESTIBULE FIRST LMS D1917 (60ft)				
845	10	1936	Derby	7515-7524
909	14	1936	Wolverton	7525-7538
995	27	1937	Wolverton	7539-7565 #

* Nos.7507-9 modified with 'air conditioning' roof ducts, luxury finish and blue/silver livery for the 1937 'Coronation Scot' sets

\# No.7555 remodelled in 1947 to D2118 with experimental loose seating (individual chairs &c) for dining purposes - also withdrawn in 1965

The three pictures here are almost self explanatory: 65ft full first No.7495 in full livery; 60ft equivalent No.7519 in simple livery and the 'one-off' post-war experimental 60ft No.7555 in the genuine (but rare) 1946 livery - see also page 7

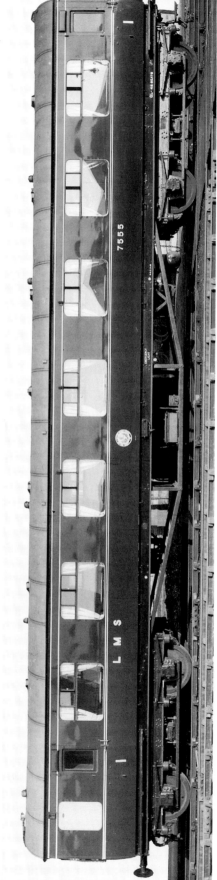

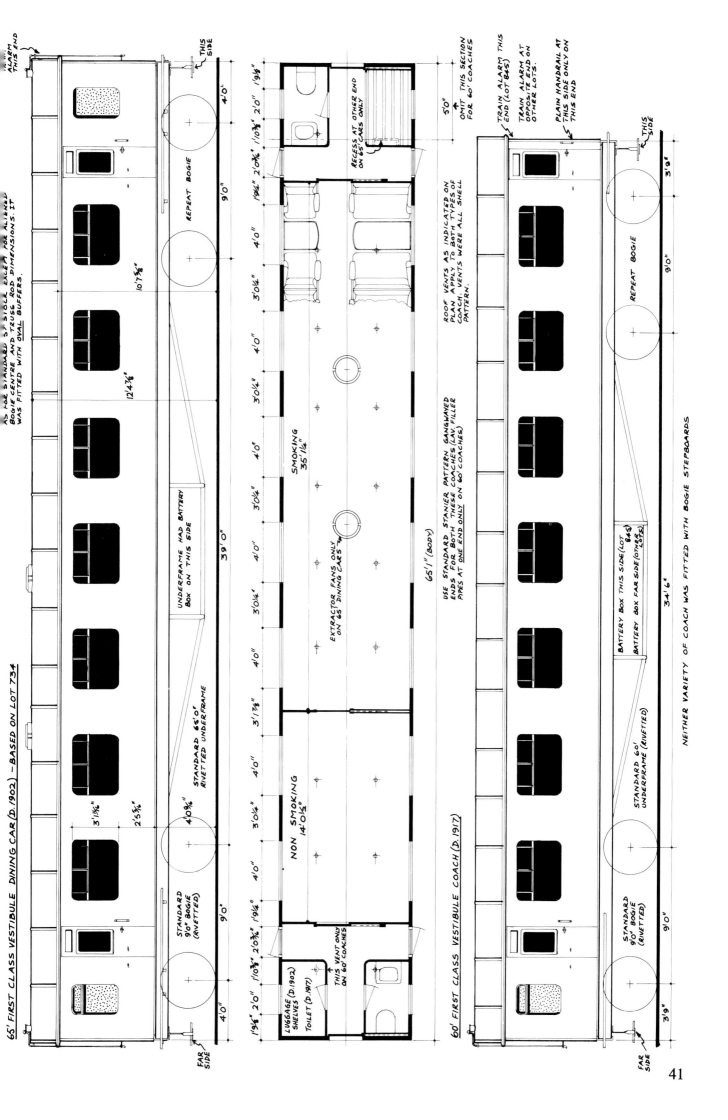

ALARM THIS END

65' FIRST CLASS VESTIBULE DINING CAR (D.1902) — BASED ON LOT 734

AS FOR STANDARD 57 SIDGE EXCEPT FOR ALTERED BOGIE CENTRE AND TRUSS ROD DIMENSIONS. IT WAS FITTED WITH OVAL BUFFERS.

THIS SIDE

REPEAT BOGIE

9'0"

10'7⅝"

124⅞"

3'1½"

2'5⅞"

4'0⅞"

UNDERFRAME HAD BATTERY BOX ON THIS SIDE

STANDARD 65'0" RIVETTED UNDERFRAME

STANDARD 9'0" BOGIE (RIVETTED)

9'0"

4'0"

FAR SIDE

39'0"

5'0"

OMIT THIS SECTION FOR 60' COACHES

RECESS AT OTHER END ON 65' CARS ONLY

1'9¾" 2'0⅜" 1'10¾" 2'0" 4'0" 3'0¼" 4'0" 4'0" 3'0¼" 4'0" 4'0" 3'0¼" 4'0" 4'0" 3'0¼" 4'0" 3'1⅞"

SMOKING 35'1¼"

EXTRACTOR FANS ONLY ON 65' DINING CARS

65'1" (BODY)

NON SMOKING 14'0½"

1'9¾" 2'0" 1'10⅜" 2'0⅜" 1'9¾"

LUGGAGE (D.1902) SHELVES

TOILET (D.1917)

THIS VENT ONLY ON 60' COACHES

ROOF VENTS AS INDICATED ON PLAN APPLY TO BOTH TYPES OF COACH. VENTS WERE ALL SHELL PATTERN.

USE STANDARD STANIER PATTERN GANGWAYED ENDS FOR BOTH THESE COACHES (LAV. FILLER PIPES AT ONE END ONLY ON 60' COACHES)

60' FIRST CLASS VESTIBULE COACH (D.1917)

TRAIN ALARM THIS END (LOT 845)

TRAIN ALARM AT OPPOSITE END ON OTHER LOTS.

PLAIN HANDRAIL AT THIS SIDE ONLY ON THIS END

THIS SIDE

3'9"

REPEAT BOGIE

9'0"

BATTERY BOX THIS SIDE (LOT 845)

BATTERY BOX FAR SIDE (OTHER LOTS)

STANDARD 60' UNDERFRAME (RIVETTED)

34'6"

STANDARD 9'0" BOGIE (RIVETTED)

9'0"

3'9"

FAR SIDE

NEITHER VARIETY OF COACH WAS FITTED WITH BOGIE STEPBOARDS

41

LMS Standard Period III Articulated Stock

The LMS built very many high seating capacity open carriages for excursion use, the majority being 57ft eight-wheelers, but for this review, the articulated version has been selected.

The LMS articulated vehicles are less well known than those on the LNER and nothing like as many were built. They were introduced to save weight and displayed only two basic body styles, arranged in three types of pairing - see plans. They were devised as eleven 10-car sets arranged (BTO+TO)=(TO+TO)=(CO+TO)=(TO+TO)=(TO+BTO) and 'loose' kitchen cars could be inserted between the pairs if desired. In fact, they rarely ran as set trains and could be found in general service on many parts of the system.

The drawings are reasonably self-explanatory but supplementary points are worth making since space does not permit a full set of underframe drawings, though pictures can be offered. Overall height was lower than normal for Period III stock (because of the form of chassis construction) and the eaves panel a trifle deeper than usual. The articulation pivot was a sort of 'male and female' joint above the central bogie pivot, while the solebars (part concealed by the lower body side panels) were cantilevered from the two longitudinal centre trusses. The battery boxes and regulators were suspended directly from the floor of the carriages on fairly rudimentary brackets set outside the central trusses and positioned opposite the central portion of truss - ie off-centre in relation to the whole body length. To save the cost of a new body design, the first class sections, uniquely for any form of LMS standard gangwayed stock, were the same length as the thirds.

The sets were built at Derby in 1937, running numbers are given with the plan views and all were extinct early in 1965.

Underframe arrangement of the LMS articulated stock, showing the central trussing (with lateral extensions) and the articulation pivot

Close-up view of the 'join' between the two elements, showing the close-coupled arrangement.

The first articulated 'twin composite', Nos. 55000/1. The third class version was externally identical save for the 2+2 seating (see plans) and lack of window curtains at the far end.....

42

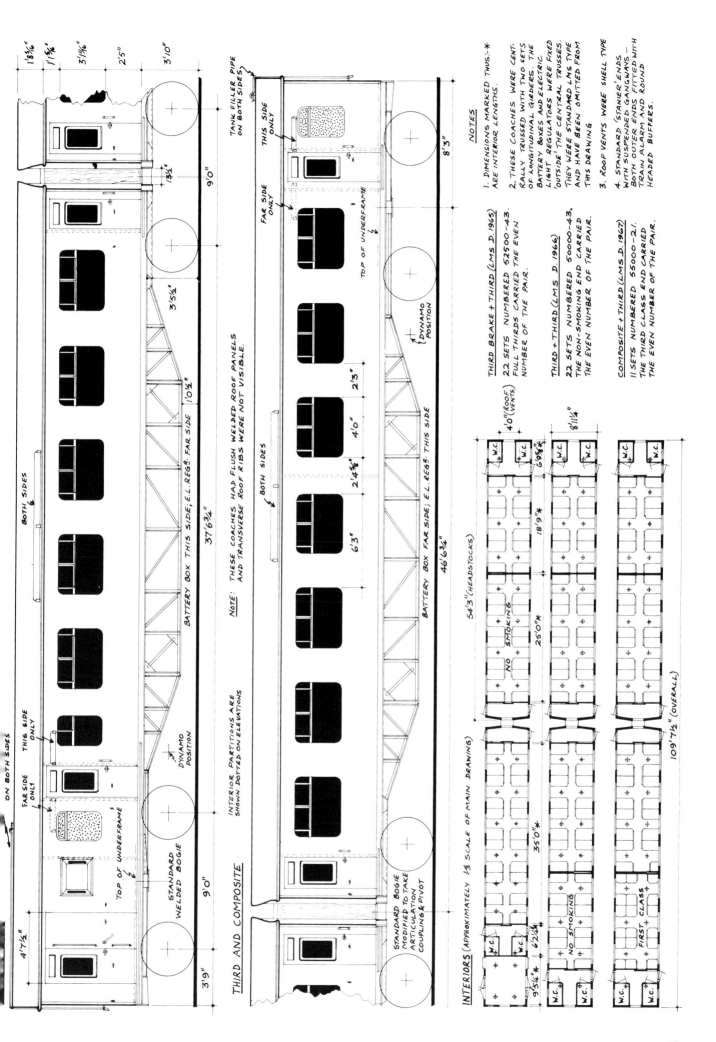

BOTH SIDES

THIS SIDE
ONLY

FAR SIDE
ONLY

4'-1½"

ON BOTH SIDES

18⅝"
11⅝"
3 11/16"
2'5"
3'10"

TANK FILLER PIPE
ON BOTH SIDES

THIS SIDE
ONLY

FAR SIDE
ONLY

TOP OF UNDERFRAME

9'0"

13½"

9'0"

3'5½"

DYNAMO
POSITION

STANDARD
WELDED BOGIE

STANDARD BOGIE
MODIFIED TO TAKE
ARTICULATION
COUPLING & PIVOT

3'9"

TOP OF UNDERFRAME

TOP OF UNDERFRAME

8'3"

DYNAMO
POSITION

BATTERY BOX THIS SIDE; E.L. REGS. FAR SIDE

BATTERY BOX FAR SIDE; E.L. REGS. THIS SIDE

37'6¾"

46'6¾"

NOTE: THESE COACHES HAD FLUSH WELDED ROOF PANELS
AND TRANSVERSE ROOF RIBS WERE NOT VISIBLE.

INTERIOR PARTITIONS ARE
SHOWN DOTTED ON ELEVATIONS

10½"

2'3"

4'0"

2'4⅝"

6'3"

THIRD AND COMPOSITE

NOTES

1. DIMENSIONS MARKED THUS:- *
ARE INTERIOR LENGTHS.

2. THESE COACHES WERE CENT-
RALLY TRUSSED WITH TWO SETS
OF LONGITUDINAL GIRDERS. THE
BATTERY BOXES AND ELECTRIC
LIGHT REGULATORS WERE FIXED
OUTSIDE' THE CENTRAL TRUSSES.
THEY WERE STANDARD LMS TYPE
AND HAVE BEEN OMITTED FROM
THIS DRAWING

3. ROOF VENTS WERE SHELL TYPE

4. STANDARD (STANIER) ENDS
WITH SUSPENDED GANGWAYS —
BOTH OUTER ENDS FITTED WITH
TRAIN ALARM AND ROUND
HEADED BUFFERS.

THIRD BRAKE + THIRD (LMS. D. 1965)

22 SETS NUMBERED 52500-43.
FULL THIRDS CARRIED THE EVEN
NUMBER OF THE PAIR.

THIRD + THIRD (LMS. D. 1966)

22 SETS NUMBERED 50000-43.
THE NON-SMOKING END CARRIED
THE EVEN NUMBER OF THE PAIR.

COMPOSITE + THIRD (LMS. D. 1967)

11 SETS NUMBERED 55000-21.
THE THIRD CLASS END CARRIED
THE EVEN NUMBER OF THE PAIR.

INTERIORS (APPROXIMATELY ⅓ SCALE OF MAIN DRAWING)

W.C.

4'0" (ROOF VENTS)

6'9⅝"

8'1¼"

18'9"

25'0" *

NO SMOKING

54'3" (HEADSTOCKS)

35'0" *

NO SMOKING

6'2¼"

9'3¼" *

FIRST CLASS

109'7½" (OVERALL)

43

LMS Standard Period I First Class Sleeping Car

Early LMS Sleeping Cars mostly followed traditional LNWR 12-wheel styling, but comparison of this drawing with the pre-group 12-wheelers on pages 86-93 reveals that vertical panel dimensions were changed - especially the waist panel. Two very similar designs were produced of which the drawing represents the later and far more common version to LMS Diagram 1705, all built at Wolverton. The two examples built in 1927 for M&NB Joint Stock use (ie before its division between LMS and LNER in 1928), both came to the LMS in due course. Panel end detail was not standard so an end elevation has been included. The underframe itself was orthodox but the positioning of some ancillary detail varied from normal and is shown on the drawing. They became extinct late in 1962.

M&NB No.2 was one of two examples built to D1705 in 1927 for the Midland main line services to Edinburgh via the Settle & Carlisle line. After 1928, it went into LMS stock as No.4031, later No.321

PROTOTYPE DETAILS

Lot	Quantity	Date	First LMS Numbers	Final LMS Numbers #
146	10	1925	2768-2777	310-319
297	10	1927	2785; 10371-7; 10381-2	322-331
341	2	1927	2778; 4031	320-321 *
381	5	1928	10367-8; 10378-80	337-341
401	5	1928	8412-6	332-336
441	5	1929	3792-3; 4087; 4090; 8420	342-346
489	4	1929	2766; 10355; 10369-70	348-351
521	1	1930	8406	347

\# For some unknown reason, the 1933 LMS running numbers were not always allocated in strict Lot Number sequence

* M&NB Nos.1/2 until 1928

During the building of D1705, a slight simplification in panelling took place - see notes on drawings. These two views show both the corridor and compartment sides respectively of this variation in the shape of No.10370 (later No.351) and No.3792 (later No.342), both built in 1929. Between the two, the LMS had changed from the first to the second type of numerical insignia (page 6)

LMS STANDARD FIRST CLASS
SLEEPING CAR :— 1925-30

UPPER ELEVATION BASED ON LOT 489
LOWER ELEVATION BASED ON LOT 341

THERE WAS A SLIGHT CHANGE OF STYLING DURING THE BUILDING OF THESE CARS. EARLY LOTS HAD DOUBLE PANELS BETWEEN WINDOWS AS ON LOWER ELEVATION. LATER LOTS HAD SINGLE PANELS OF DOUBLE WIDTH AS ON UPPER ELEVATION. THE CHANGE WAS PROBABLY INTRODUCED ON LOT 381.

TRAIN ALARM AT THIS END

END STEPS AT THIS END

NOTE: WINDOWS TO COMPARTMENTS WERE FRAMELESS DROPLIGHTS

68' 1" (BODY)

STANDARD 12'6" BOGIE

REPEAT BOGIE

UNDERFRAME HAD BATTERY BOX ON FAR SIDE

VAC. RESRS, 2'3" FROM ℄

E.I. REG. (FAR SIDE) ALSO DIAGONALLY OPPOSITE

VAC. CYL.

DYNAMO POSITION

32'6"

5'3"   6'3"   6'3"   6'3"

6'3"   6'10"   6'10"   6'10"

2'0"   6'3"   4'10½"   2'0¾"   3'11⅝"   5'3"

END ELEVATION (SEE NOTE BELOW)

12' 4¾"
10' 7½"
4' 10½"
8' 10¼"

8'4"
9'0"
9'3"

OPPOSITE END TO ELEVATION DRAWN HAD SHORT HANDRAILS EITHER SIDE, NO END STEPS AND WAS FITTED WITH TRAIN ALARM WARNING APPARATUS.

9' 0"

20¾"   5⅝"
2'5"   2'0"   11½"   2'5⅞"
6'10⅛"
4'10"
2'0 6"
6'10"
2'0"   10"   2'0"
9'4¾"
4'6¾"
4'10"
2'4⅝"
5'11 9/16"

28'2¼"

FOUR BERTHS MORE IN THE OMITTED SECTION-ARRANGED IN INTERCONNECTING PAIRS.

ROOF VENT POSITIONS (MARKED ON PLAN WITH SMALL CIRCLES) ARE BASED ON PHOTOGRAPHS.

MIRROR

HINGED FLAPS

VENTILATING UNIT

W.C.

DIMENSIONS GIVEN ON PLAN HAVE BEEN OBTAINED BY MEASUREMENT AND CALCULATION OF VALUES FROM ORIGINAL DRAWING WHICH WAS NOT FULLY DIMENSIONED.

LMS Standard Period I Third Class Sleeping Car

Third class sleeping cars were introduced to Britain in 1928 and the drawing represents the first LMS examples which, *inter alia*, also introduced the 60ft carriage length to the LMS. They were the most numerous LMS sleeping car type and very like an orthodox corridor third. Being fully convertible for day use, they were never branded SLEEPING CAR on the side. All were built to D1709, Lot 579 coming out during Period II after the change to steel panels but with the older high waist - see appended view. An example of Lot 418 is preserved at the NRM as LMS No.14241 and the type ran in service until mid-1961.

PROTOTYPE DETAILS

Lot No.	Quantity	Date	Works	Running Numbers
418	25	1928	Derby	500-524
428	25	1928/9	Derby	525-549
469	25	1929	Derby	550-574
579	10	1931	Derby	575-584 *

* Steel panelled with high waist - see text/picture

Pre-1933 numbers:
Lot 418: 14225-14249; **Lot 428:** 14419-14443
Lot 469 (samples): 846-7; 1815-6; 10651; **Lot 579 (samples):** 8615-21

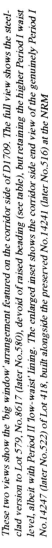

Compartment side view of No.14229 (later No.504), one of the earlier examples to D1709 at Euston c.1929. It is perhaps worth noting that these carriages were the only LMS types to retain the traditional 'three window' compartment arrangement after the elimination of individual outside compartment doors

These two views show the 'big window' arrangement featured on the corridor side of D1709. The full view shows the steel-clad version to Lot 579, No.8617 (later No.580), devoid of raised beading (see table), but retaining the higher Period I waist level, albeit with Period II 'low-waist' lining. The enlarged inset shows the corridor side end view of the genuinely Period I No.14241 (later No.516) at the NRM. No.14247 (later No.522) of Lot 418, built alongside the preserved No.14241 (later No.516) at the NRM

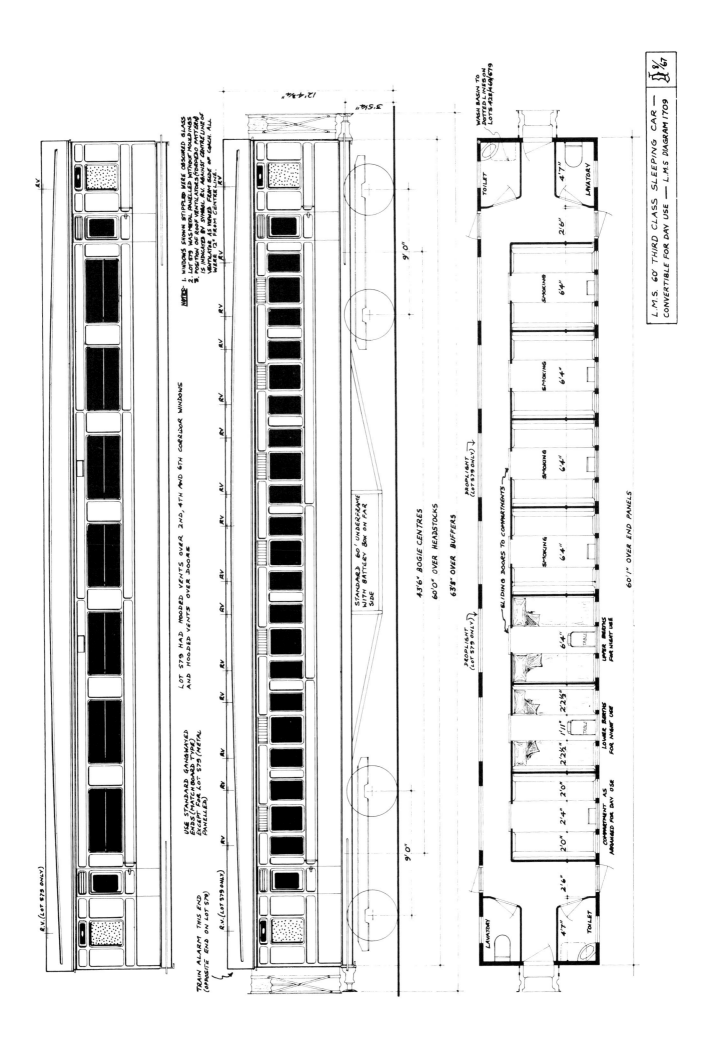

L.M.S. 60' THIRD CLASS SLEEPING CAR —
CONVERTIBLE FOR DAY USE — L.M.S DIAGRAM 1709

8/67

47

These two ex-works official views show both sides of the first example of D1781 to be built, No.10548, later No.700. Note how the fully lined LMS livery tends to reflect the essentially 'LNWR' style of the carriage

LMS Standard Period II Composite Sleeping Car

This design (LMS Diagram 1781 and all built at Wolverton) was quite unique and is shown in full on this very detailed drawing by Arthur Whitehead. Internally, it combined the features of the first class sleeping cars (page 44) with the convertible third class compartments of D1709 (page 46), while externally, the LMS came up with a sort of up-dated 'LNWR' styling, quite unlike anything else which ever appeared during 1923-47 and whose attractively 'modern' appearance is well seen on the accompanying views - note that even fixed lights did not have wooden bolection mouldings. During the mid-1930s (probably at first full overhaul), the third class was altered to fixed berth (after the style of the Period III thirds on page 52), an extra toilet (for first class use) being inserted between the first and third class sections, replacing the two third class berths immediately to the left of the first class as seen from the compartment side and thus reducing the third class to three full compartments plus a twin-berth coupé.

The ends were non-standard, but in order to show the full interior, the end elevation has been transferred to page 11. The underframe was generally as for the first class sleeping cars (page 44) and the cars ran in their modified form until late 1963

PROTOTYPE DETAILS

Lot	Quantity	Date	First LMS Numbers	Final LMS Numbers
543	6	1930	10548-51; 10555-6	700-705
571	6	1931	10558-9; 10636-9	706-711

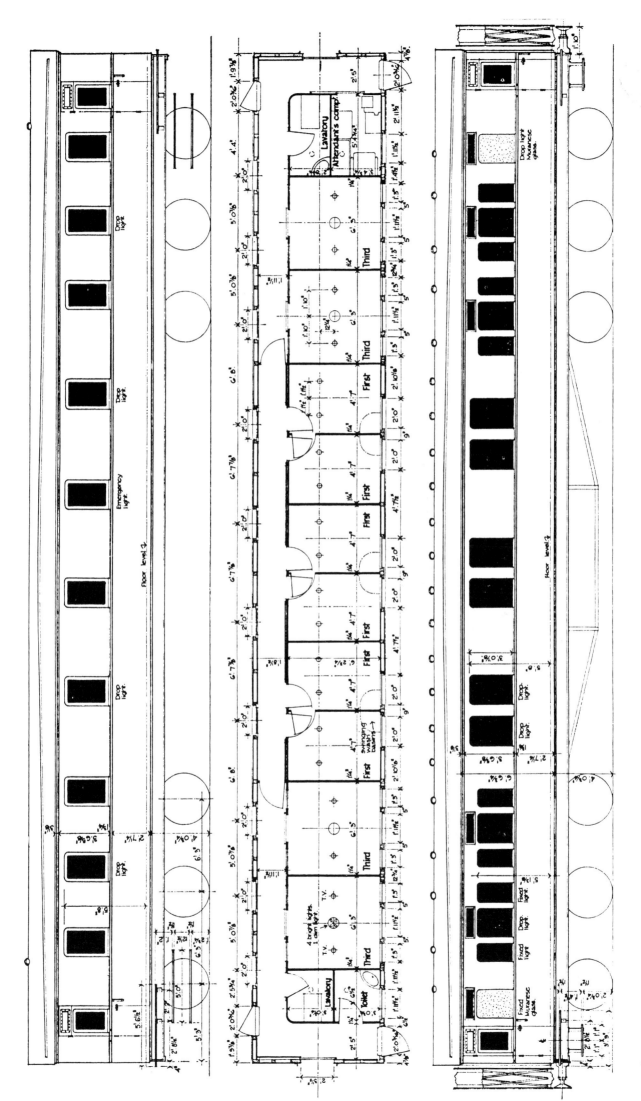

49

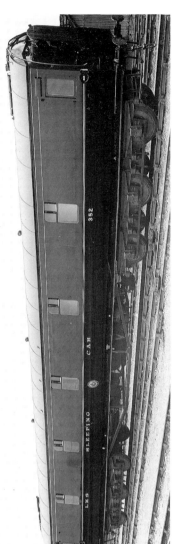

LMS Standard Period III First Class Sleeping Car

This was the final style of LMS first class sleeping car, first built in 1935/6 but repeated by BR with very few changes as late as 1951/2. It was to a new 69ft length and the drawing shows the 1935 version. For model purposes, a near-correct version of the BR-built cars could be made by omitting the hinged ventilators over the toilet window and fitting a dummy air-conditioning duct along the roof. For this reason, details of both versions are given in the summary. Most of the pre-war cars had gone by the end of 1966 (No.376 was a late survivor because of the premature accident withdrawal of No.397) but the later examples mostly lasted to receive BR blue/grey livery and ran until the 1970s. The cars were wider than the usual Period III types and had recessed door handles, mainly to allow a slight increase in berth length - see plan view - and for this reason the non-standard end elevation is given.

These three official views show (above) both sides of the first example to D1926, No.352 and (below) the compartment side of D2166, No.M386, all three taken when brand new. The BR red/cream livery (applied from new to D2166) has the interesting side-effect of making the differences between the two varieties seem greater than was, in fact, the case

PROTOTYPE DETAILS

Lot No.	Quantity	Date	Works	Running Numbers
FIRST CLASS SLEEPING CAR LMS D1926 (as drawn)				
876	20	1935/6	Wolverton	352-371
935	6	1935	Wolverton	372-377 *
FIRST CLASS SLEEPING CAR LMS series D2166				
1570	5	1951	Wolverton	378-382
1584	20	1951/2	Wolverton	383-402

* Car 377 refurbished and painted crimson/gold for 'Coronation Scot' visit to USA in 1937

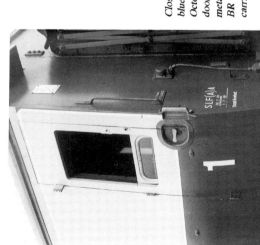

Close-up detail of M387M in BR blue-grey livery at Wolverton in October 1968, showing the recessed door handle and the replacement metal-framed droplight - a common BR alteration to many Period III carriages (D.Jenkinson)

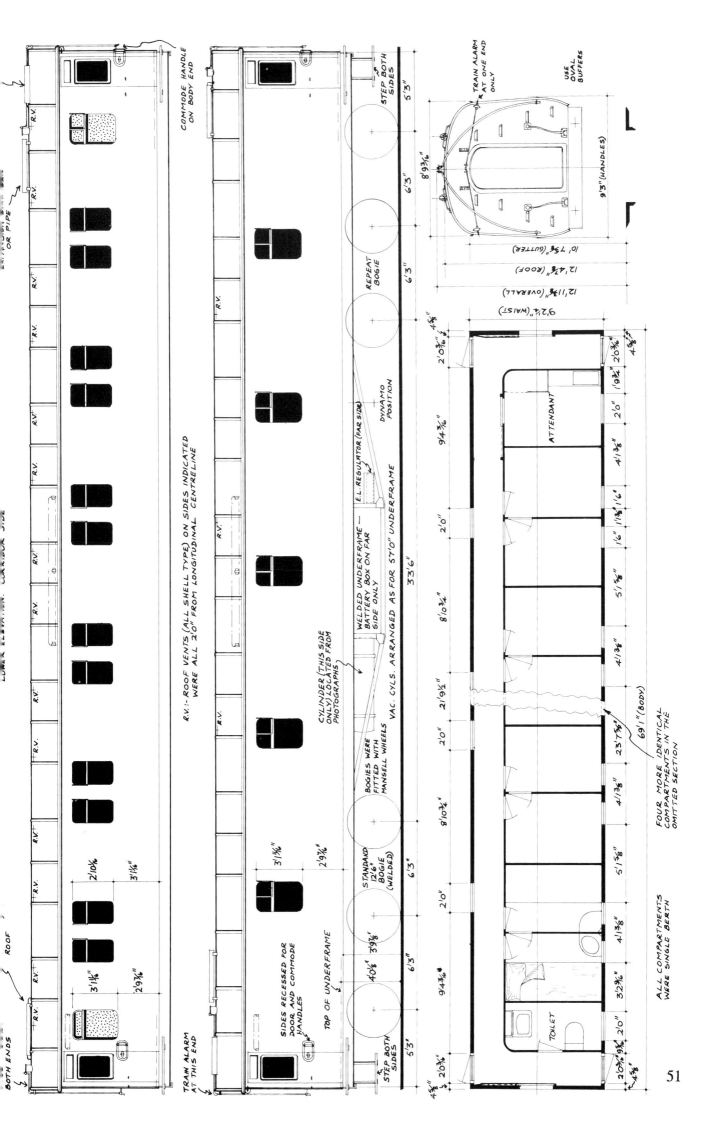

ROOF

ENTRANCE ↓ PIPE
OR PIPE

R.V.
R.V.

BOTH ENDS

R.V. R.V. R.V. R.V. R.V. R.V. R.V. R.V. R.V. R.V.

3'1¼"
2'9¾"

2'10⅜"
3'1¼"

COMMODE HANDLE
ON BODY END

TRAIN ALARM
AT THIS END

R.V.: ROOF VENTS (ALL SHELL TYPE) ON SIDES INDICATED
WERE ALL 2'0" FROM LONGITUDINAL CENTRELINE

R.V. R.V. R.V.

3'1¼"

2'9¾"

SIDES RECESSED FOR
DOOR AND COMMODE
HANDLES

TOP OF UNDERFRAME

STEP BOTH
SIDES

CYLINDER (THIS SIDE
ONLY) LOCATED FROM
PHOTOGRAPHS

WELDED UNDERFRAME —
BATTERY BOX ON FAR
SIDE ONLY

VAC. CYLS. ARRANGED AS FOR 57'0" UNDERFRAME

E.L. REGULATOR (FAR SIDE)

DYNAMO
POSITION

BOGIES WERE
FITTED WITH
MANSELL WHEELS

40⅛" 3'9⅜"

STANDARD
12'6"
BOGIE
(WELDED)

5'3"   6'3"   6'3"   6'3"   33'6"   6'3"   6'3"   5'3"

REPEAT
BOGIE

STEP BOTH
SIDES

TRAIN ALARM
AT ONE END
ONLY

USE
OVAL
BUFFERS

8'9³⁄₁₆"

9'3" (HANDLES)

10'7⅝" (GUTTER)

12'4⅞" (ROOF)

12'11⅞" (OVERALL)

9'2¼" (WAIST)

4⅝" 2'0³⁄₁₆" 2'0³⁄₁₆" 1'9¼"
9'4³⁄₁₆" 2'0" 4'1⅞" 1'6" 1'1⅞" 1'6" 5'1⅝" 4'1⅜"

8'10¾" 2'0" 21'9½" 2'0" 23'5⅝"

4'1⅜" 8'10¾" 5'1⅝" 2'0" 9'4³⁄₁₆" 3'2³⁄₁₆" 2'0"

69'1" (BODY)

4⅝" 2'0³⁄₁₆" 2'0³⁄₁₆" 9¾"

ATTENDANT

TOILET

ALL COMPARTMENTS
WERE SINGLE BERTH

FOUR MORE IDENTICAL
COMPARTMENTS IN THE
OMITTED SECTION

51

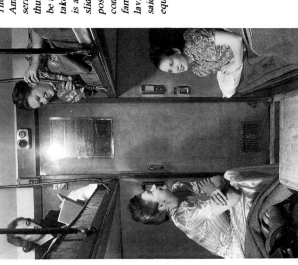

The prototype D1863 third class sleeping car car was sent to North America with the 'Royal Scot' tour train in 1933 and given a 1933 series running number in older style 'stretched' numerals. All carriages thus involved were similarly finished and were the only LMS types to be thus treated as far as is known. That apart, this superb view can be taken as definitive for the full livery on Period III gangwayed stock. It is also useful, along with the drawing, in showing the shallow depth sliding ventilators used on pre-1934 period III stock. The typically posed interior view with its delighful 'period' flavour (single sex compartment occupation was 'de rigeur' in these carriages except for family groups!), shows the somewhat spartan interior; yet this was lavish provisioning for third class at the time and the Americans are said to have been amazed at the contrast between this car and their equivalent 'coach' class accommodation

LMS Standard Period III Third Class Sleeping Car

These handsome cars were an early product of the new Stanier thinking and were the first LMS design to use the eight-wheel 65ft underframe. They also displayed the shallow depth sliding ventilators at the window top which gave way to the deeper type on carriages built from 1934. Fixed berth from the start, they were always branded SLEEPING CAR and enjoyed the services of a full time attendant. The corridor side was fitted with external ventilator 'scoops' so as to force fresh air into the interior: the nearest thing to air conditioning in those days. All told, given the date of building, they were distinctly up-market for a third class carriage. Built to D1863, they lasted until the end of 1963

PROTOTYPE DETAILS

Lot No.	Quantity	Date	Works	Running Numbers
699	15	1933	Derby	585-599

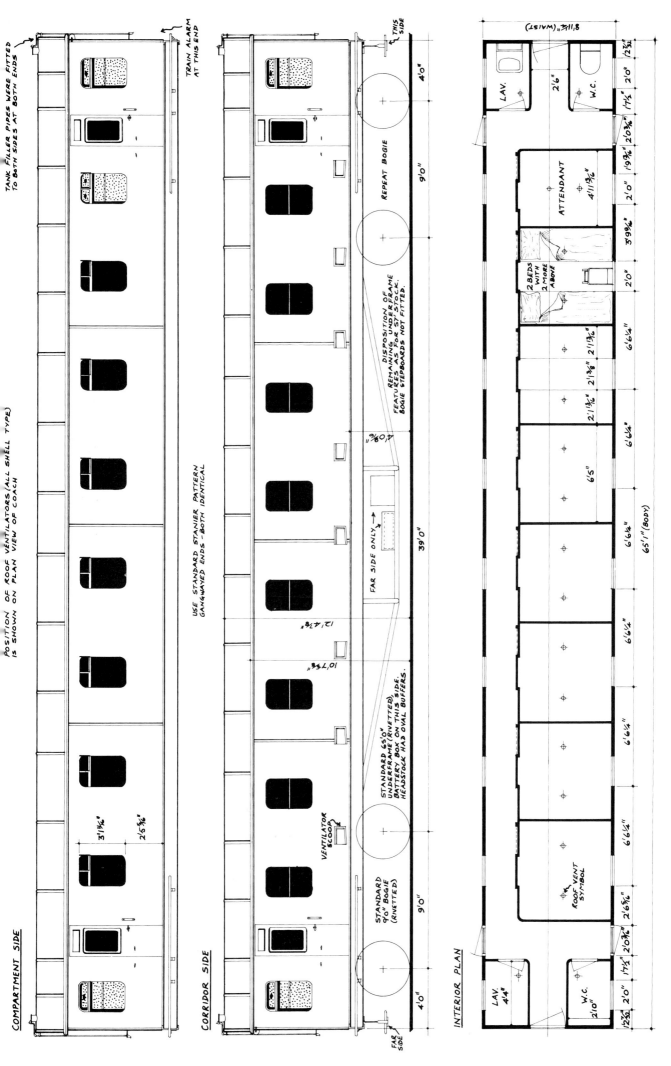

COMPARTMENT SIDE

TANK FILLER PIPES WERE FITTED TO BOTH SIDES AT BOTH ENDS

TRAIN ALARM AT THIS END

POSITION OF ROOF VENTILATORS (ALL SHELL TYPE) IS SHOWN ON PLAN VIEW OF COACH

3'1½"

2'5⅜"

CORRIDOR SIDE

USE STANDARD STANIER PATTERN GANGWAYED ENDS – BOTH IDENTICAL

THIS SIDE

REPEAT BOGIE

DISPOSITION OF REMAINING UNDERFRAME FEATURES AS FOR 57' STOCK. BOGIE STEPBOARDS NOT FITTED.

4'0"

9'0"

39'0"

FAR SIDE ONLY

4'0⅝"

STANDARD 65'0" UNDERFRAME (RIVETTED). BATTERY BOX ON THIS SIDE. HEADSTOCK HAD OVAL BUFFERS.

12'4⅞"

10'7⅝"

VENTILATOR SCOOP

STANDARD 9'0" BOGIE (RIVETTED)

9'0"

4'0"

FAR SIDE

INTERIOR PLAN

8'11½" (WAIST)

LAV.

2'6"

W.C.

1'2¾"

2'0"

1'7½"

2'0¾"

1'9¾"

2'0"

ATTENDANT 4'11⅜"

3'9¾"

2 BEDS WITH 2 MORE ABOVE

2'0"

6'6¼"

2'11⅝"

2'1⅜"

2'1⅞"

6'6¼"

6'5"

6'6¼"

6'6¼"

65'1" (BODY)

6'6¼"

6'6¼"

ROOF VENT SYMBOL

2'6¾"

2'0¾"

1'7½"

2'0"

1'2¾"

LAV. 4'4"

W.C. 2'0"

53

LMS Standard Period II Dining Cars

The LMS, well served by its pre-group inheritance, did not build many kitchen/dining cars until 1930-32 when the two designs featured on this and the next double page spread were put into service. Closely related in style and amenity, both types are described in a single narrative so as to allow more space for pictures.

Two basic types were built, 24 first class (drawing opposite) and 12 composite (drawing on page 57), though the latter were regarded as 'neutral' (ie either class) and did not carry class figures on the doors, having detachable 'class boards' for the windows when needed. Typical Period II (steel panelled) types, their nature should be apparent from the drawings, which are mostly self-explanatory.

Confusingly, the first class series came out to two diagrams in the later of which, some minor internal dimensional changes were made. Unfortunately, the LMS (normally quite meticulous) wrongly inserted six of the *first* type (Lot 525) onto the later modified diagram (D1810), so it needs to be pointed out that the drawing opposite shows *the first 18 cars* (all built at Derby) and the modifications only applied to Lot 616 (Wolverton-built), which variation can be derived by reducing the pantry lengths to 5ft 9in in both cases and adding the whole extra length to the toilet and luggage shelf area. The 1933 numbers reflect this difference - see summary - and it may be that the later diagram was issued to Wolverton only. There were also livery variations between the varieties as built, which may also have reflected the two carriage works and which the appended views serve to resolve.

All 36 carriages were withdrawn between 1959 and 1962.

First class 68ft dining car No.2592 (later No.4) when new in 1930, taken from the kitchen side. This view shows the first style of full livery (with lining at the window edges) adopted for these cars and is believed to have been used on all 18 of the Derby-built examples. The later form of full livery is given on page 56.

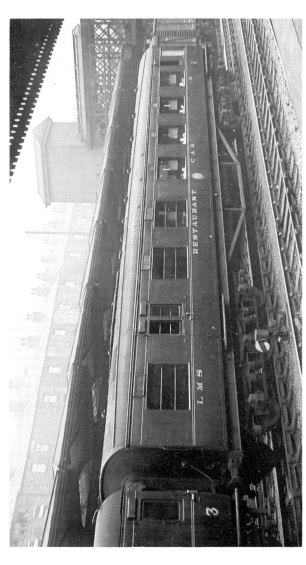

LMS No.14 (formerly No.10435) at Sheffield Midland in July 1948, taken from the corridor side. The livery is of simple style, but note some post-war changes - see also page 7. The branding is now 'RESTAURANT CAR' and there are large '1s' on the passenger windows, but the insignia is traditional. The base colour could be either crimson lake or the fairly newly introduced darker maroon shade; the probability is the former, given the insignia style (The late H.C.Casserley)

PROTOTYPE DETAILS

Lot No.	Quantity	Date	Works	Running Numbers
FIRST CLASS DINING CAR LMS D1718				
478	12	1930	Derby	4-7, 11-18
FIRST CLASS DINING CAR LMS D1810				
525	6	1930	Derby	1-3, 8-10 *
616	6	1932	Wolverton	19-24 #
COMPOSITE DINING CAR LMS D1811				
617	12	1932	Derby	228-239

* Identical in style and dimension to D1718 and probably on wrong diagram - see text
# With different internal dimensions and original livery - see text/pictures

Sample pre-1933 numbers:
Lot 478: 3128-9; 10432-5; 15333-5. Lot 525: 2557-8/91; 10413-5. Lot 616: 1864-5; 2074-7. Lot 617: 2082-3; 10436-41

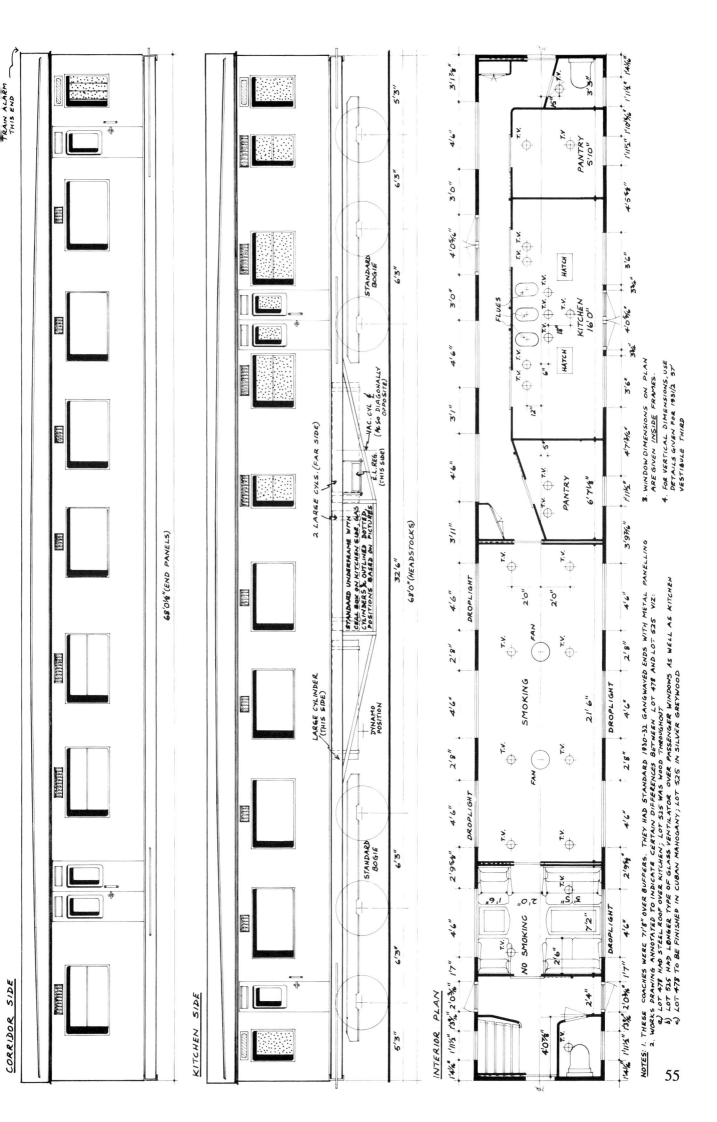

NOTES: 1. THESE COACHES WERE 7⅛" OVER BUFFERS. THEY HAD STANDARD 1930-32 GANGWAYED ENDS WITH METAL PANELLING
2. WORKS DRAWING ANNOTATED TO INDICATE CERTAIN DIFFERENCES BETWEEN LOT 478 AND LOT 525 VIZ:
   a) LOT 478 HAD STEEL ROOF OVER KITCHEN; LOT 525 WAS WOOD THROUGHOUT
   b) LOT 525 HAD LONGER TYPE OF GLASS VENTILATOR OVER PASSENGER WINDOWS AS WELL AS KITCHEN
   c) LOT 478 TO BE FINISHED IN CUBAN MAHOGANY; LOT 525 IN SILVER GREYWOOD
3. WINDOW DIMENSIONS ON PLAN ARE GIVEN *INSIDE* FRAMES.
4. FOR VERTICAL DIMENSIONS, USE DETAILS GIVEN FOR 1931/2 57' VESTIBULE THIRD

55

The first two pictures show both sides of the genuine D1810 first class cars Nos.1864 (later No.19) and 2074 (later No.21), both built at Wolverton in 1932 with somewhat larger luggage/lavatory space - see text page 54. Note also the slightly different livery style with a somewhat more modern 'between window' vertical lining arrangement. This may have been a 'Wolverton' variation (Derby kept the older style during the same year - below left), but was later adopted universally for the Period III stock which was given full livery during 1932-4

The next views show both sides of the composite dining cars to D1811 built in 1932. No.10440 (later No.238) shows the original LMS style with detachable class boards in the windows and full livery with 'window-edge' lining - see above. No.M234M, photographed at Euston c.1960, shows the type in BR maroon livery, with the first class end clearly and permanently marked as such with the blue BR 'sausage' emblem. There appear to have been some few changes in the position and numbers of roof ventilators at the kitchen end compared with the drawing and No.10440, but more exact information is unavailable (Martin S, Welch - 1)

1. UPPER ELEVATION SHOWS KITCHEN SIDE, LOWER ELEVATION
   . CORRIDOR SIDE OF CAR. DINING SEATS BEING ARRANGED
   CONVENTIONALLY (ie 2-1). SINGLE SEATS ON THE CORRIDOR
   SIDE. TOTAL SEATS: 12F + 18T

2. WINDOW DIMENSIONS ARE GIVEN TO OUTSIDE OF WINDOW
   FRAMES, GLAZED AREA BEING 2½in LESS IN HEIGHT/WIDTH. ALL
   FIXED LIGHTS HAD RAISED MAHOGANY BEADING, THE SO-
   CALLED 'FRAMELESS DROPLIGHTS' (MARKED ON DRAWING)
   HAVING NEAR-FLUSH ALUMINIUM BEADING.

3. LENGTH OF CARS OVER END PANELS WAS 68ft 1in, THE EXTRA
   3/16in BEING TAKEN UP BY STRENGTHENING CORNER ANGLES

4. ROOF VENTILATORS WERE ALL TORPEDO PATTERN

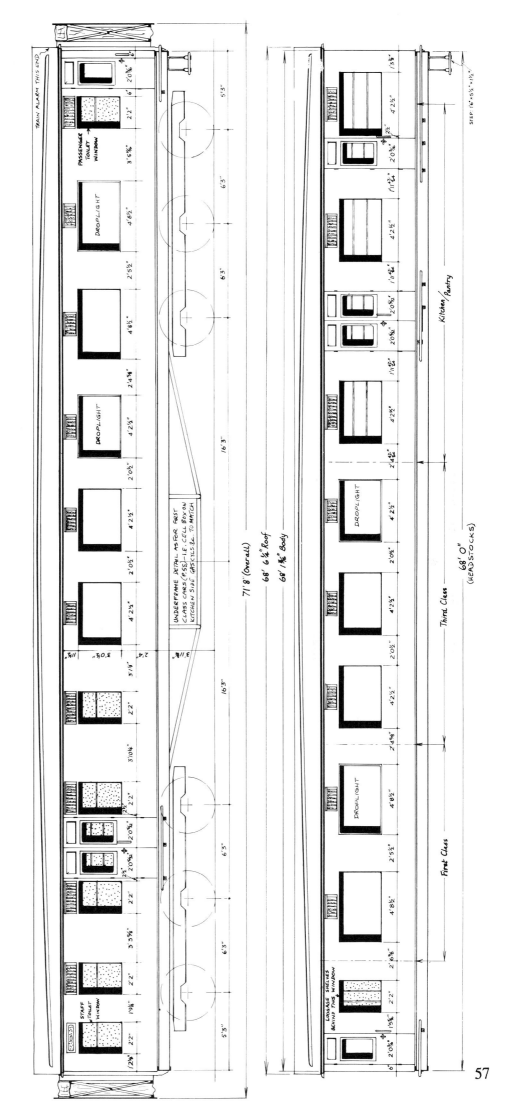

ARRANGEMENT OF VENTILATORS &c. (½ scale)

LMS Standard Period III Third Class Dining Car

This was the most numerous LMS 12-wheel dining car type, several lots being built to two diagrams (D1901 and D1923), the only real difference being the rounded interior partion corners on D1923. Prior to this, ten all but identical cars were built to D1861 with full livery and shallow sliding ventilators with one central moving element. The depth of this shallow ventilator can be taken from the third class sleeping cars (page 53) and with this variation, the earlier cars can be deduced; details are therefore appended. These cars were most often paired with open composites as given on page 38. Finally, the works drawing used for this page (D1923) lacks underframe and roof details which have, in consequence, been located from photographs and cannot therefore be 100% dimensionally guaranteed. The cars became extinct during the 1960s, viz: D1861 - 1962; D1901 - 1963; D1923 - 1964

PROTOTYPE DETAILS

Lot No.	Quantity	Date	Works	Running Numbers
LMS D1861 (shallow depth window top ventilators)				
685	10	1933	Derby	101-110 * §
LMS D1901 #				
733	10	1933	Derby	111-120
LMS D1923 (as per drawing)				
852	10	1935	Derby	121-130
903	4	1936	Derby	135-138 §
1034	10	1937	Derby	139-148

* No.105 later converted to Buffet Car by BR

As per D1923 except for minor details - see drawing

§ Missing numbers (100, 131-4) were 57ft Buffet Cars - not featured in this survey

The three types of dining car covered on this page are shown here, top to bottom:

a)   D1861 No.102 in full livery, view taken at the passenger end from the kitchen side

b)   D1901 No.118 in simplified livery, from a near-identical position

c)   D1923 No.142 in simplified livery, taken from the opposite end, and from the corridor side

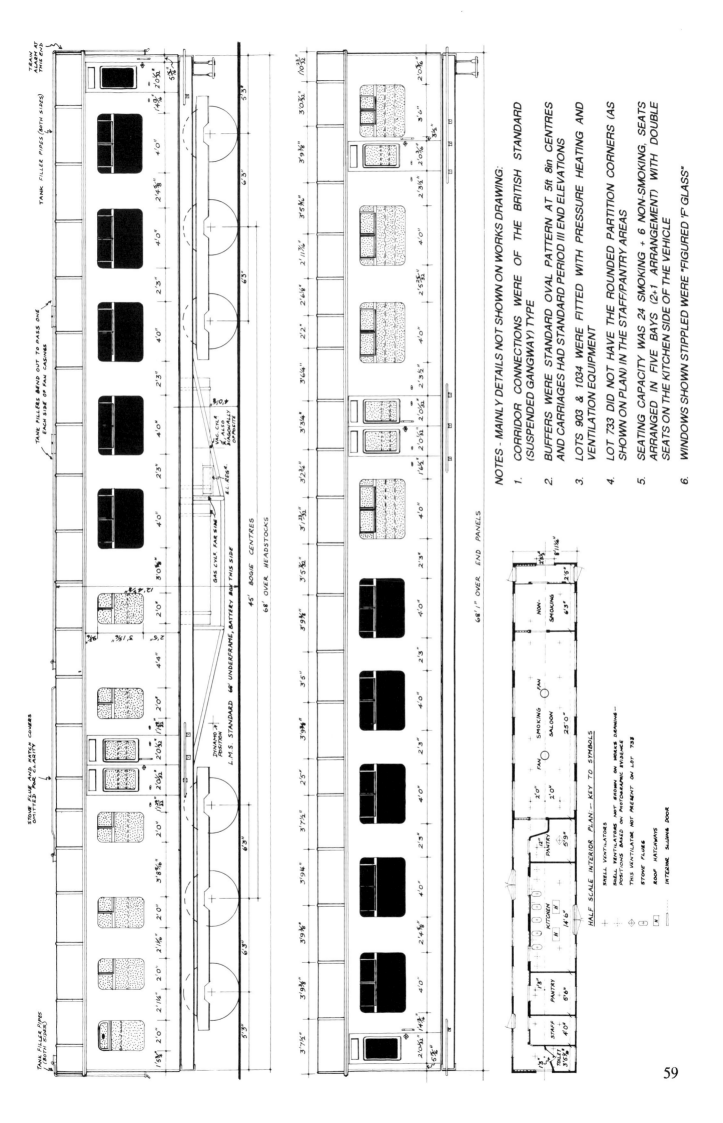

NOTES - MAINLY DETAILS NOT SHOWN ON WORKS DRAWING:

1. CORRIDOR CONNECTIONS WERE OF THE BRITISH STANDARD (SUSPENDED GANGWAY) TYPE

2. BUFFERS WERE STANDARD OVAL PATTERN AT 5ft 8in CENTRES AND CARRIAGES HAD STANDARD PERIOD III END ELEVATIONS

3. LOTS 903 & 1034 WERE FITTED WITH PRESSURE HEATING AND VENTILATION EQUIPMENT

4. LOT 733 DID NOT HAVE THE ROUNDED PARTITION CORNERS (AS SHOWN ON PLAN) IN THE STAFF/PANTRY AREAS

5. SEATING CAPACITY WAS 24 SMOKING + 6 NON-SMOKING, SEATS ARRANGED IN FIVE BAYS (2+1 ARRANGEMENT) WITH DOUBLE SEATS ON THE KITCHEN SIDE OF THE VEHICLE

6. WINDOWS SHOWN STIPPLED WERE "FIGURED 'F' GLASS"

59

LMS Standard Period II 57ft Non-Corridor Stock

LMS non-corridor stock was very standardised and Arthur Whitehead's drawings of the three basic 57ft types continued to be standard in terms of compartment layout until after nationalisation. They developed into both the Period II versions (always steel panelled) and the Period III types, both covered on page 66. The carriages shown here should be paired with standard non-gangwayed ends with matchboard panelling, only the brake end having windows. It is perhaps worth mentioning that many of these carriages were built at the old LYR carriage works at Newton Heath which was the only LMS works to be involved with new LMS carriage building outside Derby and Wolverton. All types had full livery when new and in the summary below, lot numbers have been omitted to save space. Final survivors lasted as follows: Thirds - 1964; Composites - 1965; Brake Thirds - 1966.

PROTOTYPE DETAILS

Quantity	Date	Works	Running Numbers
THIRD CLASS LMS D1700			
38	1925	Wolverton	10850-10887
62	1925	Newton Heath	10888-10949
50	1926	Newton Heath	10950-10999
50	1927/8	Newton Heath	11000-11049
150	1928	Wolverton	11050-11199
68	1928/30	Derby	11200-11267
50	1929	Wolverton	11268-11317
50	1930	Newton Heath	11318-11367
6	1930	Derby	11368-11373 *
COMPOSITE LMS D1701			
49	1925	Wolverton	16028-16076
8	1927	Derby	16077-16084
211	1926/7	Wolverton	16085-16295
BRAKE THIRD LMS D1703			
66	1927	Derby	20140-20205
81	1926/7	Newton Heath	20206-20286
100	1928	Newton Heath	20287-20386

* Built for use in North London line sets

Sample pre-1933 numbers:
Third Class: 5951-4; 14332-78; 18256-60; 19018-21
Composite: 8724-45; 9897-916
Brake Third: 13965-73; 18705-9; 18717-22

NOTE: Roof vents on these carriages were 2ft 0in from the centreline, diagonally opposed over compartments (ie always above LH quarterlight - see drawings) but directly opposite each other over the brake end

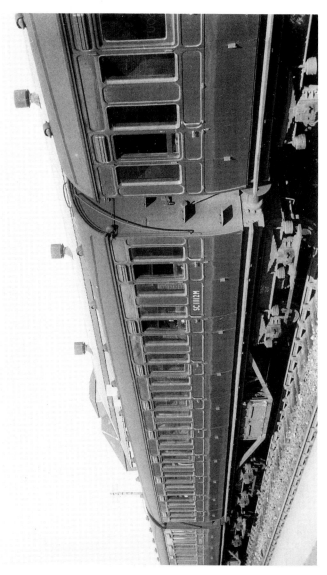

Two views of the Period I full third to D1700, quite early and relatively late in life. The LMS view shows full livery on what is believed to be No.10865, probably taken quite soon after renumbering in 1933/4. The near central position of both 'LMS' and the running number is unorthodox (see also page 6), suggesting that the older numbers (which probably appeared twice, once towards each end), had simply been painted out and the new number applied once only to balance the arrangement. The second picture is of No.Sc11112M in unlined BR red livery, probably in the late 1950s, in the middle of a set of similar carriages whose panelling is in a remarkably good state of repair. Note, however, that the original torpedo roof ventilators have been replaced by the BR 'hemispherical' type, a not uncommon but by no means widely applied modification on older LMS stock (Author's collection - 2)

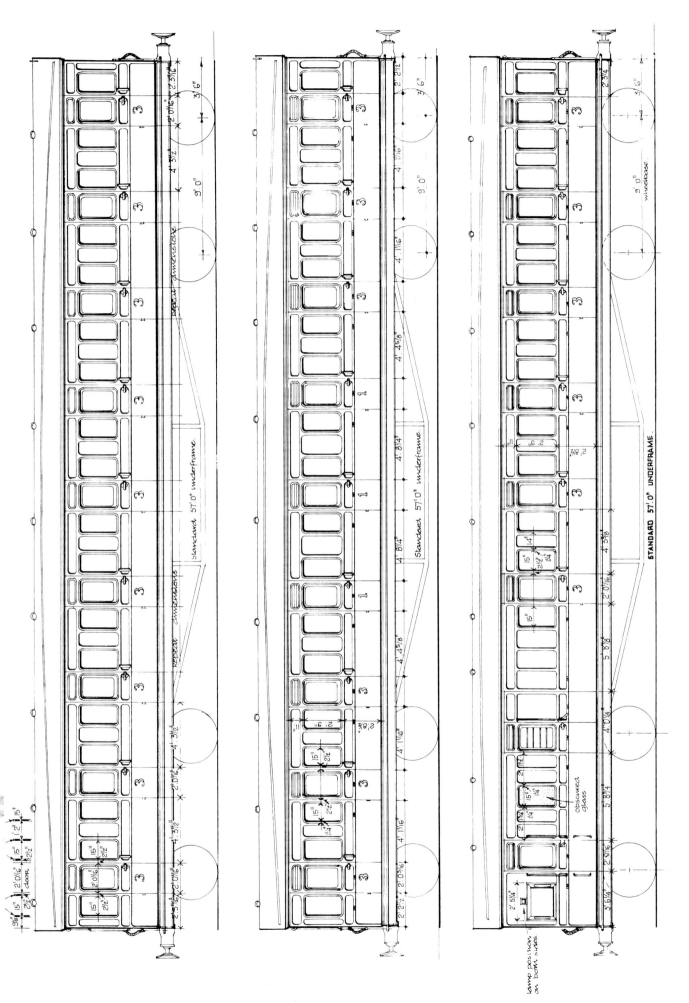

STANDARD 57'0" UNDERFRAME.

61

LMS Standard Period I 54ft & 51ft Non-Corridor Stock

Apart from one batch of thirds and brake thirds for general service (see summary), these shorter length LMS non-corridors were all intended to be formed into sets for use either on the LT&S section or the Cathcart Circle Line in Glasgow and the drawings opposite have been prepared to cover all possibilities. The Cathcart Circle carriages were contractor-built (Hurst Nelson and R.Y.Pickering) and though appearing in 1926, were 'Period II' in construction, ie steel panelling and ends. But they had full 'waist panel' lining in Period I style and apart from their lack of raised beading - and the reduction in length of the composites to 51ft (no lavatory) - were otherwise identical to the types drawn.

Sets were formed as follows, the presence of but two toilets in the eleven coach LT&S sets never having been satisfactorily explained(!):

LT&S: BT+T+T+T+CL+F+CL+T+T+T+BT (7-compartment brakes)

Cathcart Circle: BT+C+F+C+BT (7-compartment brakes)

The Tilbury sets, labelled F&S 2xx (ie for 'Fenchurch Street and Southend') lasted until 1962, the Cathcart Circle Stock until 1962-4 and the general service carriages until 1964-5.

The 'Cathcart Circle' types are depicted here by contrast with the fully beaded types opposite: 54ft first No.15368, later 10017; the unique (for the LMS) 51ft long composite No.15597, later 16007 and the 54ft 7-compartment brake third No.16236, later 20103 (Author's collection - 3)

PROTOTYPE DETAILS

Quantity	Date	Works	Sample pre-1933 numbers	1933 Numbers
FULL FIRST LMS D1762 (LT&S TYPE)				
8	1926-9	Derby	2649-50	10006-10013*§
FULL FIRST LMS D1760 (CATHCART CIRCLE: 5 per side seating!)				
7	1926	Hurst Nelson	15368; 15403	10017-10023
3	1926	Pickering	15490	10024-10026
FULL THIRD LMS D1768 (GENERAL SERVICE)				
40	1924/5	Newton Heath	14461-500	10772-10811
38	1924	Derby	950; 2735-8; 16064-7	10812-10849
FULL THIRD LMS D1769 (LT&S TYPE)				
48	1926-9	Derby	4249-60; 2347-58	10724-10771*#
51ft COMPOSITE LMS D1766 (CATHCART CIRCLE: 5 per side in firsts)				
14	1926	Hurst Nelson	15619; 15892	16007-16020
5	1926	Pickering	15990	16021-16025
LAVATORY COMPOSITE LMS D1765 (LT&S TYPE)				
16	1926-9	Derby	2495-8; 4156-9	19000-19015*§
BRAKE THIRD LMS D1772 (SEVEN-COMPARTMENT)				
4	1926	Derby	3889-92	20099-20102*@
14	1926	Hurst Nelson	16729; 16835/6	20103-20116
5	1926	Pickering	16893	20117-20121
12	1927-9	Derby	3874-7; 2721-4	20122-20133*@
BRAKE THIRD LMS D1771 (SIX-COMPARTMENT GENERAL SERVICE)				
71	1925	Derby	7606-8; 16830-3	20020-20090

* Two complete LT&S sets built in each year (Set Nos: F&S 245-52)
§ half of each batch with long/short buffers, half all short
# As D1768 but 2/3 of each batch with long/short buffers, 1/3 all short
@ LT&S Brakes had long buffers at beds and short at passenger end

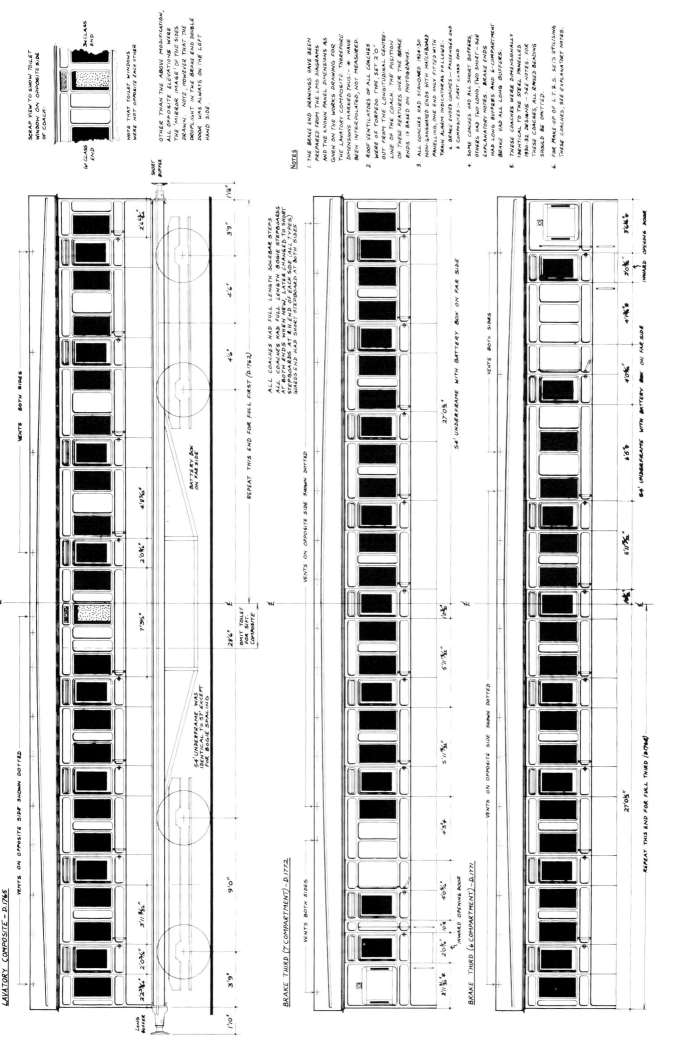

LAVATORY COMPOSITE – D.1765

BRAKE THIRD (7 COMPARTMENT) – D.1772

BRAKE THIRD (6 COMPARTMENT) – D.1771

SCRAP VIEW TO SHOW TOILET WINDOW ON OPPOSITE SIDE OF COACH.

3ʳᵈ CLASS END

1ˢᵗ CLASS END

NOTE THAT TOILET WINDOWS WERE NOT OPPOSITE EACH OTHER

OTHER THAN THE ABOVE MODIFICATION, ALL OPPOSITE ELEVATIONS WERE THE 'MIRROR IMAGE' OF THE SIDES DRAWN. NOTE, HOWEVER THAT THE DROPLIGHT IN THE BRAKE END DOUBLE DOOR WAS ALWAYS ON THE LEFT HAND SIDE.

NOTES

1. THE BRAKE END DRAWINGS HAVE BEEN PREPARED FROM THE LMS DIAGRAMS AND THE KNOWN PANEL DIMENSIONS AS GIVEN ON THE WORKS DRAWING FOR THE LAVATORY COMPOSITE. THEREFORE DIMENSIONS MARKED THUS:- ✳ HAVE BEEN INTERPOLATED, NOT MEASURED.

2. ROOF VENTILATORS OF ALL COACHES WERE OF TORPEDO TYPE, SET 2'0" OUT FROM THE LONGITUDINAL CENTRE-LINE OF THE COACH. THE POSITION OF THESE FEATURES OVER THE BRAKE ENDS IS BASED ON PHOTOGRAPHS.

3. ALL COACHES HAD STANDARD 1924-30 NON-GANGWAYED ENDS WITH MATCHBOARD PANELLING, ONE END ONLY FITTED WITH TRAIN ALARM INDICATORS AS FOLLOWS:-
   BRAKE ENDED COACHES – PASSENGER END
   COMPOSITES – FIRST CLASS END

4. SOME COACHES HAD ALL SHORT BUFFERS, OTHERS HAD TWO LONG, TWO SHORT – SEE EXPLANATORY NOTES. BRAKE ENDS HAD LONG BUFFERS AND 6-COMPARTMENT BRAKE HAD ALL LONG BUFFERS.

5. THESE COACHES WERE DIMENSIONALLY IDENTICAL TO THE STEEL PANELLED 1930-32 DESIGNS – SEE NOTES. FOR THESE COACHES, ALL RAISED BEADING SHOULD BE OMITTED.

6. FOR MAKE-UP OF L.T.&.S. SETS UTILISING THESE COACHES, SEE EXPLANATORY NOTES.

LMS Standard 57ft Non-Corridor Lavatory Stock

Compared with gangwayed stock, the LMS non-corridor contribution was somewhat basic, but the three types featured here were more lavish and, in theory, intended for use on the longer distance cross-country workings. The firsts ran intermixed with other stock but the other two were intended as 'Inter-District' sets formed BTL+CL, BTL+CL+BTL or BTL+CL+CL+BTL. Needless to say, this did not always happen!

The upper elevation shows a Period I lavatory first (confined to a single 1927 batch only) while the other two elevations show Period II versions of the Inter-District types. The fully panelled Period I version can readily be derived from these two by moving the lavatory windows on the brake third some 6in to the right of the position drawn, viewed from either side - see also pictures.

Internally, the brake thirds and full firsts had a single lavatory between two adjacent compartments only, to which they were linked by a short side corridor. The composites had back-to-back lavatories (one each class), a short corridor linking them to two compartments on each side - ie four in all. Apart from the curious LT&S composites (see previous page), these were the only lavatory non-corridors built by the LMS and none appeared after 1930. The majority had gone by the end of 1964 but a few of the brakes lasted until 1965.

Lavatory first No.15517 (later No.18003) when brand new

Fully panelled lavatory composite to D1686 in simple livery as M19034 in July 1948 (G.Coltas)

PROTOTYPE DETAILS

Lot	Quantity	Date	Works	Running Numbers
LAVATORY FIRST CLASS LMS D1761				
249	38	1927	Wolverton	18000-18029
LAVATORY COMPOSITE LMS D1686 (Period I) and D1736 (Period II)				
126	20	1926/7	Derby	19026-19045
389	50	1929	Wolverton	19046-19095
446	75	1929	Wolverton	19096-19170
529	25	1930	Wolverton	19171-19195 *
LAVATORY BRAKE THIRD LMS D1685 (Period I) and D1737 (Period II)				
127	50	1926/7	Derby	25000-25049
290	50	1927	Newton Heath	25050-25099
398	73	1928/9	Newton Heath	25100-25172
448	75	1928/9	Newton Heath	25173-25247
530	25	1930	Newton Heath	25248-25272 *

* These were the Period II lots as drawn opposite

Sample pre-1933 numbers:
D1761: 15424; 15517; 15926-7; 16195; 16871
D1686: 11606-18; 4162-4200. **D1736:** 11053-8; 11063-8
D1685: 18930-8; 14157-71; 73; 978; 6175. **D1737:** 864; 7907-9; 15524-5; 16455

64

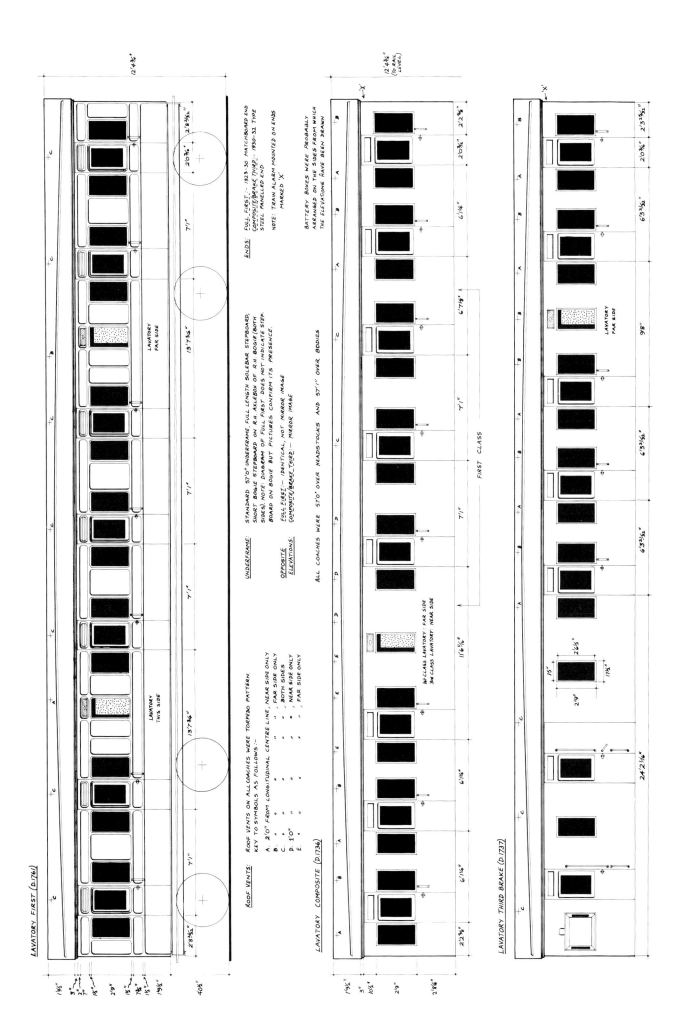

LAVATORY FIRST (D.76)

LAVATORY THIS SIDE

LAVATORY FAR SIDE

ROOF VENTS: ROOF VENTS ON ALL COACHES WERE TORPEDO PATTERN
KEY TO SYMBOLS AS FOLLOWS:-

A. 2'0" FROM LONGITUDINAL CENTRE LINE, NEAR SIDE ONLY
B. "   "   "   "   "   " , FAR SIDE ONLY
C. "   "   "   "   "   " , BOTH SIDES
D. 1'0" "   "   "   "   " , NEAR SIDE ONLY
E. "   "   "   "   "   " , FAR SIDE ONLY

UNDERFRAME: STANDARD 57'0" UNDERFRAME, FULL LENGTH SOLEBAR STEPBOARD,
SHORT BOGIE STEPBOARD ON R.H. AXLEBOX OF R.H. BOGIE (BOTH
SIDES). NOTE: DIAGRAM OF FULL FIRST DOES NOT INDICATE STEP-
BOARD ON BOGIE BUT PICTURES CONFIRM ITS PRESENCE.

OPPOSITE
ELEVATIONS:
FULL FIRST:- IDENTICAL, NOT MIRROR IMAGE
COMPOSITE/BRAKE THIRD:- MIRROR IMAGE

ALL COACHES WERE 57'0" OVER HEADSTOCKS AND 57'1" OVER BODIES

ENDS: FULL FIRST:- 1923-30 MATCHBOARD END
COMPOSITE/BRAKE THIRD:- 1930-32 TYPE
STEEL PANELLED END

NOTE: TRAIN ALARM MOUNTED ON ENDS
MARKED 'X'

BATTERY BOXES WERE PROBABLY
ARRANGED ON THE SIDES FROM WHICH
THE ELEVATIONS HAVE BEEN DRAWN

LAVATORY COMPOSITE (D.1736)

FIRST CLASS

1st CLASS LAVATORY: FAR SIDE
3rd CLASS LAVATORY: NEAR SIDE

LAVATORY THIRD BRAKE (D.1737)

LAVATORY FAR SIDE

65

LMS Standard Period II/III 57ft Non-Corridor Stock

The drawings opposite can be used to derive almost all LMS standard 57ft non-corridor types after Period I. Arthur Whitehead's side elevations show Period II versions, including the (slight) modifications for the motor fitted (Push-Pull) 'Driving' brake third, while Ken Morgan's single elevation gives all the 'specific to Period III' dimensions needed to derive the Stanier types.

End/underframe details followed standard custom and practice, while roof vents were arranged as for Period I stock (page 60), the change from torpedo to shell type taking place in 1934, just after the first of the Period III types appeared. Ex-works liveries almost always followed the 'rules' on page 6 while to further simplify matters, only the year of building is quoted and 'extinction' year(s) are tabulated.

PROTOTYPE DETAILS

Quantity	Date	Works	Running Numbers	Extinct
COMPOSITE LMS D1734 (Period II) and D1921/1921A (Period III) *f*				
143	1931/2	Wolverton	16331-16488	1965 § f
			17900-17904	1964 § #
89	1933	Derby	16496-16569	1966 * f
			17905-17919	1965 # *
45	1933/4	Derby	16570-16614	1966
59	1935/6	Derby	16615-16671	1966
			17920-17921	1964 #
36	1938	Wolverton	16672-16706	1966
			17922	1966 #
40	1939	Wolverton	16707-16746	1966
70	1949	Derby	M16747-16796	1966
			M17923-17942	1966 #
10	1950	Wolverton	M19377-19386	1966 # ¥
THIRD LMS D1784 (Period II) and D1906/1906A (Period III)				
50	1930/31	Derby	11374-11423	1948 §
78	1930	Wolverton	11424-11501	1948 §
100	1932	Derby	11506-11605	1965 §
50	1933	Derby	11628-11675	1966 *
			15858-15859	1964 # *
25	1934	Derby	11680-11704	1966
25	1935	Derby	11717-11741	1967
110	1936	Wolverton	11742-11851	1967
60	1937	Derby	11852-11911	1967
247	1937/8	Wolverton	11912-12157	1964 #
			15860	1966
70	1939/40	Wolverton	12158-12227	1966
BRAKE THIRD LMS D1735/1790# (Period II) and D1907/1856# (Period III) @				
40	1930	Derby	20540-20572	1965 §
			24403-24409	1964 § #
40	1930/31	Newton Heath	20387-20426	1965 §
110	1931/32	Derby	20427-20536	1965 §
160	1933	Wolverton	20577-20719	1967 *
			24410-24426	1965 # *
61	1934	Wolverton	20720-20780	1966
32	1935	Derby	20785-20814	1965
			24427-24428	
1	1938	Wolverton	20584	1963 †

f Including some to transitional D1849 which bridged the Period II/III changeover
§ Period II types, remainder Period III
# Motor fitted stock (ie Push-Pull), 17900-4 originally allocated 16326-30
* Early Period III with torpedo ventilators and full livery when new
¥ 'Overflow' numbers in lavatory composite series
@ From 1936, Period III third brakes had two pairs of double doors at the van end which means that they cannot be derived from these drawings
† This was a one-for-one replacement of a 1937 accident victim

Sample pre-1933 numbers (Period II stock only):
D1734: 3041-55; 13925-6; 17811. **D1784:** 704-5; 2365-93; 10669-73.
D1735: 1868-83; 6371-4; 16958-9. **D1790:** 17117-9

Standard 57ft non-corridor brake thirds: No.17194 (later No.20571) is a standard Period II example from D1735 in full livery while No.24413 is a push-pull Period III version from D1856, one of several early Period III lots which were built with the older style torpedo roof ventilators

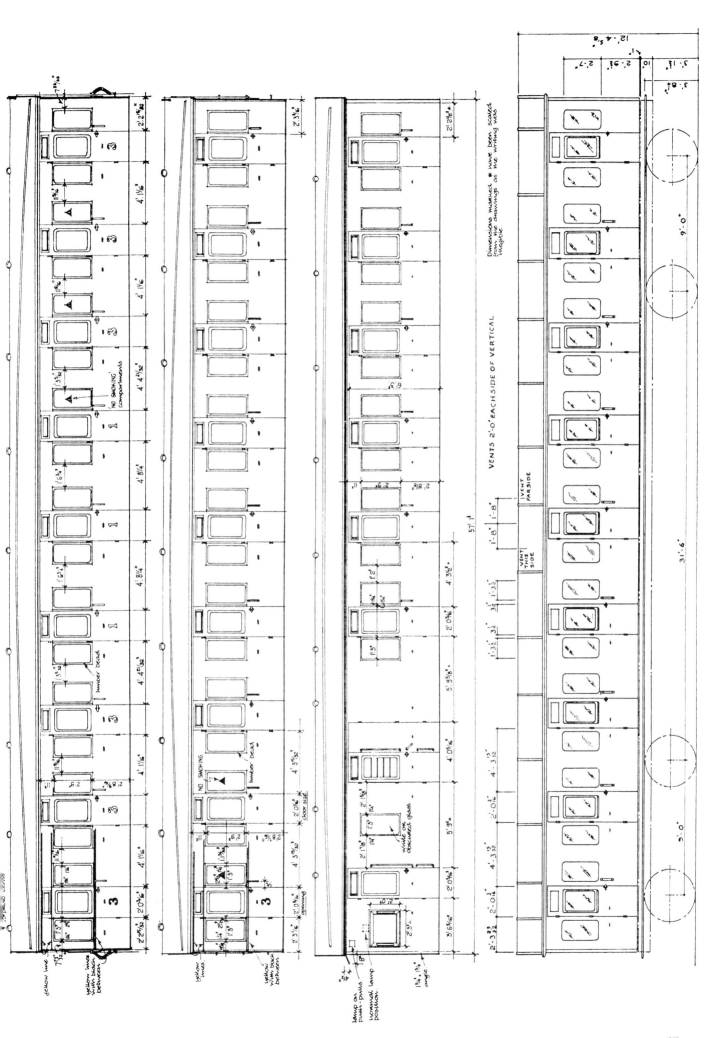

67

LMS Standard 50ft Full Brakes/50ft Underframe

The final LMS standard types featured are the two most common 50ft full brakes from Periods I and III respectively, there being no period II version. The late John Hinchliffe prepared the Period I drawing, Graham Warburton producing the underframe drawing with cross-brace detail typical of LMS practice, regardless of length. It should be noted that both elevations of both brakes were identical (not mirror images) and that end elevations were slightly different from standard. Both lasted to the end of steam (1968), but such was the nature of recording at the time that final 'extinction' dates cannot be given. The Period III examples were built to two separate diagrams (externally identical), some of those from D2007 becoming the last LMS standard types in regular BR service, many painted in all-over rail blue with their gangways removed.

Period I Full Brake No.5509 (later No.30528) in full livery when new. Although it was customary LMS practice to use gold (gilt) lining for gangwayed stock in full livery, it is thought possible that these vehicles were given the same primrose yellow lining as fully liveried non-gangwayed stock - see page 6

Period III full brake No.30965 from D2007 in simple livery. Although there was a limited build of Stanier pattern brakes during 1932-4 (D1854, Nos.30908-30963 - see table), the main series of Period III full brakes was late to appear because the LMS had also introduced a considerable number of 50ft 'All Steel' full brakes (ie without separate chassis - c.f the passenger stock given on page 28) between 1926 and 1930, thus reducing the need. The prominent side beading strips seen on this view (and present also on D1854) seem to have ended with No.31208 - see table

PROTOTYPE DETAILS

Quantity	Date	Works	Running Numbers
PERIOD I PASSENGER FULL BRAKE LMS D1778			
75	1925/6	Wolverton	30400-30474
25	1926	Newton Heath	30475-30499
49	1927/8	Wolverton	30500-30548 *
PERIOD III PASSENGER FULL BRAKE LMS D1854 #			
50	1932/3	Derby	30908-30957
6	1934	Wolverton	30958-30963
PERIOD III PASSENGER FULL BRAKE LMS D2007			
75	1938/9	Wolverton	30964-31038
20	1940	Derby	31039-31058
100	1939/41	Wolverton	31059-31158
50	1941/2	Derby	31159-31208
114	1941/4	Wolverton	31210-31323
25	1947	Wolverton	31324-31348

* Believed 50 built but only 49 renumbered in 1933

Torpedo Vents on all examples and full livery on the Derby-built batch when new, otherwise as per D2007

Sample pre-1933 numbers (D1778 only):
9; 74; 305; 5509; 6510-5; 6881-3; 7460/8

68

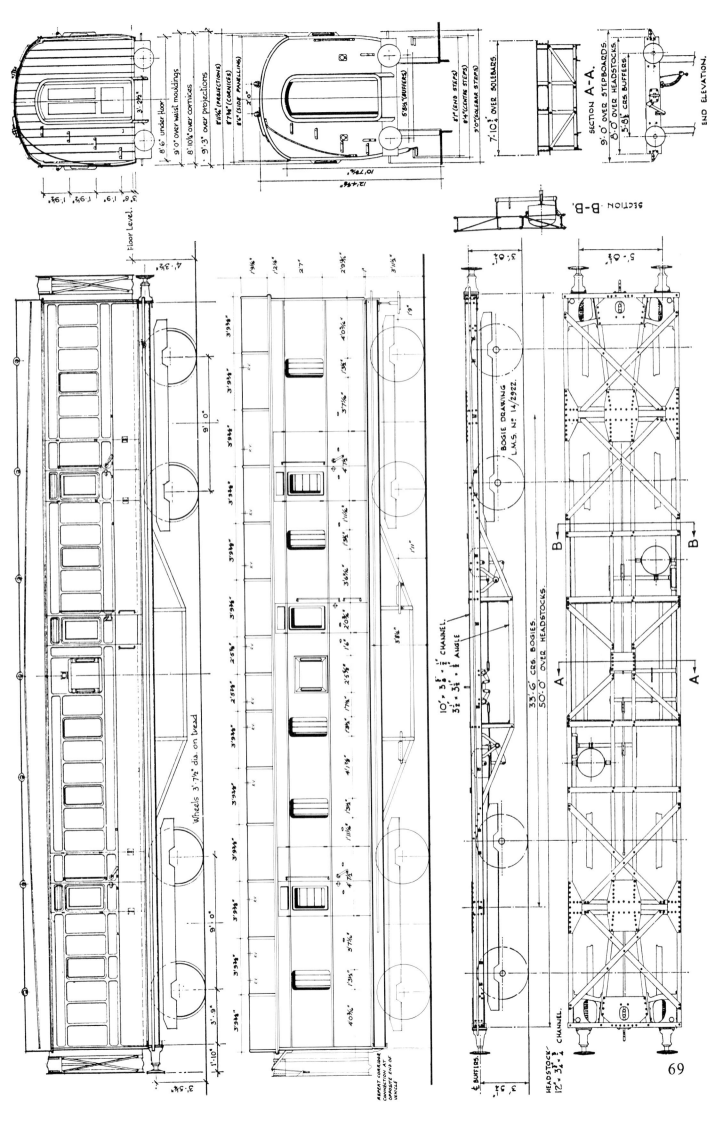

SECTION A-A.

END ELEVATION.

SECTION B-B.

69

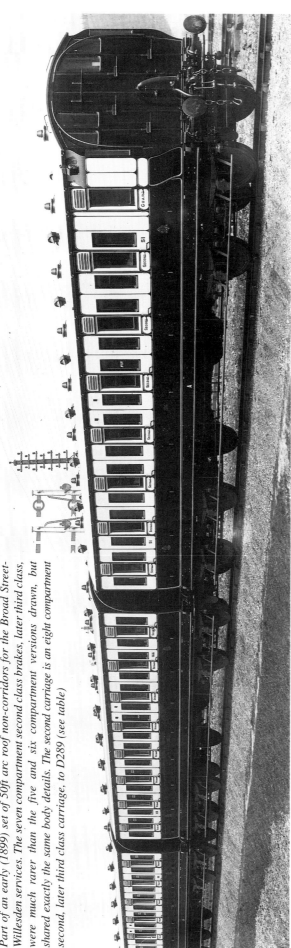

Part of an early (1899) set of 50ft arc roof non-corridors for the Broad Street-Willesden services. The seven compartment second class brakes, later third class, were much rarer than the five and six compartment versions drawn, but shared exactly the same body details. The second carriage is an eight compartment second, later third class carriage, to D289 (see table)

LNWR 50ft Arc Roof Non-Corridor Stock

The arc roof profile was characteristic of LNWR carriages until early Edwardian days and these drawings show typical 50ft non-corridor types (from the 1897-1902 period) which lasted throughout the LMS era. Most were originally gas lit (see note on drawing) but by LMS times, many had been converted to electric light. Underframe and panel dimensions are given with the 50ft corridor stock (pages 74-7).

The brake composites were built for slip working with raised 'birdcage' lookouts (D249), but converted to orthodox form at or just before the grouping (D221). The second class compartment (the central of the five) became third c.1912. The non-lavatory stock was for general service and the full third can be derived from the six-compartment brake. LNWR numbers quoted are those carried at grouping but only samples can be offered.

PROTOTYPE DETAILS

Quantity	Sample LNWR Numbers	1st LMS	2nd LMS	Extinct *
LAVATORY TRI-COMPOSITE BRAKE BUILT 1901 (LNWR D249/221)				
9	5922/68; 6087-90	9816-9826	25823-25831	to BR
COMPOSITE (4F+3T) BUILT 1897-1902 (LNWR D187)				
54	2523-4; 2756; 3816-20	9158-9209	16957-17004	to BR
FIVE COMPARTMENT BRAKE THIRD BUILT 1898-1902 (LNWR D347)				
83	6516-8; 6520-5; 7489	7472-7554	22286-22364	to BR
SIX COMPARTMENT BRAKE THIRD BUILT 1897-1902 (LNWR D345)				
68	6505/52; 6926/83; 7207; 7492	7400-7466	22493-22558	to BR
FULL THIRD BUILT 1897-1901 (LNWR D289)				
136	38; 157; 644; 1041; 1728; 2180	5563-5672	13644-13742	to BR

* Scrapping began in early LMS days but examples of all types reached BR, though exact final survival dates cannot be given for these diagrams - usually the early 1950s

BASIC LNWR CARRIAGE LIVERY

Sides: Lower panels purple (carmine) lake, upper panels in white 'broken' with ultramarine blue. Fixed window frame mouldings usually Indian Red, door/window droplights usually varnished natural wood finish

Ends: To match lower body side panels

Lining: Placed on edge of beading, chrome yellow edged with fine white line where adjacent to purple lake

Insignia: Yellow sans-serif edged black (LNW general service stock) or shaded green to right and below (all WCJS).

Roof: Generally white but sometimes grey

Chassis: All black. Wood centred wheels generally had Indian Red centres and special vehicles had white tyres

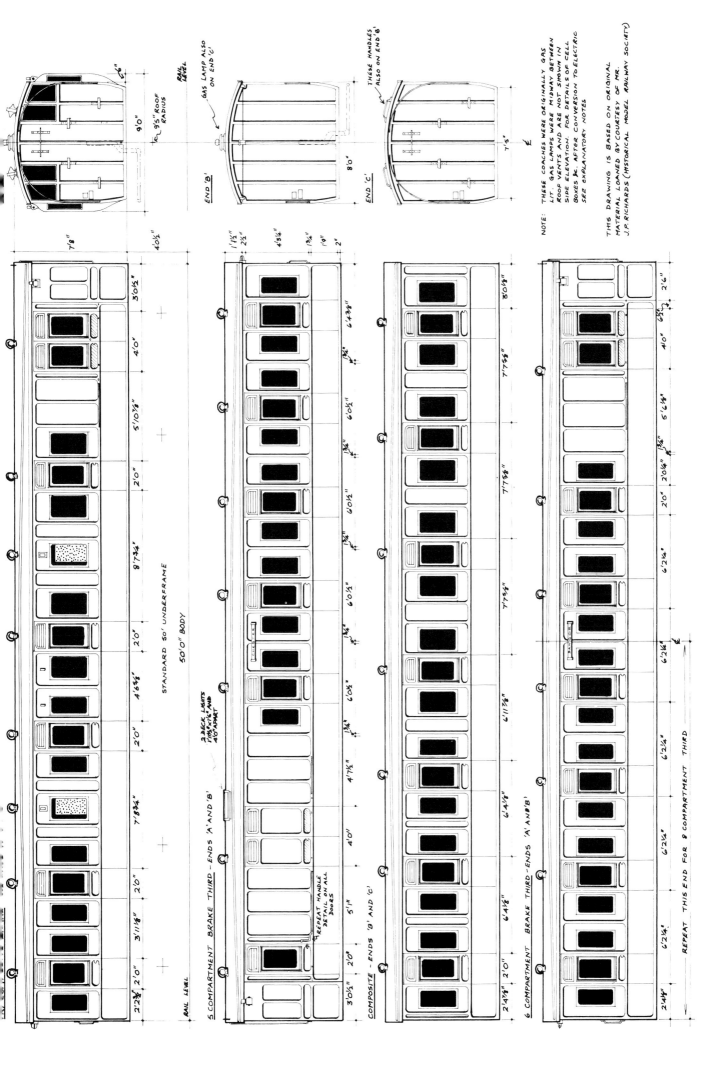

9'0"

95" ROOF RADIUS

RAIL LEVEL

GAS LAMP ALSO ON END 'C'

END 'B'

8'0"

END 'C'

7'5"

THESE HANDLES, ALSO ON END 'B'

NOTE: THESE COACHES WERE ORIGINALLY GAS LIT. GAS LAMPS WERE MIDWAY BETWEEN ROOF VENTS AND ARE NOT SHOWN IN SIDE ELEVATION. FOR DETAILS OF CELL BOXES &c. AFTER CONVERSION TO ELECTRIC SEE EXPLANATORY NOTES

THIS DRAWING IS BASED ON ORIGINAL MATERIAL LOANED (BY COURTESY OF MR. J.P. RICHARDS (HISTORICAL MODEL RAILWAY SOCIETY)

7'8"

40½"

RAIL LEVEL

STANDARD 50' UNDERFRAME

50'0" BODY

5 COMPARTMENT BRAKE THIRD — ENDS 'A' AND 'B'

2 DECK LIGHTS 1"THICK X 8¾" AND 4'0" APART

REPEAT HANDLE DETAIL ON ALL DOORS

COMPOSITE — ENDS 'B' AND 'C'

6 COMPARTMENT BRAKE THIRD—ENDS 'A' AND 'B'

REPEAT THIS END FOR 9 COMPARTMENT THIRD

71

Part of a six-coach set of 50ft cove roof non-corridor lavatory carriages, including all three types featured on this page. From the near end they are brake third, composite, full first (not drawn, but see caption to next picture) and full third, the set being completed by a further third and brake third.

LNWR 50ft Cove Roof Non-Corridor Lavatory Stock

The low elliptical or 'cove' roof was a short-lived but attractive styling phase during mid-Edwardian days, lasting from c.1903-7 and usually accompanied by an increase of carriage width to 9ft. The 50ft length remained normal for non-corridor types and the examples here typify the best non-gangwayed stock of the time - a sort of LNWR precursor of LMS Inter District lavatory sets (page 64) but more generously provisioned with toilets. The carriages were always electrically lit (one cell box each side) and the standard 50ft underframe was used, details of which can be found with the 50ft corridor stock (pages 74-7).

As can be seen from the summary, these types, albeit few in number, were very long-lived and most of them reached BR. Details are also given of the matching full first which, though not drawn opposite, is not too hard to derive - see caption to appended picture.

This picture shows the matching 50ft cove roof lavatory full first to D102 which, though not drawn here, could be derived from the offered drawings with relatively little effort. For its time it was a distinctly lavish carriage with a separate lavatory area for each individual compartment, not to mention the generous dimensions of the latter, each of which seated but seven passengers. The compartments were fractionally over 7ft 7in between partitions, the two outer lavatory sections (each containing two lavatory areas serving one each of the adjacent two compartments) were 4ft between partitions, while the central lavatory section, occupying the full width of the carriage and serving the central compartment only, was fractionally less than 3ft between partitions. The carriage is No.208, later 4636 (LMS 10091, later 18178).

PROTOTYPE DETAILS

Quantity	Sample LNWR Numbers	1st LMS	2nd LMS	Extinct *
LAVATORY COMPOSITE BUILT 1905 (LNWR D153)				
9	2538; 3862/6-7	8562-8565	19500-19503	1952
LAVATORY THIRD CLASS BUILT 1905-7 (LNWR D276)				
24	33; 269; 803; 1159-60; 1969	5259-5280	18621-641/3	1953
LAVATORY THIRD CLASS BRAKE BUILT 1905 (LNWR D326)				
8	6528; 6613; 6913; 7148	6941-6947	25515-25521	1955
LAVATORY FULL FIRST, BUILT 1905 (LNWR D102)				
10	4516; 4553; 4562; 4636	10083-10092	18172-18181	1952

* One or two pre-group withdrawals amongst the thirds/brake thirds, hence the fact that the LMS numbers do not cover the full quantity built. Planned scrapping began c.1944

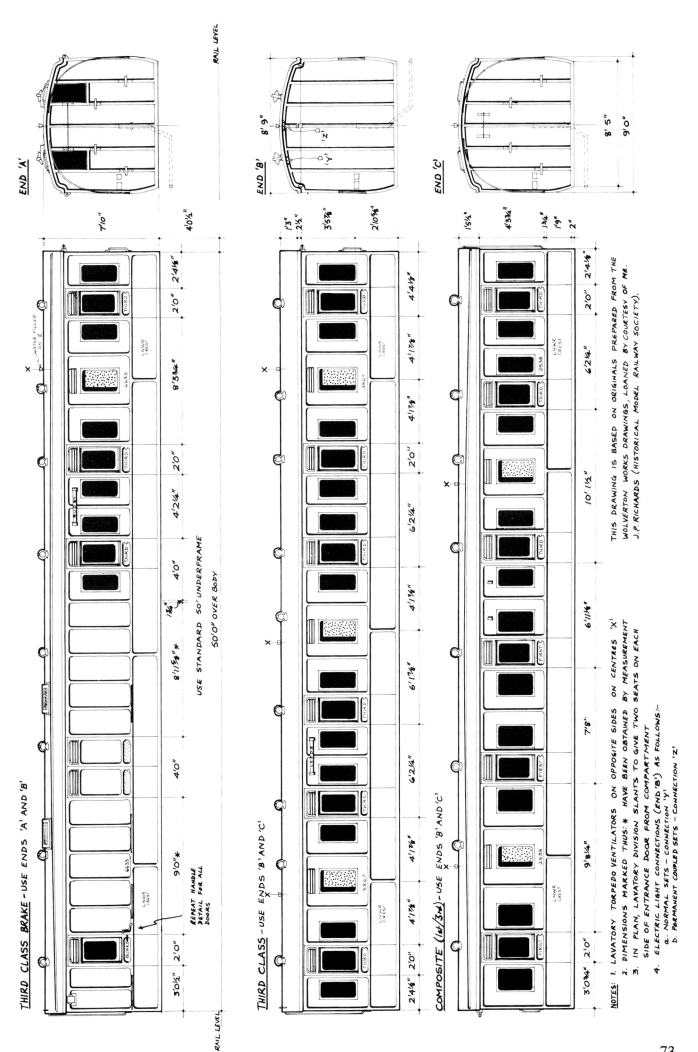

END 'A'

RAIL LEVEL

THIRD CLASS BRAKE - USE ENDS 'A' AND 'B'

7/10"

40'0½"

RAIL LEVEL

2'4⅛"

2'0"

8'3¾"

4'2¼"

2'0"

4'0"

8'11⅝"*

4'0"

9'0"*

3'0½" 2'0"

USE STANDARD 50' UNDERFRAME

50'0" OVER BODY

1¾"

WATER FILLER ON ₵

REPEAT HANDLE DETAIL FOR ALL DOORS

GUARD

6633

LNWR CREST

6633

THIRD

END 'B'

8'9"

THIRD CLASS - USE ENDS 'B' AND 'C'

1'3"
2½"

3'5⅝"

2'0⅝"

4'4½"

4'1⅞"

2'0"

6'2¼"

4'1⅞"

6'1⅞"

6'2¼"

4'1⅞"

4'1⅞" 2'0"

2'4⅛"

X

3867

LNWR CREST

3867

THIRD

END 'C'

8'5"

9'0"

COMPOSITE (1st/3rd) - USE ENDS 'B' AND 'C'

1'5½"

4'3¾"

1¾"
1'9"
2"

2'4⅛"

2'0"

6'2¼"

10'1½"

6'11⅞"

7'8"

9'3¼"

3'0¾" 2'0"

2538

2538

THIRD

FIRST

FIRST

FIRST

THIRD

LNWR CREST

NOTES:
1. LAVATORY TORPEDO VENTILATORS ON OPPOSITE SIDES ON CENTRES 'X'
2. DIMENSIONS MARKED THUS: * HAVE BEEN OBTAINED BY MEASUREMENT
3. IN PLAN, LAVATORY DIVISION SLANTS TO GIVE TWO SEATS ON EACH SIDE OF ENTRANCE DOOR FROM COMPARTMENT
4. ELECTRIC LIGHT CONNECTIONS (END 'B') AS FOLLOWS:-
   a. NORMAL SETS - CONNECTION 'Y'
   b. PERMANENT COUPLED SETS - CONNECTION 'Z'

THIS DRAWING IS BASED ON ORIGINALS PREPARED FROM THE WOLVERTON WORKS DRAWINGS, LOANED BY COURTESY OF MR. J.P. RICHARDS (HISTORICAL MODEL RAILWAY SOCIETY).

73

LNWR 50ft Arc Roof Corridor Stock

The LNWR (including its West Coast Joint operations) began to move to corridor trains during the 1890s and by the time the carriages on these and the next two pages appeared, the 'corridor revolution' was well into its stride, so much so that the full third to D268 (drawing on page 77) became the most numerous side corridor design to be built at Wolverton in pre-group days. Space permits but four types to be given in detail but dedicated enthusiasts could probably evolve a fifth version (brake third) from the featured brake composite should they so desire. Details are therefore given below for this type.

On this page, two numerous composite designs are featured along with end elevations for all types (save the full brake) and details of the characteristic 'Wolverton' style of panelling applicable to all arc roof stock, most of whose features continued through to the cove and early elliptical roof phases (pages 78-85). The featured composite to D138 was the most common arc roof example of the genre. Originally tri-composite (2F+2S+2T) - seconds in the middle and a lavatory for each class - it became First/Third c.1912 when the LNWR abolished second class. The brake composite to D216 was, however, always First/Third.

For most general purposes the matching brake third can be derived from D216 by substituting two standard third class compartments (and the corresponding smaller size 'large' windows on the corridor side) for the two firsts and adding one plain panel on both sides between the passenger area at this end and the double van door - see picture. This type (LNWR D316) was originally a 2nd/3rd composite (all third after 1912) and at a later date, some 36 of the 100 examples were altered to D317 by removal of the two original second class compartments (plus the lavatory) to produce a longer 'van' portion at that end, but still with central lookout. It has not been possible to offer exact details of this variation and the summary below includes only the 'five compartments plus centre van' version.

This fine official LMS view of an arc roof corridor third to LNWR D268 shows the vehicle after its conversion to LMS 'CARAVAN' No.46000 c.1934 ('Camping Coach' in more modern parlance); its previous numbers are not known. Apart from the sealing up of the majority of the compartment side doors, little of outward significance has changed and the picture gives a very fine impression of the fully lined LMS livery as applied to LNWR stock

A nicely posed train of 50ft arc roof corridors in LNWR days, though the reason for it having been taken is unknown. Two of the three featured carriage types on the drawing pages are shown, two composites to D138 at vehicles two and three, along with a full brake to D377 lurking in the distance. The leading carriage is a centre brake 2nd/3rd class composite arranged in identical fashion to the centre brake 1st/3rd composite featured in the drawings, save for the smaller sized second class compartments at the far end as seen in this view. This was the version which eventually became an all-third brake to D316 (see text), the extra vertical plain panel between the double 'van' doors and the far end compartments (ie compared with the drawings of the 1st/3rd type) being readily apparent

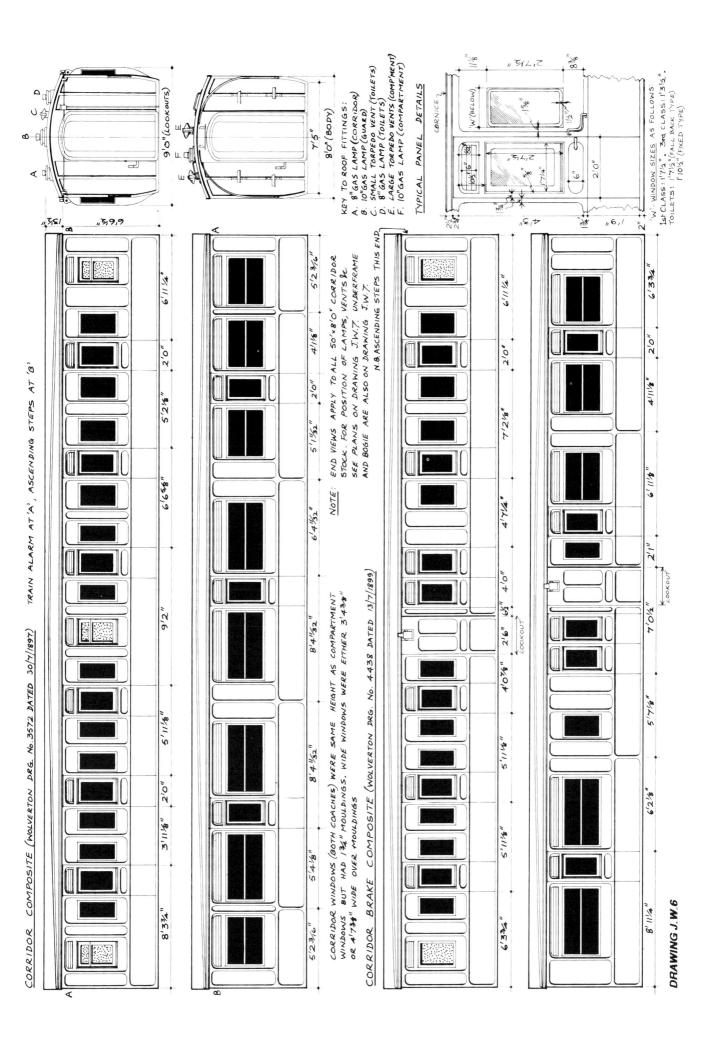

CORRIDOR COMPOSITE (WOLVERTON DRG. No. 3572 DATED 30/7/1897)   TRAIN ALARM AT 'A', ASCENDING STEPS AT 'B'

CORRIDOR BRAKE COMPOSITE (WOLVERTON DRG. No. 4438 DATED 13/7/1899)

CORRIDOR WINDOWS (BOTH COACHES) WERE SAME HEIGHT AS COMPARTMENT WINDOWS BUT HAD 1¾" MOULDINGS. WIDE WINDOWS WERE EITHER 3'4⅜" OR 4'7⅜" WIDE OVER MOULDINGS

NOTE: END VIEWS APPLY TO ALL 50'×8'0" CORRIDOR STOCK. FOR POSITION OF LAMPS, VENTS &c. SEE PLANS ON DRAWING J.W.7. UNDERFRAME AND BOGIE ARE ALSO ON DRAWING J.W.7.

N.B. ASCENDING STEPS THIS END.

KEY TO ROOF FITTINGS:
A. 8" GAS LAMP (CORRIDOR)
B. 10" GAS LAMP (GUARD)
C. SMALL TORPEDO VENT (TOILETS)
D. 8" GAS LAMP (TOILETS)
E. LARGE TORPEDO VENTS (COMP'M'ENT)
F. 10" GAS LAMP (COMPARTMENT)

TYPICAL PANEL DETAILS

'W'- WINDOW SIZES AS FOLLOWS:
1st CLASS: 1'7½". 3rd CLASS: 1'3½".
TOILETS: 1'7½"(FALL BACK TYPE)
1'10½" (FIXED TYPE)

DRAWING J.W.6

LNWR 50ft Arc Roof Corridor Stock (continued)

The second page of drawings shows the full third plus full brake, together with half scale plans of the passenger carrying types and the end elevation of the full brake which had the 8ft 6in width most commonly seen on contemporary WCJS 50ft arc roof corridors (not featured). About one third of this type were built for the WCJS and are listed separately on the summary.

The full third drawing offered shows the later variant, earlier examples having droplights on the corridor side (with louvre vents above) where double plain panels are shown, along with horizontally divided lavatory windows on the compartment side containing a fall-back upper portion. It has not been possible to determine the precise split between the two types but the change was quite early and the version as drawn seems to have been the more common.

PROTOTYPE DETAILS

Quantity	Sample LNWR Numbers	1st LMS	2nd LMS	Extinct
CORRIDOR COMPOSITE BUILT 1898-9 (LNWR D138)				
80	2513; 2620-1; 3342-3; 3701	8230-8309	4383-4458*	to BR §
CORRIDOR COMPOSITE BRAKE BUILT 1900-1 (LNWR D216)				
60	5703/25-6; 5915-6; 6011-29	9735-9794	6992-7048	to BR §
CORRIDOR THIRD CLASS BUILT 1898-1903 (LNWR D268)				
244	96; 1441; 2260-329; 2336-485	4910-5152	2773-2799	1953
CORRIDOR THIRD CLASS BRAKE BUILT 1898-1903 (LNWR D316)				
64	6919; 7657-9; 7774-9; 7884-6	6768-6831	6059-6119	to BR §
CORRIDOR FULL BRAKE BUILT 1902 (LNWR D377 & WCJS D79)				
41	8001-2; 8021-2; 8081-2; 8513	2248-2287¥	32415-32420	to BR §
			32486-32517	
			32526	
21	WCJS 212-31; 464	2291-2311#	32421-32439	to BR §

* Excluding 4409-13
§ Exact extinction dates not known, probably c.1953-5 in most cases
\# Excluding 2299
¥ Excluding 2249

Detail views of LNWR 50ft corridor stock. The view above shows two corridor thirds to D268 at Liverpool Riverside around the turn of the 19th/20th Centuries, both sides of the type being featured. The corridor side (further vehicle) shows the earlier style for this diagram wherein conventional droplights were found between the long windows compared with the plain panels of the version drawn opposite - see accompanying text. The detail view to the right shows typical LNWR corridor-end detail, specifically the method of connecting a 'slip' coach (left) to an arc roof corridor (right)

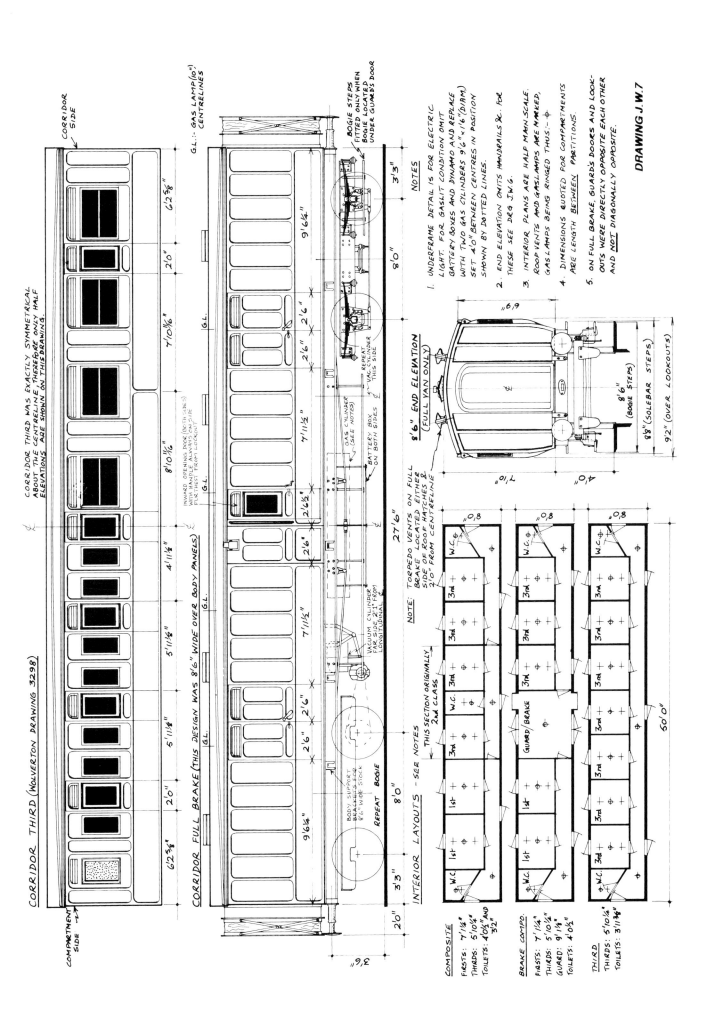

CORRIDOR THIRD (WOLVERTON DRAWING 3298)

CORRIDOR THIRD WAS EXACTLY SYMMETRICAL ABOUT THE CENTRELINE, THEREFORE ONLY HALF ELEVATIONS ARE SHOWN ON THIS DRAWING.

CORRIDOR SIDE

G.L.= GAS LAMP (10") CENTRELINES

CORRIDOR SIDE

COMPARTMENT SIDE

6'2⅝" 2'0" 5'11½" 5'11½" 4'11½" 8'10½" 7'10½" 6'2⅝"

CORRIDOR FULL BRAKE (THIS DESIGN WAS 8'6" WIDE OVER BODY PANELS)

BOGIE STEPS FITTED ONLY WHEN BOGIE LOCATED UNDER GUARD'S DOOR

9'6¼" 8'10½" 7'11½" 2'6½" 2'6" 2'6" 7'11½" 9'6¼"

INWARD OPENING DOOR (BOTH SIDES) WITH HANDLE ALWAYS ON SIDE FURTHEST FROM LOOKOUT

G.L.

G.L.

G.L.

REPEAT BOGIE

BODY SUPPORT BRACKETS FOR 8'6" WIDE STOCK

VACUUM CYLINDER FAR SIDE, 2'1" FROM LONGITUDINAL ₵

GAS CYLINDER (SEE NOTES)

BATTERY BOX ON BOTH SIDES

REPEAT VAC. CYLINDER THIS SIDE

3'3" 8'0" 27'6" 8'0" 3'3"

2'0"

3'6"

9'6¼"

8'0"

3'3"

NOTES

1. UNDERFRAME DETAIL IS FOR ELECTRIC LIGHT. FOR GASLIT CONDITION OMIT BATTERY BOXES AND DYNAMO AND REPLACE WITH TWO GAS CYLINDERS 9'6"×16" (DIAM.) SET 4'0" BETWEEN CENTRES IN POSITION SHOWN BY DOTTED LINES.

2. END ELEVATION OMITS HANDRAILS &c. FOR THESE SEE DRG. J.W.G.

3. INTERIOR PLANS ARE HALF MAN SCALE. ROOF VENTS AND GASLAMPS ARE MARKED, GAS LAMPS BEING RINGED THUS:-

4. DIMENSIONS QUOTED FOR COMPARTMENTS ARE LENGTH BETWEEN PARTITIONS.

5. ON FULL BRAKE GUARD'S DOORS AND LOOK-OUTS WERE DIRECTLY OPPOSITE EACH OTHER AND NOT DIAGONALLY OPPOSITE.

DRAWING J.W.7

8'6" END ELEVATION (FULL VAN ONLY)

9'6"

7'10"

4'10"

8'6" (BOGIE STEPS)

8'8" (SOLEBAR STEPS)

9'2" (OVER LOOKOUTS)

INTERIOR LAYOUTS - SEE NOTES

NOTE: TORPEDO VENTS ON FULL BRAKE LOCATED EITHER SIDE OF ROOF HATCHES & 2'0" FROM CENTRELINE

THIS SECTION ORIGINALLY 2nd CLASS

W.C. | 1st | 1st | 3rd | 3rd | W.C. | 3rd | 3rd | 3rd | 3rd

8'0"

W.C. | 1st | 1st | 3rd | 3rd | GUARD/BRAKE | 3rd | 3rd | 3rd

8'0"

W.C. | 3rd | 3rd | 3rd | 3rd | 3rd | 3rd | 3rd | 3rd | 3rd

8'0"

50'0"

COMPOSITE
FIRSTS: 7'1¼"
THIRDS: 5'10¼"
TOILETS: 4'0½" AND 3'2"

BRAKE COMPO.
FIRSTS: 7'1¼"
THIRDS: 5'10¼"
GUARD: 9'1¼"
TOILETS: 4'0½"

THIRD
THIRDS: 5'10¼"
TOILETS: 3'11¾"

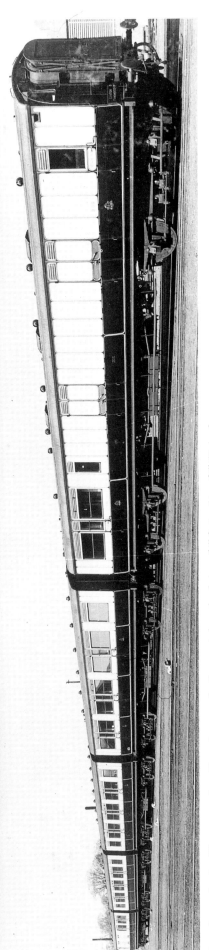

A neatly posed train of five cove roof corridors when new, the three central coaches being a full first and two full thirds of the types drawn on page 80. The leading vehicle is a rare two compartment brake first. Only four were built, two of which were rebuilt with clerestory roofs in 1923 for the Royal Train and are now preserved by the NRM

LNWR Cove Roof Corridor Stock

Apart from the first design of all (a neat 50ft Brake Composite for the Central Wales and similar services), the cove roof period was to see the establishment of a 57ft length for LNWR corridor stock which, with a few exceptions, became the LNWR standard. Many varieties appeared and to cover them more fully, this section consists of three pages of fully annotated drawings (which should be self explanatory) but only one page of text. The 50ft carriages used the underframe on page 77, the 57ft underframe appearing on page 81 along with plans of the five types featured. Some of them catered for the second class until 1912 - see floor plans. Two types were repeated in the elliptical roof period and may be derived by using the end elevations given on page 84. Details of these two are given in the summary below - see footnotes. There were also cove roof versions of some of the elliptical roof types on pages 83-5, details of which will be found on page 82.

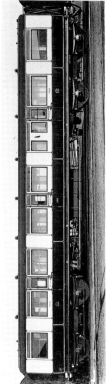

PROTOTYPE DETAILS

Quantity	Sample LNWR Numbers		1st LMS		2nd LMS		Extinct
50ft CORRIDOR COMPOSITE BRAKE BUILT 1903 (LNWR D214)							
10	5715; 5752; 5843; 5885; 5718		9725-9734		7049-7058		1953 *
57ft CORRIDOR COMPOSITE BRAKE BUILT 1906 (LNWR D208)							
40	6092/6; 6101/4; 6110-45		9575-9614		7086-7124		1956 §
57ft CORRIDOR FIRST CLASS BUILT 1906-7 (LNWR D95)							
9	4632-3/8-9; 4651-2/6-7/60		10036-10044	1143-51			#
¥ 3	4537; 4551; 4561		10033-10035	1152-4			# ¥
57ft CORRIDOR THIRD CLASS BUILT 1906-7 (LNWR D264)							
30	131; 224; 362; 739; 1478; 1612		4313-4339		2773-2999		1953 †
¥ 7	721; 804/6-7; 1469; 1636/49		4306-4312		2800-2806		1956 ¥
57ft CORRIDOR COMPOSITE BUILT 1907 (LNWR D134)							
9	2670; 3706-7; 3888-90; 4030		8145-8153		4656-4664		1956

* One example (5718-9734-7058) had a typing compartment replacing the first class compartment adjacent to the brake van. LMS 7057 later to all third as LMS 6429

§ One example (6132-9601-7111) had a typing compartment replacing the third class compartment adjacent to the firsts. Fitted with 8ft bogies. Some to all third later

To full thirds in 1936 as 2241-8 (cove roof)/2249; 2236-7 (high roof) in same order as listed in summary (final withdrawal dates not known). One early cove roof casualty

¥ Elliptical roof equivalents built 1908 (Firsts - D94; Thirds - D263)

† Three converted for push-pull use before grouping

Two more types featured on the drawings page. Above is the 57ft composite No.1815 to D134 featured on page 81 (later numbers not known) and to the left is the first of the cove roof corridor types in the form of a 50ft brake composite to D214, No.900 (Later LNWR 5885; LMS 9733/7057). The drawing for this design is opposite

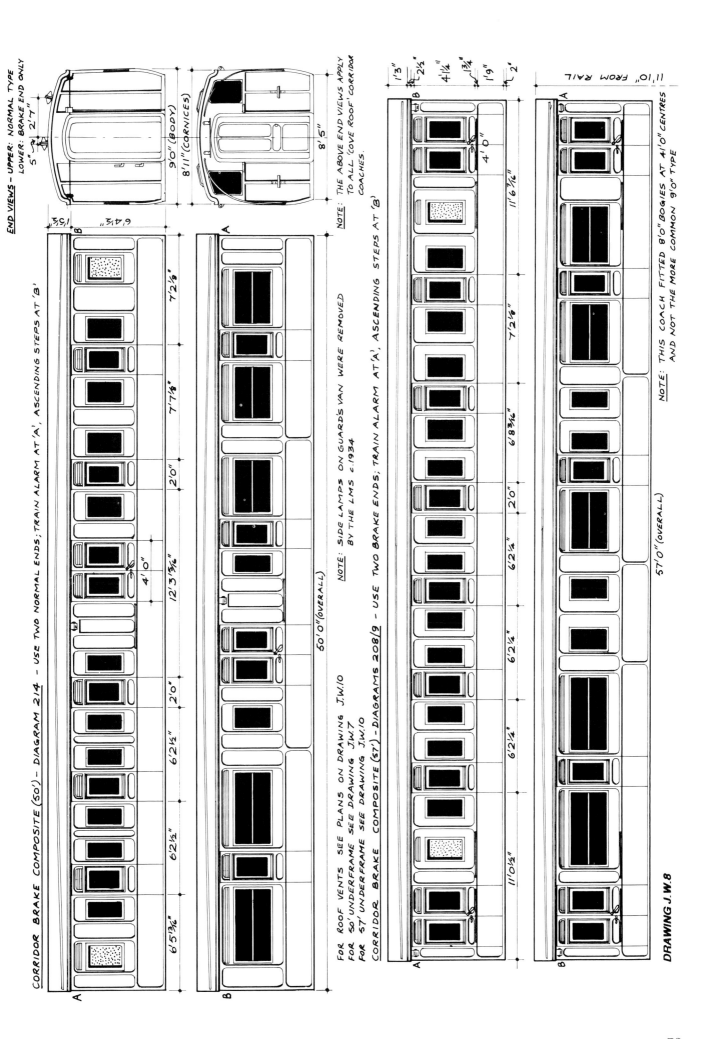

END VIEWS – UPPER: NORMAL TYPE
LOWER: BRAKE END ONLY

5" 2'-7"

9'0"(BODY)
8'11"(CORNICES)

8'5"

NOTE: THE ABOVE END VIEWS APPLY TO ALL 'COVE ROOF' CORRIDOR COACHES.

CORRIDOR BRAKE COMPOSITE (50') – DIAGRAM 214 – USE TWO NORMAL ENDS; TRAIN ALARM AT 'A', ASCENDING STEPS AT 'B'

1'3½"
6'4½"

7'2⅝"
7'7⅛"
2'0"
12'3⁵⁄₁₆"
4'0"
2'0"
6'2½"
6'2½"
6'5³⁄₁₆"

50'0"(OVERALL)

NOTE: SIDE LAMPS ON GUARD'S VAN WERE REMOVED BY THE LMS c.1934

FOR ROOF VENTS SEE PLANS ON DRAWING J.W.10
FOR 50' UNDERFRAME SEE DRAWING J.W.7
FOR 57' UNDERFRAME SEE DRAWING J.W.10

CORRIDOR BRAKE COMPOSITE (57') – DIAGRAMS 208/9 – USE TWO BRAKE ENDS; TRAIN ALARM AT 'A', ASCENDING STEPS AT 'B'

1'3"
2½"
4'¼"
3¾"
1'9"
2"

4'0"

11'6½"

7'2½"
2'0"
6'8³⁄₁₆"
6'2½"
6'2½"
11'0½"

11'10" FROM RAIL

NOTE: THIS COACH FITTED 8'0" BOGIES AT 4'0" CENTRES AND NOT THE MORE COMMON 9'0" TYPE

57'0"(OVERALL)

DRAWING J.W.8

79

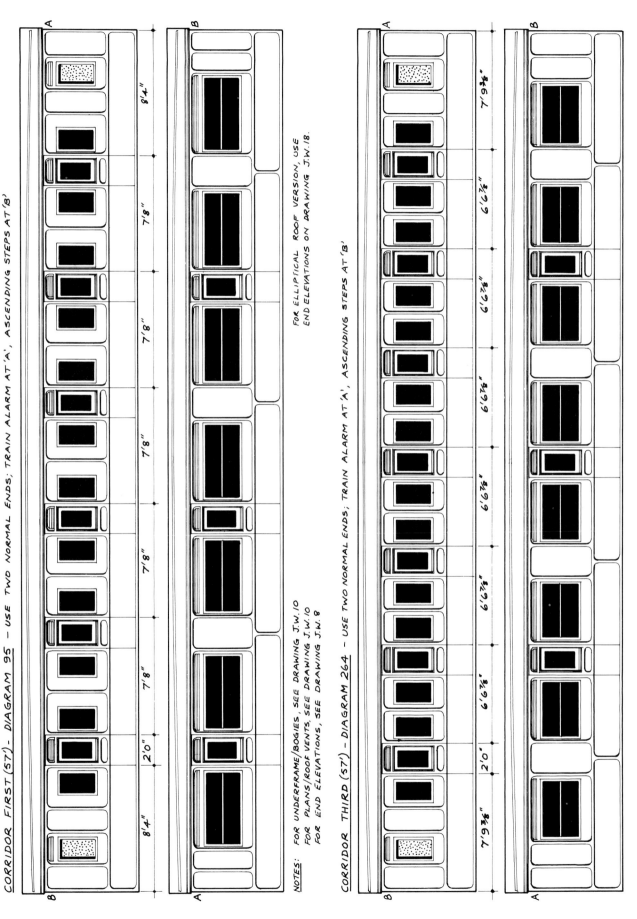

CORRIDOR FIRST (57') – DIAGRAM 95 – USE TWO NORMAL ENDS; TRAIN ALARM AT 'A', ASCENDING STEPS AT 'B'

NOTES: FOR UNDERFRAME/BOGIES, SEE DRAWING J.W.10
FOR PLANS/ROOF VENTS, SEE DRAWING J.W.10
FOR END ELEVATIONS, SEE DRAWING J.W. 8

FOR ELLIPTICAL ROOF VERSION, USE
END ELEVATIONS ON DRAWING J.W.18.

CORRIDOR THIRD (57') – DIAGRAM 264 – USE TWO NORMAL ENDS; TRAIN ALARM AT 'A', ASCENDING STEPS AT 'B'

DRAWING J.W.9

80

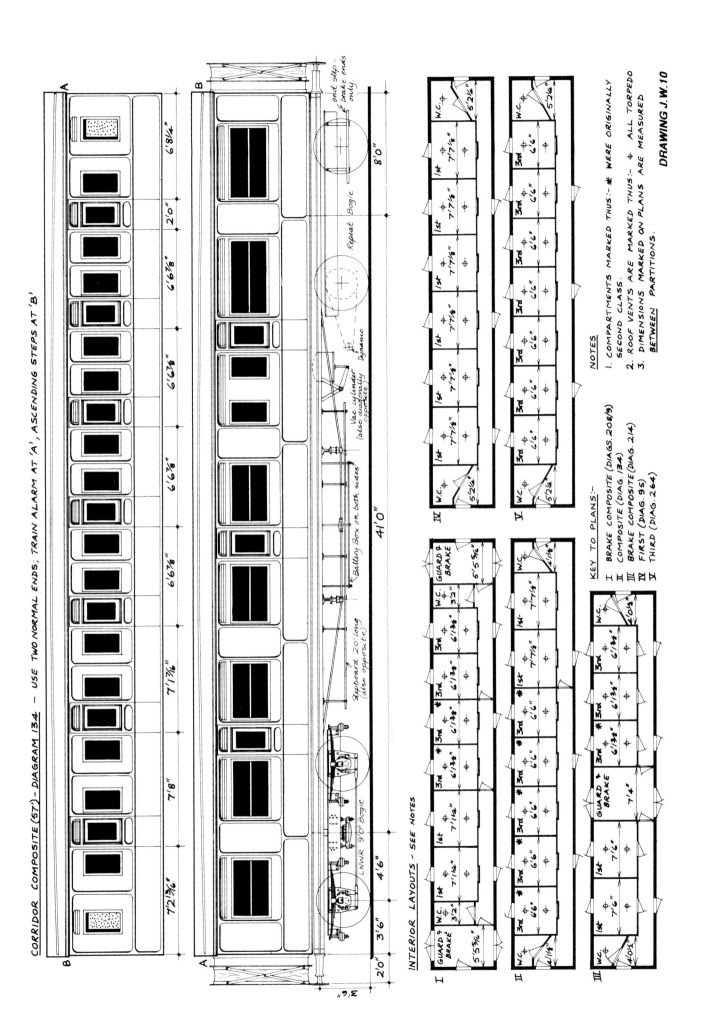

CORRIDOR COMPOSITE (57) - DIAGRAM 134. - USE TWO NORMAL ENDS; TRAIN ALARM AT 'A', ASCENDING STEPS AT 'B'

INTERIOR LAYOUTS - SEE NOTES

KEY TO PLANS:-

I   BRAKE COMPOSITE (DIAGS. 208/9)
II   COMPOSITE (DIAG. 134)
III BRAKE COMPOSITE (DIAG. 214)
IV   FIRST (DIAG. 9s)
V   THIRD (DIAG. 264)

NOTES

1. COMPARTMENTS MARKED THUS :- ✱ WERE ORIGINALLY
   SECOND CLASS.
2. ROOF VENTS ARE MARKED THUS :- ⊕ ALL TORPEDO
3. DIMENSIONS MARKED ON PLANS ARE MEASURED
   BETWEEN PARTITIONS.

DRAWING J.W.10

81

LNWR 57ft Elliptical Roof Corridor Stock

The carriages in this next section cover the period 1907-10 and were in direct continuation of the cove roof types on the previous four pages. Once again, so as to allow more comprehensive coverage, three pages of drawings and only one page of notes are offered. The cove/elliptical roof phase was continous so, as with elliptical roof types derived from cove roof drawings already offered, this section includes near-identical cove roof types which preceded those given here. Such differences as did exist (apart from the roof profile) are given on the drawings.

Five varieties are again offered (with interior plans), underframes were as shown on page 81 and the cove roof variants are given in the summary table. Note however that in this series, the full thirds were 8ft 6in wide (for greater route availability) and had one extra compartment.

PROTOTYPE DETAILS

Quantity	Sample LNWR Numbers	1st LMS	2nd LMS	Extinct
57ft CORRIDOR COMPOSITE BUILT 1907-8(LNWR D133)				
32	2640; 3160; 3929-58	8113-8144	4626-55/65-6	*
57ft CORRIDOR COMPOSITE BRAKE BUILT 1908-10 (LNWR D205)				
18	6093/7/9/100/2-3/5-9; 6152-8	9544-9561	7125-34/41-8	1953
57ft CORRIDOR THIRD CLASS BRAKE BUILT 1908 (LNWR D312)				
49	6657/82-3; 7062; 7285-7; 7307	6627-6674	6177/81-227	1958 §
¥ 12	6658; 6660-70	6675-6686	6168-76/8-80	1955 ¥
57ft CORRIDOR THIRD CLASS BUILT 1908 (LNWR D265)				
174	15; 394; 540; 1450-2; 2214	4422-4595	2828-2987	#
57ft CORRIDOR FIRST CLASS BRAKE BUILT 1908 (LNWR D125)				
2	5601/3	9681-9682	7079-7080	1948 †
¥ 20	5604-23	9661-9680	7059-7078	1953 † ¥

* Final extinction dates unavailable, but during mid-1950s
§ One pre-group casualty and LMS 6177 confused with D313 at the 1933 renumbering!
¥ Cove roof predecessors built 1906-7 (Brake Thirds - D313; Brake Firsts - D126)
8ft 6in wide carriages
† Converted to brake composite (2F+2T) in 1922 - details of consequential bodywork changes are on page 85 (D210 - elliptical roof/D210A - cove roof). LNWR numbers are in first class series, LMS numbers are as brake composites

The picture at the top of the page shows an 8ft 6in wide corridor third No.1488 to D265 (drawing on page 84). It later became LMS 4549/2958 and was withdrawn in 1951.

The view to the left shows the corridor side of LMS No.4627, a 9ft wide composite to D133 in somewhat scruffy full LMS livery - drawings opposite. Originally a tri-composite, this was the first type of elliptical roof corridor to appear and the example

CORRIDOR COMPOSITE – DIAGRAM 133 — USE TWO NORMAL 9'0" ENDS; TRAIN ALARM AT 'A', ASCENDING STEPS AT 'B'

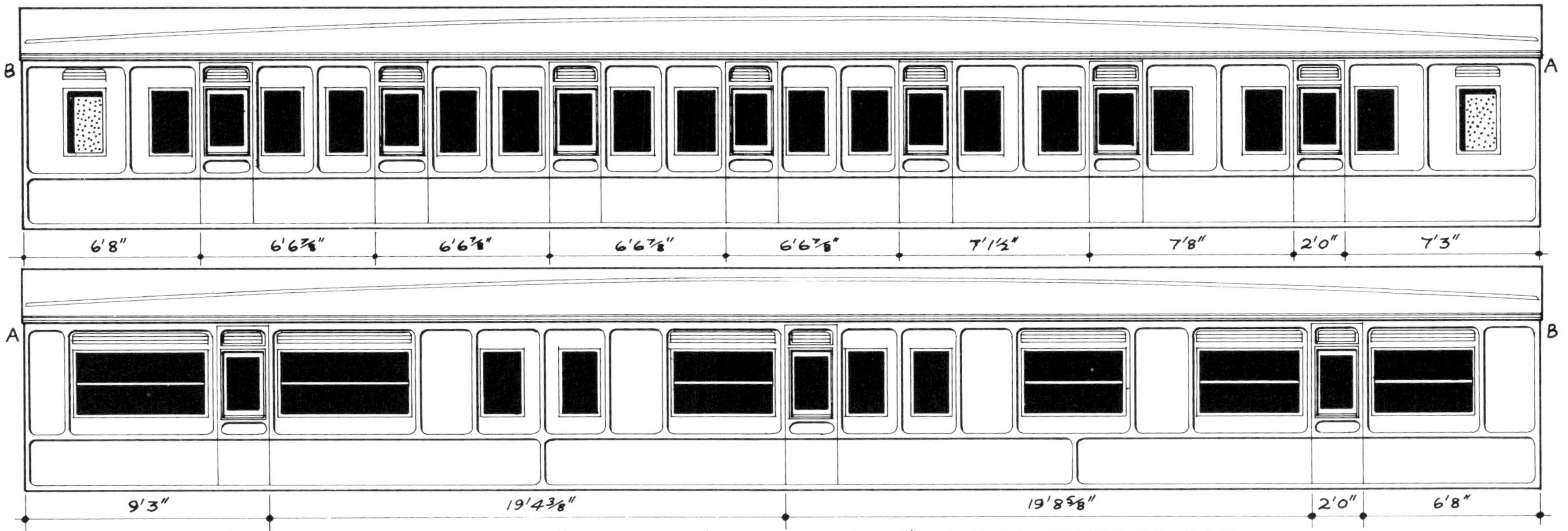

NOTES: 1. UNDERFRAME/BOGIES AS FOR COVE ROOF STOCK (DRAWING J.W.10). FOR PLANS/ROOF VENTS, SEE DRAWING J.W.19.
2. FOR END ELEVATIONS, SEE DRAWING J.W.18.

CORRIDOR BRAKE COMPOSITE – DIAGRAM 205 — USE TWO BRAKE ENDS (9'0"); TRAIN ALARM AT 'A', ASCENDING STEPS AT 'B'

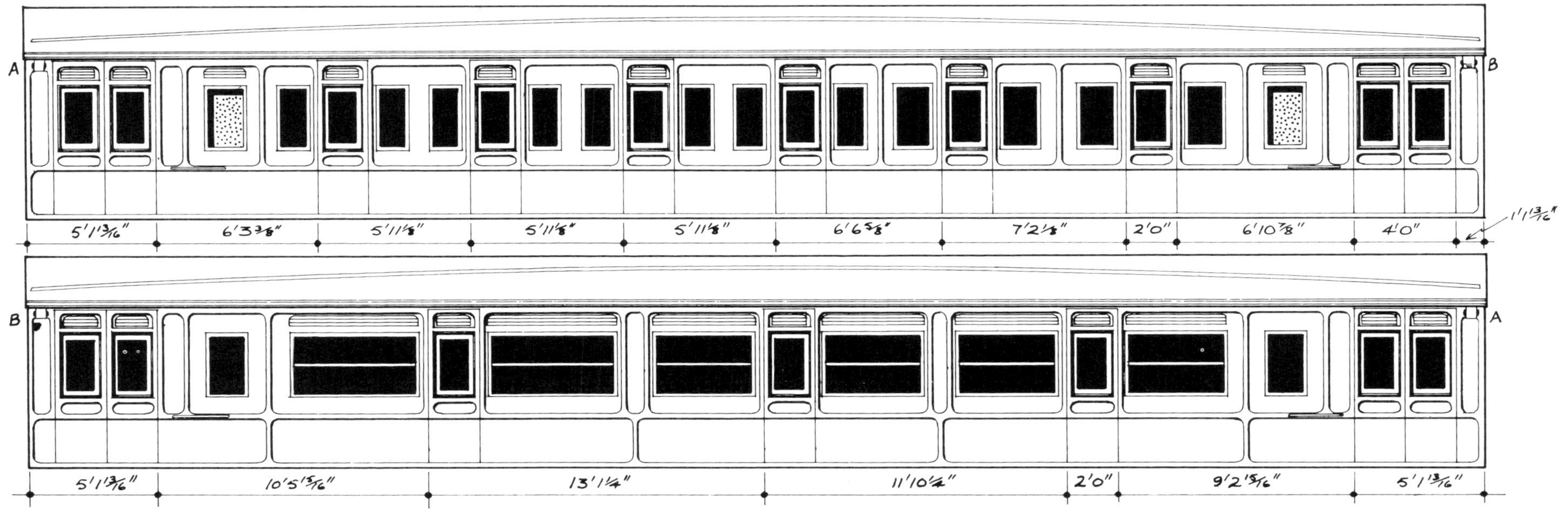

DRAWING J.W.17

83

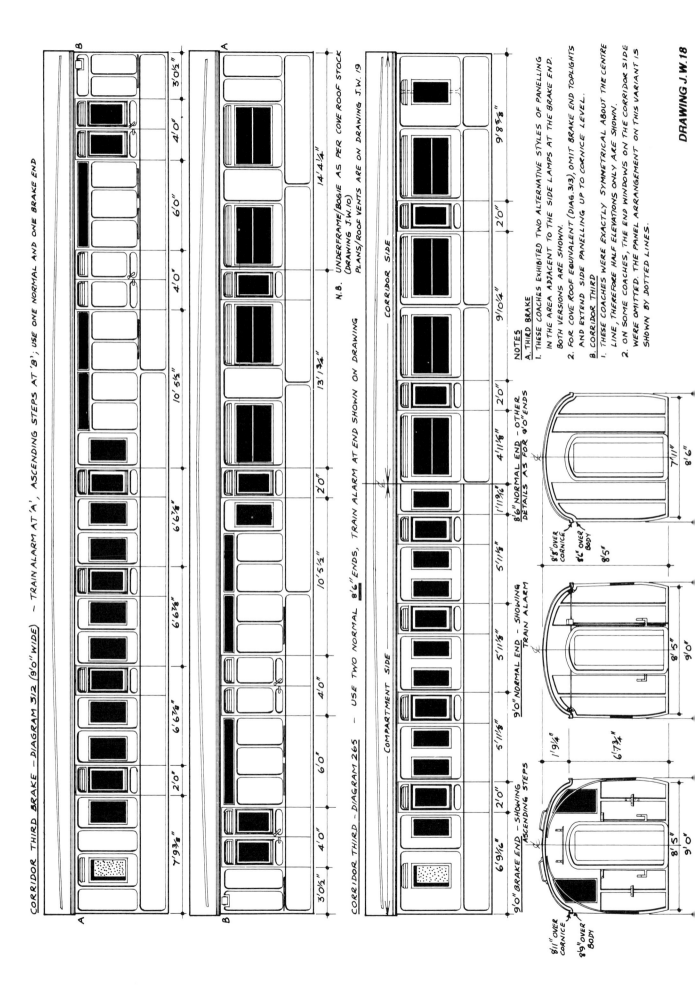

CORRIDOR THIRD BRAKE — DIAGRAM 312 (9'0" WIDE) — TRAIN ALARM AT 'A', ASCENDING STEPS AT 'B'; USE ONE NORMAL AND ONE BRAKE END

| 3'0½" | 4'0" | 6'0" | 4'0" | 10'5½" | 6'6⅞" | 6'6⅞" | 6'0" | 2'0" | 6'6⅞" | 4'0" | 7'9⅜" |

CORRIDOR THIRD — DIAGRAM 265 — USE TWO NORMAL 8'6" ENDS, TRAIN ALARM AT END SHOWN ON DRAWING

| 14' 4¼" | 6'0" | 4'0" | 13' 7¼" | 2'0" | 10'5½" | 6'6⅞" | 4'0" | 6'0" | 2'0" | 3'0½" |

N.B. UNDERFRAME/BOGIE AS PER COVE ROOF STOCK (DRAWING J.W.10)
PLANS/ROOF VENTS ARE ON DRAWING J.W.19

CORRIDOR SIDE

| 9'8⅝" | 2'0" | 9'10¼" | 4'11⅛" | 2'0" | 5'11⅛" | 5'11⅛" | 6'9½" | 2'0" |

COMPARTMENT SIDE

9'0" BRAKE END — SHOWING ASCENDING STEPS

1'9¼"

6'7¾"

8'5"
9'0"

8'11" OVER CORNICE
8'9" OVER BODY

9'0" NORMAL END — SHOWING TRAIN ALARM

8'5"
9'0"

8'6" NORMAL END — OTHER DETAILS AS FOR 9'0" ENDS

1'11 9/16"

7'11"
8'6"

8'8" OVER CORNICE
8'6" OVER BODY
8'5"

NOTES

A. THIRD BRAKE
1. THESE COACHES EXHIBITED TWO ALTERNATIVE STYLES OF PANELLING IN THE AREA ADJACENT TO THE SIDE LAMPS AT THE BRAKE END. BOTH VERSIONS ARE SHOWN.
2. FOR COVE ROOF EQUIVALENT (DIAG.3.3), OMIT BRAKE END TOPLIGHTS AND EXTEND SIDE PANELLING UP TO CORNICE LEVEL.

B. CORRIDOR THIRD
1. THESE COACHES WERE EXACTLY SYMMETRICAL ABOUT THE CENTRE LINE, THEREFORE HALF ELEVATIONS ONLY ARE SHOWN.
2. ON SOME COACHES, THE END WINDOWS ON THE CORRIDOR SIDE WERE OMITTED. THE PANEL ARRANGEMENT ON THIS VARIANT IS SHOWN BY DOTTED LINES.

DRAWING J.W.18

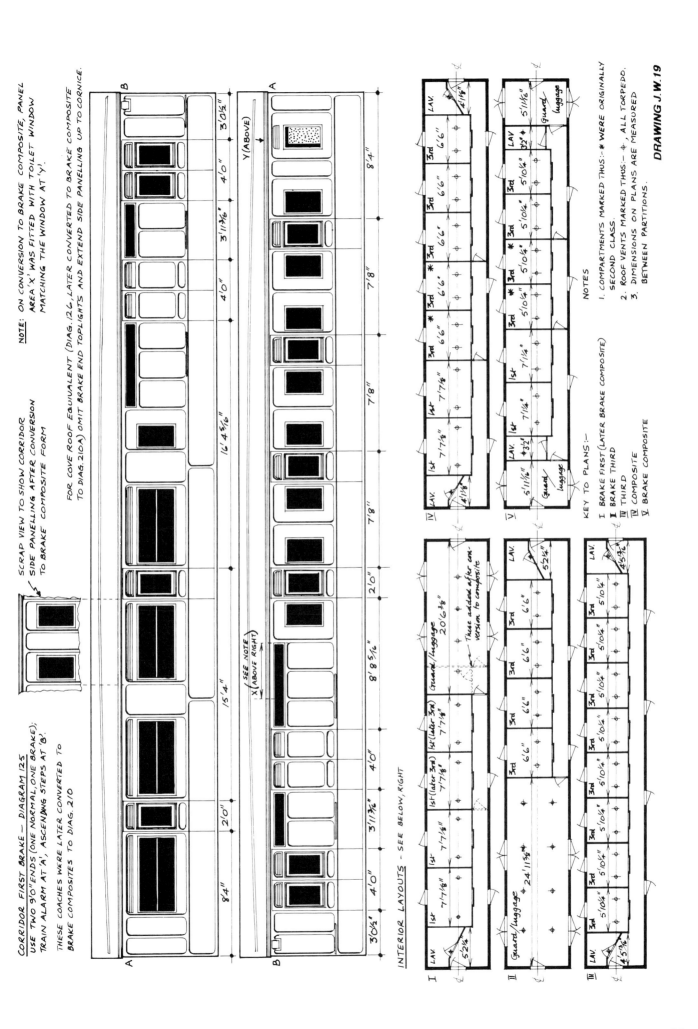

CORRIDOR FIRST BRAKE — DIAGRAM 125
USE TWO 9'0" ENDS (ONE NORMAL, ONE BRAKE).
TRAIN ALARM AT 'A', ASCENDING STEPS AT 'B'.

THESE COACHES WERE LATER CONVERTED TO
BRAKE COMPOSITES TO DIAG. 210

SCRAP VIEW TO SHOW CORRIDOR
SIDE PANELLING AFTER CONVERSION
TO BRAKE COMPOSITE FORM

NOTE: ON CONVERSION TO BRAKE COMPOSITE, PANEL
AREA 'X' WAS FITTED WITH TOILET WINDOW
MATCHING THE WINDOW AT 'Y'.

FOR COVE ROOF EQUIVALENT (DIAG. 126, LATER CONVERTED TO BRAKE COMPOSITE
TO DIAG. 210A) OMIT BRAKE END TOPLIGHTS AND EXTEND SIDE PANELLING UP TO CORNICE.

INTERIOR LAYOUTS - SEE BELOW, RIGHT

NOTES

1. COMPARTMENTS MARKED THUS:-* WERE ORIGINALLY
SECOND CLASS.

2. ROOF VENTS MARKED THUS:- φ, ALL TORPEDO.

3. DIMENSIONS ON PLANS ARE MEASURED
BETWEEN PARTITIONS.

KEY TO PLANS:-
I   BRAKE FIRST (LATER BRAKE COMPOSITE)
II   BRAKE THIRD
III THIRD
IV   COMPOSITE
V   BRAKE COMPOSITE

DRAWING J.W.19

85

LNWR/WCJS Clerestory Sleeping & Dining Cars

The famous 65ft 6in Wolverton 12-wheelers began to appear in 1895 and continued building for almost 20 years in many varieties, but space allows only a representative sample to be offered, starting on this page with two significant types. The sleeping car was the older of the two, identical examples being built for LNWR and WCJS use. They were 8ft 6in wide and utilised the narrow entrance lobby and ornate scrollwork which was characteristic of these earlier types. The dining car was a wholly WCJS type and had the later 9ft width, wider entry lobbies and modified clerestory roof shape. The WCJS preferred to use composite dining cars with central kitchens and two of this type were rostered into the famous 1908 '2pm' 12-wheel sets featured on page 90.

Note that underframe detail on these and all the featured LNWR and WCJS 12-wheel types has had to be obtained from pictures and by assuming known standard practices. There were also slight detail changes with the passage of time and photographs may show variations from the details as drawn. It should also be noted that the rather florid (and large) style of early lettering seen on some of the pictures did not last beyond early Edwardian days.

NOTE: For space reasons, some of the pictures illustrating this section have been placed on page 88.

These two pictures show opposite side views of the 8ft 6in wide clerestory sleeping cars to WCJS D5 (No.265 - above) and LNWR D20 (No.129, later 5129 - below), both displaying the florid 'turn of century' lettering along the headboard. The cars became LMS 10381 and 10371 respectively after 1922 (withdrawn late 1932 and late 1927) and are also believed to have been the first cars built to this type. Compared with the drawings, they show double windows throughout, a feature believed to have been confined to the first two examples only on each of the two diagrams (ie LNWR 129/30; WCJS 256/489), the rest being built as per the drawing. It is not known if the earlier carriages were later converted to match, though it is quite probable. Over time, LNWR/West Coast sleeping cars were regularly updated and modernised, often with changes to the window arrangement

After the grouping, the LMS continued to modernise some of the Wolverton 12-wheelers and this is former WCJS D9 No.10421, resplendent in fully lined LMS livery at the time of a complete interior refurbishment with standard LMS pattern fittings and simplified decor. It started life as WCJS No.484, fixed seating replaced the individual chairs (see plan) before the grouping, it became LMS No.274 after 1933 and was withdrawn at the end of 1947

PROTOTYPE DETAILS

Quantity	Pre-Group Numbers	1st LMS	2nd LMS	Extinct
65ft 6in FIRST CLASS SLEEPING SALOON BUILT 1897-9 (LNWR D20; WCJS D5)				
5	LNWR 5129-30/4-6	10371-10375	438-440	c.1933-4 *
7	WCJS 142-6; 265; 489	10376-10382	441-446	1932 *
65ft 6in COMPOSITE DINING SALOON BUILT 1905 (WCJS D9)				
12	WCJS 483-8; 527-32	10420-10431	273-284	1950 §

* These cars were mostly replaced by new LMS standard types from c.1927 but exact 'final survival' dates cannot be offered for LNWR D20. The second LMS series numbers were allocated to all survivors in 1932 but apart from Nos.438-40 and No.443, none of the other cars carried them. Many went into departmental use as 'staff dormitory cars'.

§ Apart from two earlier 8ft 6in wide end-kitchen types retained for Royal Train use (not featured in this review) which ran until 1956 and 1966, the WCJS D9 carriages were, by some margin, the last Wolverton pre-group clerestory dining cars to run in general service. Latterly used as 'spare' and/or 'extra' diners (eg LMS 273-8 were allocated to the through summer services to Ramsgate just before the war), it seems unlikely that they had much post-war use, given the slow reinstatement of full catering facilities.

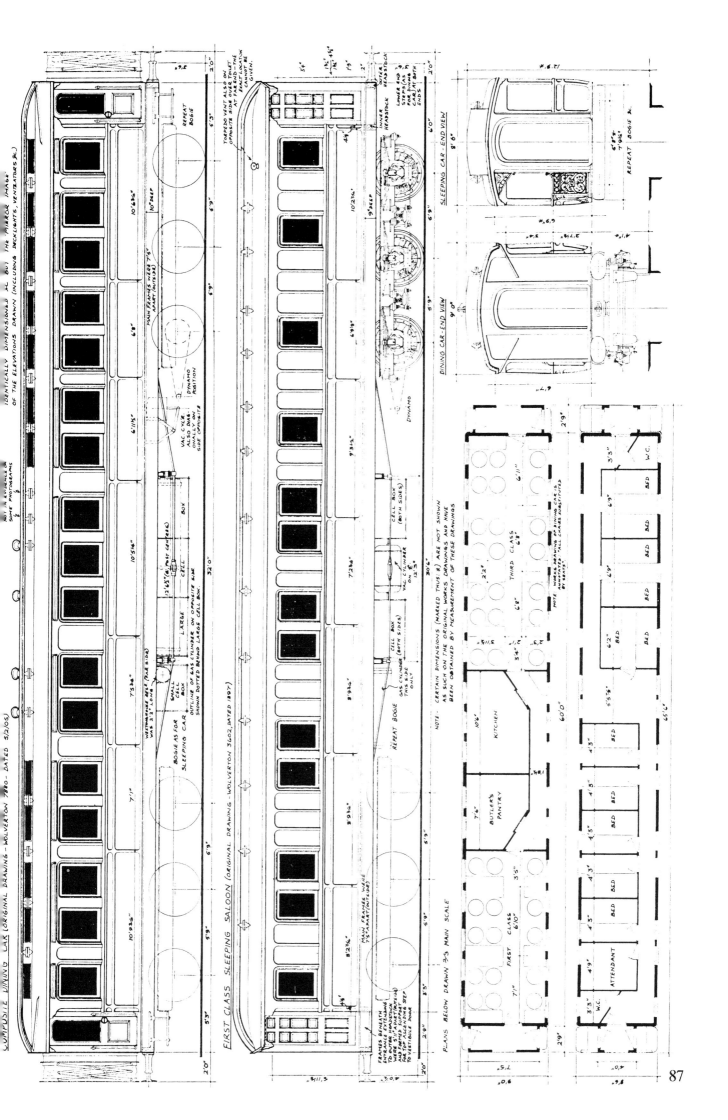

COMPOSITE DINING CAR (ORIGINAL DRAWING - WOLVERTON 7280 - DATED 5/2/03)

NOT IN EVIDENCE ON SOME PHOTOGRAMS

IDENTICALLY DIMENSIONED & BUT THE MIRROR IMAGE OF THE ELEVATIONS DRAWN (INCLUDING DECKLIGHTS, VENTILATORS &.)

FIRST CLASS SLEEPING SALOON (ORIGINAL DRAWING - WOLVERTON 3602, DATED 1897)

SLEEPING CAR-END VIEW

DINING CAR-END VIEW

PLANS BELOW DRAWN ⅓ MAIN SCALE

NOTE:- CERTAIN DIMENSIONS (MARKED THUS:-*) ARE NOT SHOWN AS SUCH ON THE ORIGINAL WORKS DRAWINGS AND HAVE BEEN OBTAINED BY MEASUREMENT OF THESE DRAWINGS

87

LNWR Clerestory Composite Dining Car

For its 'domestic' (ie non-WCJS) services, the LNWR preferred the end-kitchen form of dining car and regularly rostered two (or more) such vehicles into its trains for the different classes, one of them always being a dedicated first class only car. Before the abolition of second class in 1912, it was common for the additional diner to be a 2nd/3rd class composite and the type featured here was built in that form during 1903-4, the first dining cars to display the new 9ft width and styling. In 1912, eight of them were reclassified 1st/3rd (LNWR D35A), the rest being marked down to all third (LNWR D39), almost certainly all of them without any significant internal changes. They reached the LMS in this configuration and did not long withstand the onslaught of new Period III types in the 1930s (see page 58). In 1938, LMS 178/180-1 were converted into mobile ARP (Air Raid Precaution) lecture cars.

PROTOTYPE DETAILS

Quantity	LNWR Numbers	1st LMS	2nd LMS	Extinct
20	5281-300	10451-10458*	265-272*	1935
		10481-10492§	171-182§	1938

* 1st/3rd Composites
§ 3rd Class cars

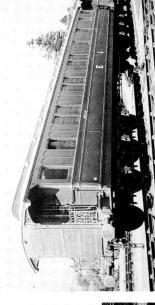

Composite dining car to D35A/D39 No.290 (later 5290) as built. This was one of eight which remained composite - see text - becoming LMS 10455, later 269 and being withdrawn in 1936

After withdrawal from normal service, it was common for the old 12-wheelers to go into service stock, their robust construction giving them many years of extra life. These pictures show former WCJS D9 dining car No.485 (LMS 10422/275) as converted to Emergency Mess Room No.0024 and a pre-war conversion of a narrow entrance sleeping car as engineers' sleeping van No.297238. This was a later type to the version drawn, having its corridor along one side only, but the removal of the gangways allows the detail of the entrances to be seen clearly

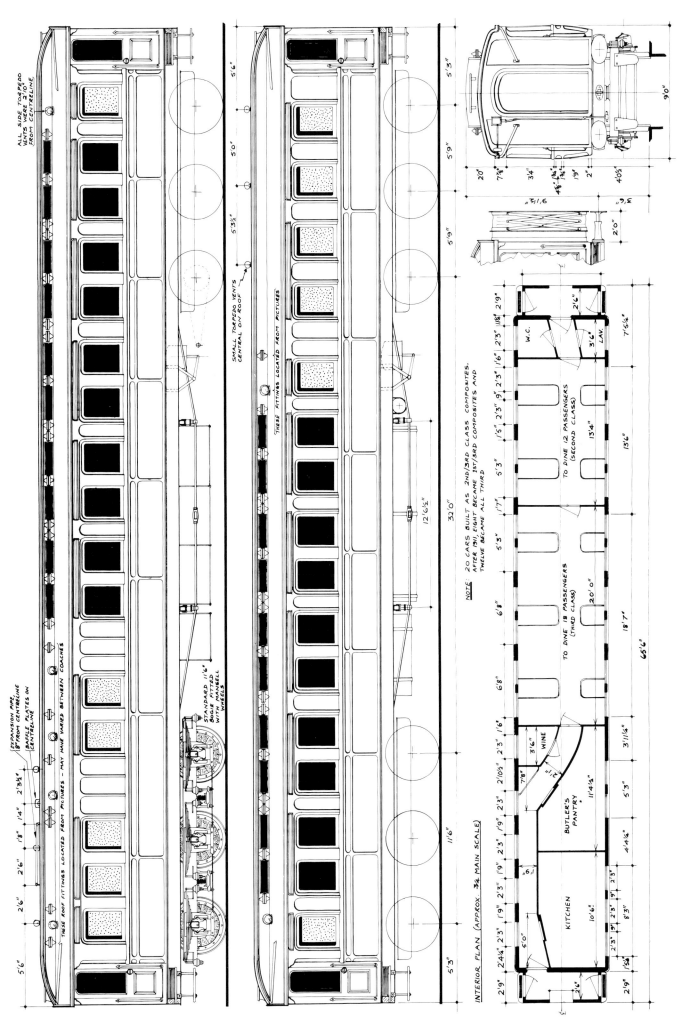

ALL SIDE TORPEDO VENTS WERE 2'0" FROM CENTRELINE

EXPANSION PIPE 8" FROM CENTRELINE

BAFFLE PLATES ON CENTRELINE

THESE ROOF FITTINGS LOCATED FROM PICTURES - MAY HAVE VARIED BETWEEN COACHES

STANDARD 11'6" BOGIE FITTED WITH MANSELL WHEELS

SMALL TORPEDO VENTS CENTRAL ON ROOF

THESE FITTINGS LOCATED FROM PICTURES

NOTE: 20 CARS BUILT AS 2ND/3RD CLASS COMPOSITES. AFTER 1911, EIGHT BECAME 1ST/3RD COMPOSITES AND TWELVE BECAME ALL THIRD

INTERIOR PLAN (APPROX. ¾ MAIN SCALE)

W.C.

LAV.

TO DINE 12 PASSENGERS (SECOND CLASS)

TO DINE 18 PASSENGERS (THIRD CLASS)

WINE

BUTLER'S PANTRY

KITCHEN

WCJS Special 12-wheel '2pm' Corridor Stock

Although not very numerous, the 65ft 6in 12-wheel day carriages built at Wolverton in 1908-9 for the WCJS '2pm' Anglo-Scottish train were so well-known and long-lived that no excuses are offered for giving them ample, albeit not fully comprehensive coverage here. Nicknamed 'Corridor' in 1893 when it was the first WCJS train to embody through gangways, this soubriquet remained in use for the 2pm departure from Euston for a generation or more, long after most other long distance trains also had corridors. The LMS later called it 'The Mid-Day Scot' and continued to use the 1908 carriages for several years after 1922.

Three types were built in no fewer than six varieties according to destination (one brake composite, two composite and three brake third variants), three of which are given here. Opposite is the 'Glasgow' composite while on the next spread are the 'Glasgow' brake third and 'Aberdeen' brake composite types, together with further underframe details and interior plans. Advantage has been taken of the slight extra space to offer information on the omitted 'Edinburgh' types which dedicated modellers could probably evolve should they so wish....

The 12-wheelers ran in an eight coach formation northbound only (supplemented by 'ordinary' stock if needed), arranged as follows, the sections being for Glasgow, Edinburgh and Aberdeen respectively:

BTK+CK+RC+BTK/=RC+CK+BTK/=BCK

The Aberdeen brake was worked forward separately from Preston, while the main train divided at Symington. Southbound, the sets came back in their three separate parts for operational reasons. The two diners were of the clerestory type described on page 86.

Individual variations were a little complex. Two of the Glasgow brake thirds (the 'north' end example in each set) were built opposite handed to the version drawn so as to keep the corridor on the West side of the train, while the Edinburgh brake third had four compartments and the composite 4F+3T rather than the 4½F+2T of the Glasgow type drawn. All are given in the summary from which it can be seen that the only 'spares' were of the types drawn, so it seems probable that the Glasgow types may have been used in the Edinburgh portion at times.

The '2pm' carriages remained in regular use on their designated service for about 20 years until replaced by some of the new 'luxury' stock with big windows built from 1928 onwards - see earlier pages. Thereafter for another 20 years or so, and in spite of their heavy and non-standard nature, they could be found running singly in all manner of LMS expresses and were still mostly in use in early BR days.

These two views show the brake-ended '2pm' stock featured on page 93, viewed from the corridor side. Above is 'Aberdeen' brake composite to Diagram W38 No.386 (LMS 9699/7213) seen from the same side as the drawing while the lower view shows the more common of the two Glasgow' brake thirds to Diagram W62 No.390 (LMS 6464/6390) from the opposite side to that shown on the drawing. In both cases, of course, the compartment side had twin windows throughout, rather than the alternating twin and double-width windows shown here.

The opposite handed 'Glasgow' brake thirds to Diagram W63 can be evolved quite easily by simply transposing the two side elevations shown here and on page 93, leaving all other details and dimensions unchanged

PROTOTYPE DETAILS

Type/Diag.	Qty.	WCJS Nos.	1st LMS	2nd LMS	Extinct
CK/W22	2	383-384	7989-7990	4778-4779	1951 *
CK/W23	4	379-382	7985-7988	4780-4783	1953 # @
BCK/W38	3	385-387	9698-9700	7212-7214	1953 § @
BTK/W62	5	390-394	6461-6465	6390-6394	¥ # @
BTK/W63	2	388-389	6468-6469	6395-6396	¥ # @ †
BTK/W64	2	395-396	6466-6467	6388-6389	¥ *

* Edinburgh carriages
\# Glasgow carriages
§ Aberdeen carriages
@ Drawings appended (opposite handed to get W63 from W62 as drawn)
¥ Extinction dates not known, probably c.1953
† Identically dimensioned to W62 but opposite handed

This excellent official view shows 'Glasgow' corridor composite to Diagram W23 No.381 (LMS 7987/4782) taken from the opposite side to the drawing given below - note the single window for the first class coupé at the left hand end. Note too, compared with the other '2pm' stock featured in this review, that the roof is clearly grey not white. This may have been a later change because the shade seems too dark to be 'degraded white'

NOTES 1. THIS ELEVATION SHOWS THE CORRIDOR SIDE. THE COMPARTMENT SIDE WAS A 'MIRROR IMAGE' BUT HAD STANDARD DOUBLE WINDOWS IN PLACE OF THE THREE OF THE FOUR LARGE SINGLE WINDOWS. THE ARRANGEMENT OPPOSITE THE FOURTH LARGE WINDOW IS SHOWN INSET.
2. END ELEVATIONS, BOGIE DETAILS AND INTERIOR PLAN OF THIS COACH ARE INCLUDED ON THE DRAWING OF THE MATCHING W.C.J.S. BRAKE THIRD AND BRAKE COMPOSITE.

ARRANGEMENT OF PANELLING
& ON COMPARTMENT SIDE

FOR FITTINGS ON OPPOSITE SIDE ELEVATION
OF UNDERFRAME REFER TO BRAKE THIRD

* ON COMPARTMENT SIDE, THESE DIMENSIONS
WERE 7'8" AND 9'11½₆" RESPECTIVELY

These two views show the omitted 'Edinburgh' types which should not be too difficult to evolve from the offered drawings. The upper view shows composite No.384 to Diagram W22 (LMS 7990/4779) which had a 4F + 3T layout. Compartment sizes were identical to those in the Glasgow version but the toilets were reduced by six inches to 4ft 0½in. The brake third No.395 to Diagram W64 (LMS 6466/6338) was identically dimensioned to the Glasgow version save for the reduction by one compartment and a corresponding increase in length at the van end. Note, however, that on this design only, vertical beading below the waist was centred under the windows, not the panels

The 'Glasgow' portion of the '2pm' leaving Glasgow Central behind the famous Caledonian 4-6-0 No.903 CARDEAN, an engine which virtually monopolised this service north of Carlisle (in both directions) for many years. Out of sight on the left behind the four-coach 12-wheel set would be additional ordinary stock for the less fortunate.....

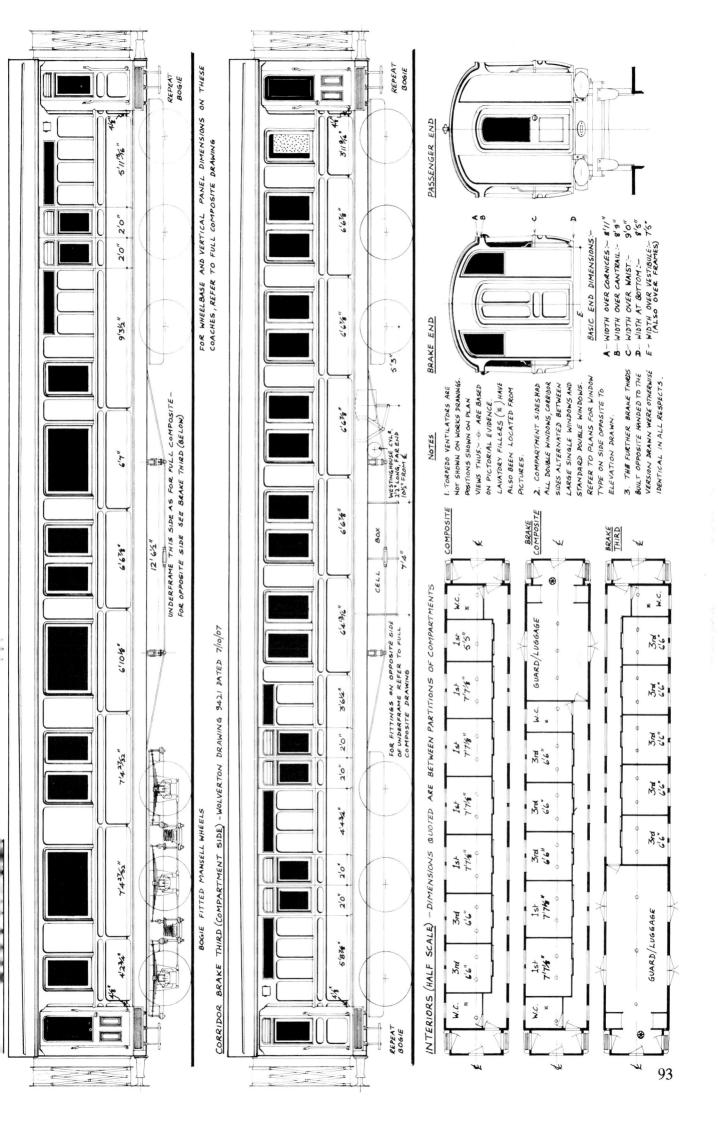

BOGIE FITTED MANSELL WHEELS

CORRIDOR BRAKE THIRD (COMPARTMENT SIDE) - WOLVERTON DRAWING 9421 DATED 7/10/07

FOR WHEELBASE AND VERTICAL PANEL DIMENSIONS ON THESE COACHES, REFER TO FULL COMPOSITE DRAWING

REPEAT BOGIE

UNDERFRAME THIS SIDE AS FOR FULL COMPOSITE - FOR OPPOSITE SIDE SEE BRAKE THIRD (BELOW)

FOR FITTINGS ON OPPOSITE SIDE OF UNDERFRAME REFER TO FULL COMPOSITE DRAWING

WESTINGHOUSE CYLR. 21" LONG, FAR END (10½" FROM C̲L̲)

CELL BOX

REPEAT BOGIE

PASSENGER END

BRAKE END

NOTES

1. TORPEDO VENTILATORS ARE NOT SHOWN ON WORKS DRAWINGS. POSITIONS SHOWN ON PLAN VIEWS THUS:- ⊕ - ARE BASED ON PICTORIAL EVIDENCE. LAVATORY FILLERS (⊗) HAVE ALSO BEEN LOCATED FROM PICTURES.

2. COMPARTMENT SIDES HAD ALL DOUBLE WINDOWS, CORRIDOR SIDES ALTERNATED BETWEEN LARGE SINGLE WINDOWS AND STANDARD DOUBLE WINDOWS. REFER TO PLANS FOR WINDOW TYPE ON SIDE OPPOSITE TO ELEVATION DRAWN.

3. THE FURTHER BRAKE THIRDS BUILT OPPOSITE HANDED TO THE VERSION DRAWN WERE OTHERWISE IDENTICAL IN ALL RESPECTS.

BASIC END DIMENSIONS:-

A - WIDTH OVER CORNICES:- 8'11"
B - WIDTH OVER CANTRAIL:- 8'9"
C - WIDTH OVER WAIST:- 9'0"
D - WIDTH AT BOTTOM:- 8'5"
E - WIDTH OVER VESTIBULE:- 7'5" (ALSO OVER FRAMES)

INTERIORS (HALF SCALE) - DIMENSIONS QUOTED ARE BETWEEN PARTITIONS OF COMPARTMENTS

COMPOSITE

BRAKE COMPOSITE

BRAKE THIRD

93

Midland Railway Six-wheel Stock

The MR was a huge user of six-wheel stock until the turn of the 19th/20th Centuries and in consequence many varieties lasted well into LMS days, some of which are featured here. The main drawing (based on the preserved example at the NRM) is a typical Clayton arc roof luggage composite of c.1884 while the other drawings (by the late Ralph Lacy) show other common types, together with an end elevation of the brake-ended arc roof type contemporary with the composite.

The arc roof carriages were built from 1883 to 1896 in two main series, short- and long-buffered. The short buffered stock had all gone before LMS times but the latter consisted of 31ft composites and third brakes (as drawn), plus 31ft thirds, derived by replacing the brake end with two more compartments, all types having steps/lamp brackets at each end. They were used on all kinds of trains and several hundred came to the LMS, some surviving until 1935-7.

The clerestory six-wheelers, dating from 1898-9, were 33ft 6in long and built for main line express use, just before the more familiar types shown on the next page and similar in both style and amenity. There were not too many of them (bogie types being about to appear) but the composites were both long-lived and typical, being built in two variants (see drawings) and two heights, both of which are shown.

To save space and since many old Midland numbers are lost from the records, the summary below makes no mention of numbers built, precise dates and/or diagrams and sample numbering only is offered - but see Bibliography (page 136) for more detailed MR sources.

The Clayton arc roof style was one of the most consistent in visual terms from the time of its introduction to its final demise just after the turn of the 19th/20th Centuries and this picture shows most of the relevant detail. It features the full third type which can be derived from the brake third drawing. M.S.J.S No.8 was one of many such carriages built for Anglo-Scottish services, this example being additionally interesting in having been constructed to Midland design by the G&SWR at its Kilmarnock works. Though very comfortable by mid/late Victorian standards, one cannot help but comment on the lack of lavatories and other amenities for a vehicle designed to operate over many hundreds of miles.....

PROTOTYPE DETAILS

Type	Last MR/1st LMS numbers	2nd LMS numbers	Extinct
ARC ROOF 31ft TYPES			
Luggage Composite	901; 3675-3712	none	pre-1933 #
Third	1709-1781	26459-63/6-71	1934
Third Brake	204; 865; 971; 1182; 1383	27720-27733	1937
CLERESTORY ROOF 33ft 6in TYPES			
Lavatory Composite	3056-3063	27443-27445	1936 *
	3108-3111	27446-27448	1936 §
Luggage Composite	3064-3073	27198-27202	1938 *
	3112-3116	27203-27204	1935 §

Some undoubtedly to LMS but no known post-1932 survivors
* 13ft 3in high
§ 13ft 1in high

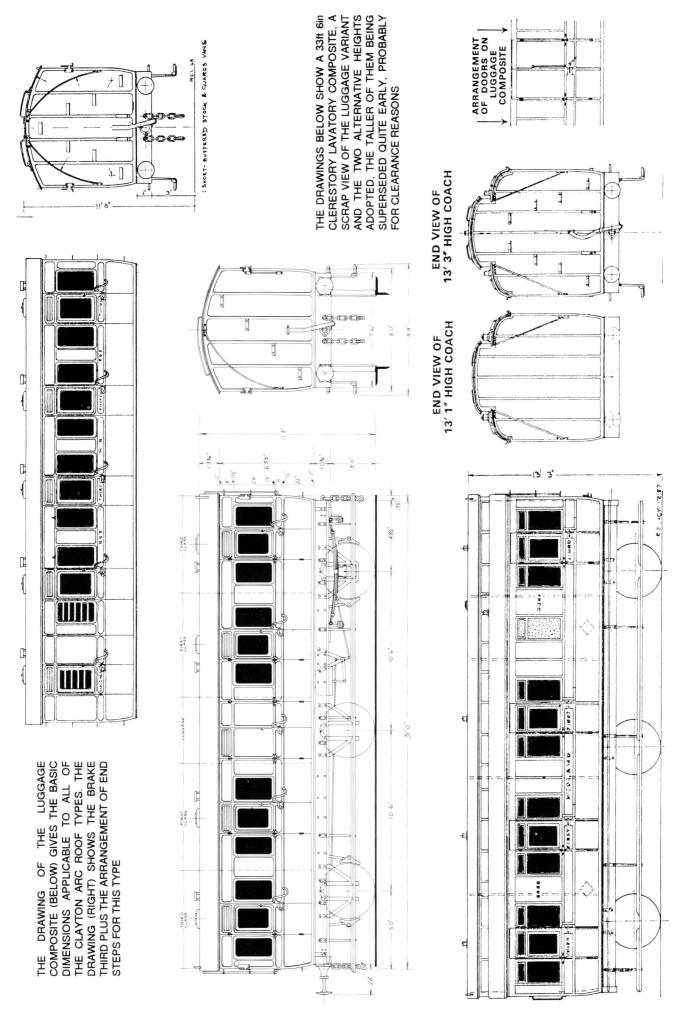

THE DRAWING OF THE LUGGAGE
COMPOSITE (BELOW) GIVES THE BASIC
DIMENSIONS APPLICABLE TO ALL OF
THE CLAYTON ARC ROOF TYPES. THE
DRAWING (RIGHT) SHOWS THE BRAKE
THIRD PLUS THE ARRANGEMENT OF END
STEPS FOR THIS TYPE

THE DRAWINGS BELOW SHOW A 33ft 6in
CLERESTORY LAVATORY COMPOSITE, A
SCRAP VIEW OF THE LUGGAGE VARIANT
AND THE TWO ALTERNATIVE HEIGHTS
ADOPTED, THE TALLER OF THEM BEING
SUPERSEDED QUITE EARLY, PROBABLY
FOR CLEARANCE REASONS

ARRANGEMENT
OF DOORS ON
LUGGAGE
COMPOSITE

END VIEW OF
13' 3" HIGH COACH

END VIEW OF
13' 1" HIGH COACH

SHORT-BUFFERED STOCK & GUARDS VANS

Midland Railway 48ft Lavatory Clerestory Stock

The Midland was slow to introduce corridor carriages and these types were built during 1897-1901 for main line use. After corridor types came on the scene they remained in use on secondary longer distance work until the mid-1930s and a few until 1948, most remaining gaslit throughout their lives. The clerestory top handrail (dating from c.1900) had mostly been replaced by a series of shorter rails on the side of the clerestory roof by c.1920.

From c.1910, many carriages had the transverse bogie springing replaced by coil springs and a few were given replacement 8ft bogies. Most lower stepboards were removed by the LMS in the later 1920s. A detail point to note (not shown on the drawings) is that from c.1906, part of the top moulding near the centre of the carriages was made deeper to carry the word 'MIDLAND' and this modification, though by now redundant, was retained after 1922. On many examples, probably most of them, the door toplight was later replaced by a conventional four-element louvre type ventilator and most LMS survivors displayed this change, though it canot be precisely dated.

These drawings should therefore be taken as typifying the type and not representative of any individual carriage. As usual, only sample pre-1933 numbers can be offered.

The view to the right shows close-up detail of typical square-panelled Midland clerestory stock (vehicles unidentified) while below is lavatory brake composite No.3052 (later cyphered 03052, final LMS No.25862) in LMS days showing replacement 8ft bogies and louvre ventilators above the doors. Note, however, that it is still gas-lit

PROTOTYPE DETAILS

Quantity	MR/1st LMS Numbers	2nd LMS numbers	Extinct
	LAVATORY THIRD CLASS BUILT 1898-1900 (MR D486)		
122	119; 286/9; 345; 1994-2043	18664-18777	1948
	LAVATORY THIRD CLASS BRAKE BUILT 1898-1900 (MR D499)		
61	103; 145; 164; 590; 1616; 2090-2114	25571-25628	1946
	LAVATORY COMPOSITE BUILT 1898-1901 (MR D509)		
49	3074-86; 3156; 3207-22; 3603; 3635	19683-19719	1948
	LAVATORY COMPOSITE BRAKE BUILT 1897-1901 (MR D508)		
68	3026-3055; 3719-38; 3256-64	25840-25907	1944 *

* There were approximately 100 further examples of this type listed on the same MR diagram with luggage compartment only and no brake, These included MR/1st LMS Nos. 3015-25/3748-72. Later survivors included 2nd LMS Nos.19617-19682 and this variant became extinct in 1946

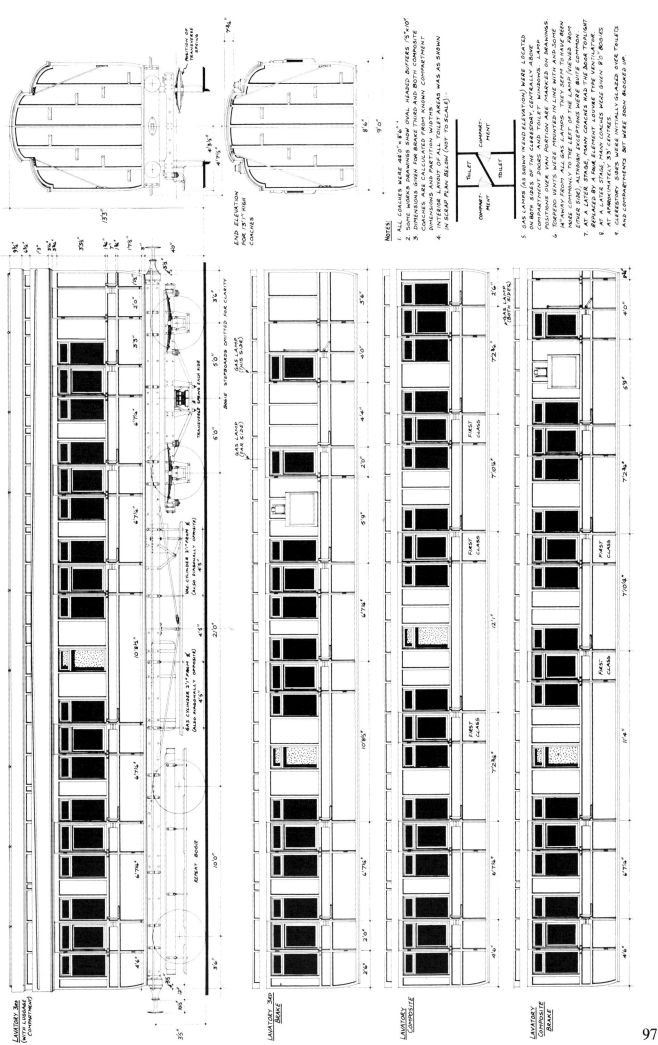

LAVATORY 3RD
(WITH LUGGAGE COMPARTMENT)

LAVATORY 3RD
BRAKE

LAVATORY COMPOSITE

LAVATORY COMPOSITE BRAKE

END ELEVATION FOR 131'11" HIGH COACHES

NOTES:

1. ALL COACHES WERE 48'0" × 8'6".

2. SOME WORKS DRAWINGS SHOW OVAL HEADED BUFFERS 1'5"×10".

3. DIMENSIONS GIVEN FOR BRAKE THIRD AND BOTH COMPOSITE COACHES ARE CALCULATED FROM KNOWN COMPARTMENT DIMENSIONS AND PARTITION WIDTHS.

4. INTERIOR LAYOUT OF ALL TOILET AREAS WAS AS SHOWN IN SCRAP PLAN BELOW (NOT TO SCALE):-

5. GAS LAMPS (AS SHOWN IN END ELEVATION) WERE LOCATED ON BOTH SIDES OF THE CLERESTORY, CENTRALLY ABOVE COMPARTMENT DOORS AND TOILET WINDOWS. LAMP POSITIONS OVER VAN PORTION ARE MARKED ON DRAWINGS.

6. TORPEDO VENTS WERE MOUNTED IN LINE WITH AND SOME 14" AWAY FROM ALL GAS LAMPS. THEY SEEM TO HAVE BEEN MORE COMMONLY TO THE LEFT OF THE LAMP (VIEWED FROM EITHER SIDE) ALTHOUGH EXCEPTIONS WERE QUITE COMMON.

7. AT A LATER STAGE, MANY COACHES HAD THE DOOR TOPLIGHT REPLACED BY A FIXED ELEMENT LOUVRE TYPE VENTILATOR.

8. AT A LATER STAGE, MANY COACHES WERE GIVEN 9'0 BOGIES AT APPROXIMATELY 33' CENTRES.

9. CLERESTORY SIDES WERE INITIALLY GLAZED OVER TOILETS AND COMPARTMENTS BUT WERE SOON BLOCKED UP.

97

Ex-works views of 'Sheffield' full third No.809 (2nd LMS 14138), above, and 'Sheffield' brake third No.1563 (2nd LMS 22953). Note the 8ft bogies and shallower depth eaves panels - see foootnote on drawings page opposite

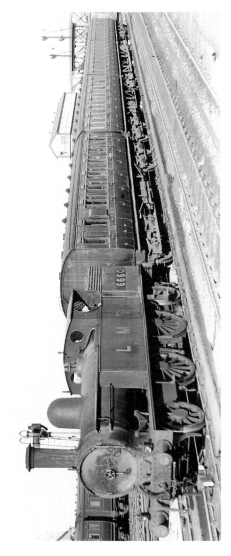

The accompanying picture shows a six compartment Metropolitan area brake third of the 9ft wide type in front of an experimental articulated 'triplet' set of similar stock, built by the LMS to gain experience prior to introducing its own new articulated designs in 1937

Midland Railway 48ft Low Roof Bain Suburban Stock

These carriages were built for use in close-coupled suburban sets, replacing many 19th Century Clayton six-wheelers on the way. They were all very similar in appearance though there were variations in type, width, panel depth and underframe depending on the area to which allocated. The drawings allow most permutations to be covered and the summary is by area not by type/diagram - see also notes on drawings. They were later converted to electric light and most lasted well into BR days. As usual, numbers quoted from the Midland and 1st LMS series are generally samples only.

PROTOTYPE DETAILS

Type/Diag.	Qty.	MR/1st LMS Numbers	2nd LMS	Extinct
MANCHESTER SETS (BUILT 1903, 8ft 6in wide, 10ft bogies)				
BT/D501*	14	1450-4/6-64	23082-23095	1947
T/D487	21	1465-1485	14065-14085	1947
F/D481	28	2561-7/9-74/6-90	10443-10463	1943 §
			14058-14064	1947 #
BIRMINGHAM SETS (BUILT 1907-9, 8ft 6in wide, 10ft bogies)				
BT/D501*	34	88; 91; 120; 527	23096-23128	1957
BT/D552	12	597; 627; 631; 673	22867-22878	1953
T/D487	37	22; 33; 350; 447	14086-14120	1957
C/D551	11	3299; 3300; 3353	17318-17326	1956
F/D481	26	2502-5/7/11-30/61/84; 2664	10464-10485	1956
SHEFFIELD SETS (BUILT 1912, 8ft 6in wide, 8ft bogies) ¥				
BT/D552	58	1526-1572	22912-22966	1958
T/D487	22	451; 660; 741; 809; 863	14121-14141	1957
C/D551	29	3794-3822	17327-17353	1958
METROPOLITAN LINE SETS (BUILT 1910, 9ft wide, 8ft bogies)				
BT/D604*	24	404; 597; 680; 1623	23129-23152	1956
T/D605	24	126; 1513-5/7-9; 2135-7	14142-62/70-2	1957
C/D606	24	2801-2; 2820-5/7-8/31-3; 3387	17373-17396	1957
NOTTINGHAM SETS (BUILT 1911-3, 9ft wide, 8ft bogies)				
BT/D603	40	594; 1036; 1573-88; 1613	22879-22911	1958
T/D605	16	550; 635; 1588-1596;	14163-9/90-7	1958
C/D602	16	2837-8; 3361/84; 3415	17354-61/5-72	1957 †

* Six-compartment brake thirds, other BT diagrams were four compartment types
§ Date is withdrawal of last full first. Most of the Manchester district carriages were downgraded to composite (eg 16917-21) or third before and after 1933 and ran until 1947
# Downgraded to third before 1933
¥ Sheffield sets had revised later panel depths and 8ft bogies of the 9ft wide series
† Nottingham District composites were all 4F+3T - see note on drawings

98

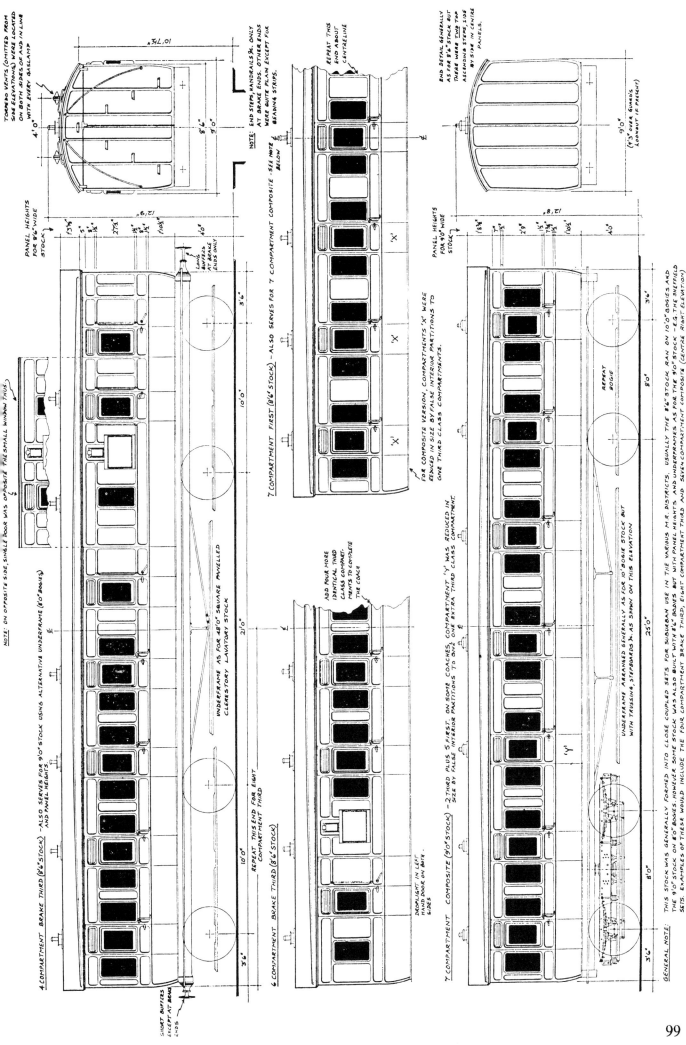

NOTE: ON OPPOSITE SIDE, SINGLE DOOR WAS OPPOSITE THE SMALL WINDOW THUS :-

TORPEDO VENTS (OMITTED FROM SIDE ELEVATIONS) WERE LOCATED ON BOTH SIDES OF AND IN LINE WITH EVERY GASLAMP.

NOTE: END STEPS, HANDRAILS &c. ONLY AT BRAKE ENDS. OTHER ENDS WERE QUITE PLAIN EXCEPT FOR BEARING STRIPS.

END DETAIL GENERALLY AS FOR 8'6" STOCK BUT THERE WERE TWO TOP ASCENDING STEPS, SIDE BY SIDE IN CENTRE PANELS.

4 COMPARTMENT BRAKE THIRD (8'6" STOCK) —ALSO SERVES FOR 9'0" STOCK USING ALTERNATIVE UNDERFRAME (8'0" BOGIES) AND PANEL HEIGHTS.

SHORT BUFFERS EXCEPT AT BRAKE ENDS

REPEAT THIS END FOR EIGHT COMPARTMENT THIRD

UNDERFRAME AS FOR 48'0" SQUARE PANELLED CLERESTORY LAVATORY STOCK

6 COMPARTMENT BRAKE THIRD (8'6" STOCK)

DROPLIGHT IN LEFT HAND DOOR ON BOTH SIDES

7 COMPARTMENT FIRST (8'6" STOCK) —ALSO SERVES FOR 7 COMPARTMENT COMPOSITE - SEE NOTE BELOW

FOR COMPOSITE VERSION, COMPARTMENTS 'X' WERE REDUCED IN SIZE BY FALSE INTERIOR PARTITIONS TO ONE THIRD CLASS COMPARTMENTS.

REPEAT THIS END ABOUT CENTRELINE

ADD FOUR MORE IDENTICAL THIRD CLASS COMPART- MENTS TO COMPLETE THE COACH

7 COMPARTMENT COMPOSITE (9'0" STOCK) - 2 THIRD PLUS 5 FIRST. ON SOME COACHES, COMPARTMENT 'Y' WAS REDUCED IN SIZE BY FALSE INTERIOR PARTITIONS TO ONE ONE EXTRA THIRD CLASS COMPARTMENT.

UNDERFRAME ARRANGED GENERALLY AS FOR 10' BOGIE STOCK BUT WITH TRUSSING, STEPBOARDS &c. AS SHOWN ON THIS ELEVATION

REPEAT BOGIE

GENERAL NOTE: THIS STOCK WAS GENERALLY FORMED INTO CLOSE COUPLED SETS FOR SUBURBAN USE IN THE VARIOUS M.R. DISTRICTS. USUALLY THE 8'6" STOCK RAN ON 10'0" BOGIES AND THE 9'0" STOCK ON 8'0" BOGIES. HOWEVER, SOME STOCK WAS ALSO BUILT WITH 8'6" BODIES BUT WITH PANEL HEIGHTS AND UNDERFRAMES AS FOR THE 9'0" STOCK - E.G. THE SHEFFIELD SETS. EXAMPLES OF THESE WOULD INCLUDE THE FOUR COMPARTMENT BRAKE THIRD, EIGHT COMPARTMENT THIRD AND SEVEN COMPARTMENT COMPOSITE (CENTRE RIGHT ELEVATION)

PANEL HEIGHTS FOR 8'6" STOCK

PANEL HEIGHTS FOR 9'0" WIDE STOCK

Midland/MSJS Bain Corridor Clerestory Stock

Although the Midland (including its Joint Stock activities) operated far fewer corridor carriages than the LNWR and WCJS, the types, styles and subtle variations were probably larger in proportion to the total; but the most common types were the Bain 54ft round-panelled clerestories featured in the next four pages. Built for the Midland, M&GSW and M&NB fleets during the 1905-7 period, they exhibited a number of minor variations, to cover which necessitates more notes than the total quantity of carriages may seem to merit(!). This is made no simpler by the extreme paucity of official views of the types in question, so it seems appropriate at this point to make it clear that I am deeply indebted to the late Ralph Lacy for helping me to unravel their complications many years ago.

Arthur Whitehead's drawings cover four of the five types built, the omitted variety being the brake first, a wholly Midland type which was never built for the Joint Stock fleets. It is, however, illustrated alongside and *en passant*, full firsts were never built to this style at all. This spread incorporates the basic drawing of the brake composite together with underframe and bogie for all types, while overleaf are detailed end elevations and panel details applicable to all, together with elevations of the three additional generic types.

Within the 'build', four recognisable but minor variations were to be seen, identified below by the following unofficial 'shorthand'. As far as possible, the summary table takes account of these differences:

Type A: 13ft 1in high with 8in deep eaves panel and four-element louvre vents as in panel detail drawing on page 103.

Type B: As Type A but 12ft 11½in high - see alternative end views on page 103.

Type C: As Type B but on the corridor side, louvre vents were now confined to doors only, not intermediate droplights

Type D: As Type C but vertical panel dimensions revised to the values given on the side elevation of the full composite

It should also be noted that although shown on some of the works drawings and therefore incorporated in these transcripts, such pictorial evidence as does survive indicates that louvre ventilators were always located over toilet windows but not located over the corresponding end windows on the corridor side! Also, even though the official drawings show the clerestory windows as indicated over the first class compartments in the composite (page 103), they actually matched the compartment window spacing - see pictures on page 102.

On all varieties, a vertical beading strip was added at the extreme ends of the sides between waist and solebar c.1910, whilst some time after building, torpedo ventilators were added c.14in to the left of the gas lamps. On conversion to electric light (not

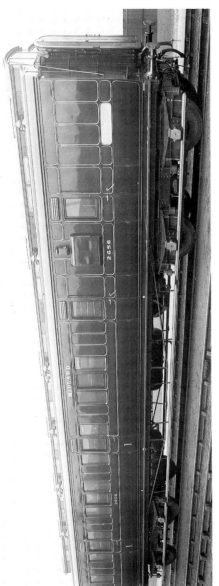

Most official views of the first generation round panelled clerestory corridor stock are believed to have been lost, but one survivor is this very clear corridor-side view of the brake first to D576 of which 18 were built in 1907, all for the Midland. It displays Type C details (see text) and its general body characteristics were common to all varieties. Given that the opposite side elevation was almost an exact mirror image (save for doors to all compartments and left hand droplights to all the brake end double doors), this type could be derived from the information given by using the following internal dimensions: Brake Van - 19ft 7½in; four compartments - 7ft 4in; toilet - 4ft 0in. This example was MR/1st LMS No.2656 (2nd LMS 5184). Midland numbers included 2655-63; 2779-84, the final LMS numbers being 5180-97

dated but before the 1923 grouping - see pictures, p.102 - and undoubtedly the normal LMS condition), gas lamps were removed, torpedo ventilators centred over compartments and battery boxes replaced the gas cylinders.

Finally, quite a number of these carriages went into ambulance use during WWI and did not reach the LMS, so it should not be assumed that the summary table includes all examples built. All told, as with the 48ft Lavatory stock (pp 96-7), these drawings are typical of the type and not representative of individual carriages. The table also includes ex-M&NB types which went to the LNER in 1928 and as usual, pre-1933 Midland number detail is often in the form of samples only.

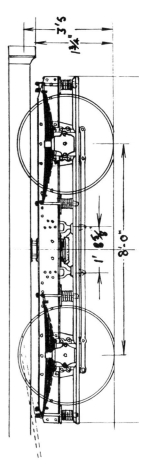

ENLARGED SIDE ELEVATION OF THE BAIN 8ft BOGIE DRAWN AT 7mm = 1ft SCALE

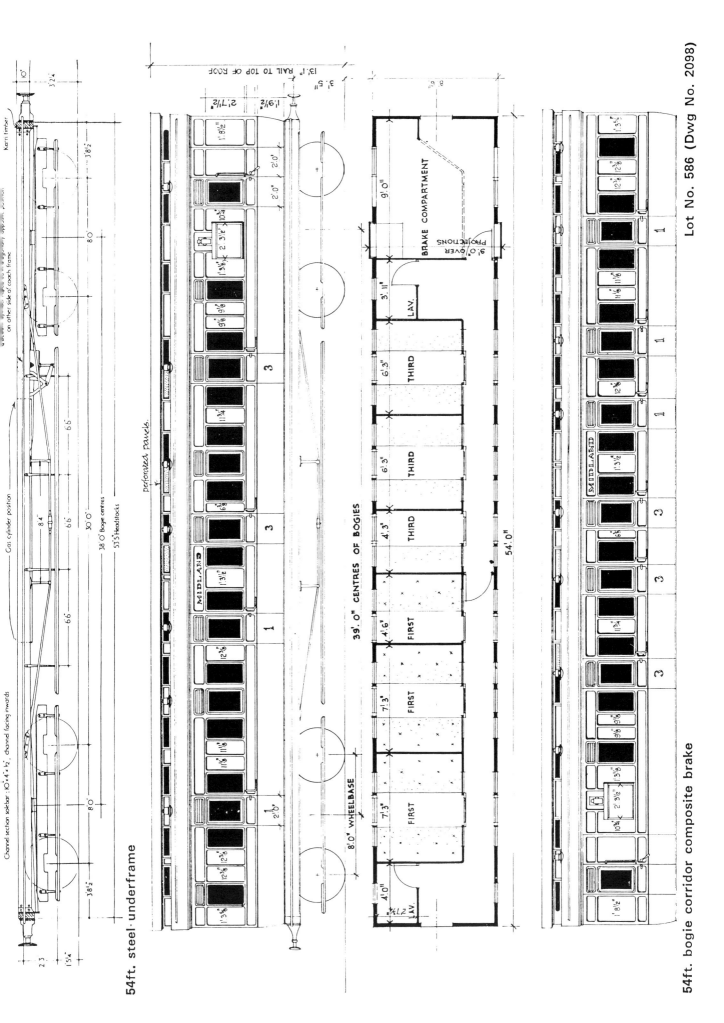

54 ft. steel · underframe

13'1" RAIL TO TOP OF ROOF

MIDLAND

39'0" CENTRES OF BOGIES

8'0" WHEELBASE

LAV. | FIRST | FIRST | FIRST | THIRD | THIRD | THIRD | LAV. | BRAKE COMPARTMENT

9'0" OVER PROJECTIONS

54'0"

MIDLAND

54ft. bogie corridor composite brake   Lot No. 586 (Dwg No. 2098)

101

PROTOTYPE DETAILS

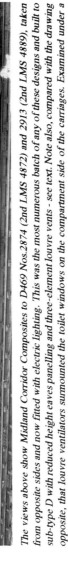

Quantity	Type#	Pre-Group Nos.*	1st LMS	2nd LMS	Extinct
CORRIDOR BRAKE COMPOSITE D559, BUILT 1904-6					
2	A	M&GSW 275-276	3958-3959	7283-7284	1944
10	A	MR 3301 plus nine§	as MR	7282	1948
6	C	M&NB 61-63/78-80	LNER 32539-40		unknown
			4086/101-3	7285-7288	1950
CORRIDOR THIRD CLASS D473, BUILT 1905-6					
4	A	M&GSW 366-369	4000-4003	3174-3177	1945
20	A	MR 15; 54/6; 104	as MR	3154-3161	1946
4	A?B	M&GSW 342; 359	3976/3793	3172-3173	1946
		M&GSW 377-8	4011-4012	3178-3179	
14	C	MR 575/8; 615/34	as MR	3180-3188	1951
6	C?	M&NB 125-130	LNER 3894-5/9; 3904/6		unknown
CORRIDOR COMPOSITE D469, BUILT 1905-7					
10	A	M&GSW 259;277-84	3942/60-7	4843-4851	1946
		M&NB 11	4034	4852	1945
15	C	M&NB 54-60/70-7	4077-83/93-5	4853-4862	1947
			LNER 32535-8		unknown
40	D	MR 2872-4; 2910-3	as MR	4863-4902	1948
CORRIDOR BRAKE THIRD 476¥/D561. BUILT 1904-6					
7	A	M&GSW 371-376	4005-4010	6438-6443	1950
30	A?	MR 115/7; 224/7	as MR	6420-6437	1947
30	D	MR 4; 897; 1488-99	as MR	6444-6466	1953
12	C(?B)	M&NB 113-124	4117/23-28	6467-6473	1947
			LNER 3907/13/16-7		unknown

\# Type variation letters as per summary in main narrative

* As at 1922. A number of these carriages (especially Joint Stock vehicles) were renumbered at least once before that time

§ To ambulance use, never returned. A further 22 examples from this diagram (probably Type B) also to ambulance use and not returned

¥ This diagram applies to one batch built without brake-end gangways (later LMS 6420-37), which were altered to conventional D561 type before grouping

The views above show Midland Corridor Composites to D469 Nos.2874 (2nd LMS 4872) and 2913 (2nd LMS 4889), taken from opposite sides and now fitted with electric lighting. This was the most numerous batch of any of these designs and built to sub-type D with reduced height eaves panelling and three-element louvre vents - see text. Note also, compared with the drawing opposite, that louvre ventilators surmounted the toilet windows on the compartment side of the carriages. Examined under a magnifying glass, these pictures also show the additional vertical beading strip between waist and solebar added at the extreme carriage ends c.1910 - see text

The picture to the left is the only known official view of this type - corridor brake third to D561, M&NB No.123, taken after the dreadful Ais Gill accident on the Settle and Carlisle line in September 1913. Viewed from the compartment side, it shows the extra window to the left of the guard's lookout which some examples received. These carriages are thought to have been Type C (see text) but no corridor-side view has been found to confirm this 100%. After repair, this was one of the four examples which eventually passed into LNER ownership (probably as LNER No.3916)

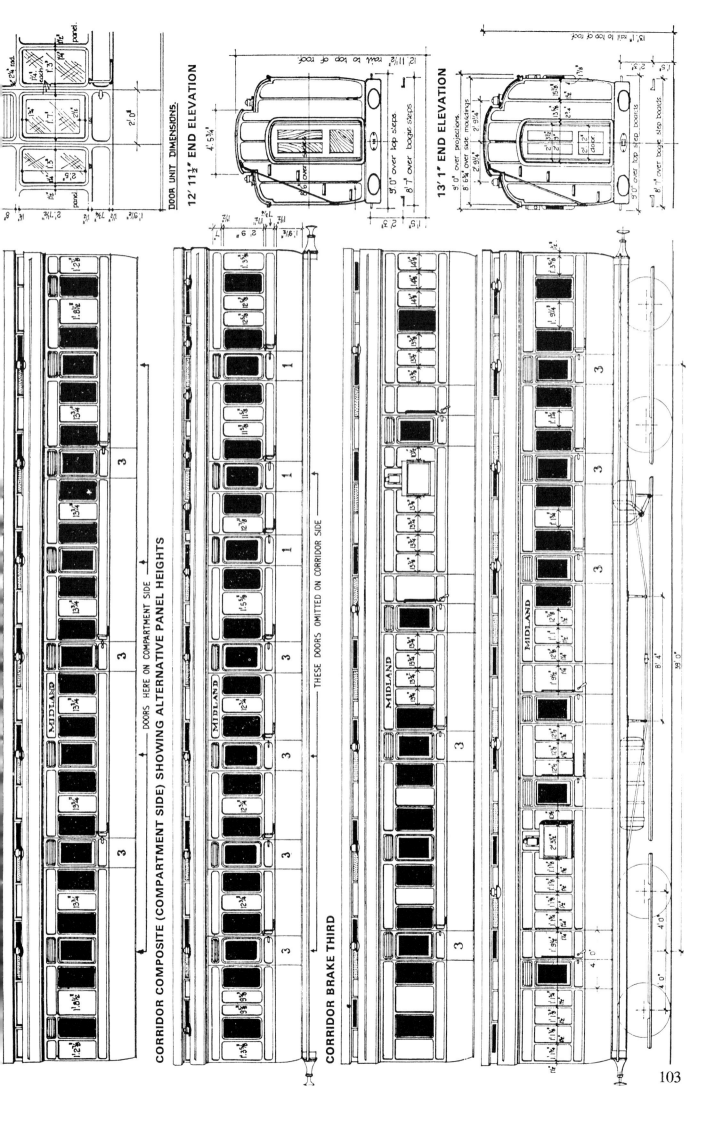

DOOR UNIT DIMENSIONS.

12′ 11½″ END ELEVATION

13′ 1″ END ELEVATION

CORRIDOR COMPOSITE (COMPARTMENT SIDE) SHOWING ALTERNATIVE PANEL HEIGHTS

DOORS HERE ON COMPARTMENT SIDE

THESE DOORS OMITTED ON CORRIDOR SIDE

CORRIDOR BRAKE THIRD

MIDLAND

103

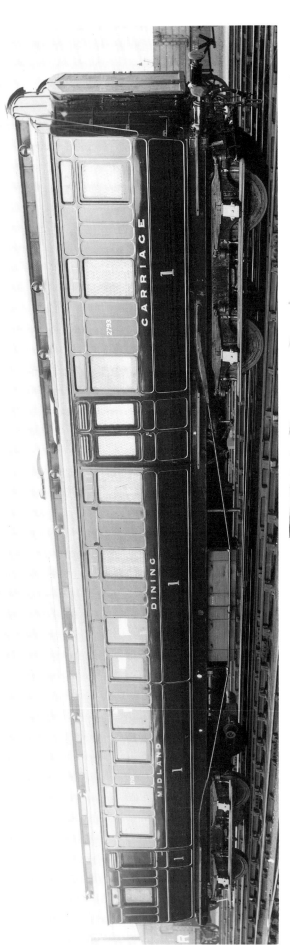

Midland Railway 59ft First Class Clerestory Dining Car

The Midland built many specialised vehicles, but mostly rather few in number, so it seems appropriate to select a numerically larger type for this review, moreover a design which lasted for a long time and which (in LMS days) was seen well outside its native heath. Notwithstanding the more celebrated 12-wheel types, the 59ft eight-wheel first class dining cars were the most common of this Midland genre and lasted longer than any other ex-MR clerestory dining cars.

Built in 1908, and originally designed to run with matching open thirds, the cars were very modern in their contemporary context, having pressed steel bogies and displaying a considerable length for an eight-wheel vehicle. They came to the LMS as first class cars and although only eight in total were not relegated to the 'Second Division' until the turn of the LMS/BR period when a few (but not all) were downgraded to third class, an especially interesting post-grouping sphere of activity being on the former Highland lines.

Built to D436 in 1908, they were numbered MR/1st LMS 2787-94, becoming LMS 89-96 in 1933, still in the first class series. There was an early casualty (LMS No.91) at Little Salkeld on the Settle-Carlisle line in 1935 and in 1946, three of them were downgraded to all third (LMS Nos.180-2) as LMS Nos.180-2 but in reverse numerical order! The last first class example was withdrawn in May 1950 and the last of the downgraded thirds lasted until October 1952

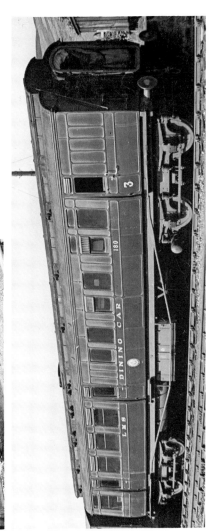

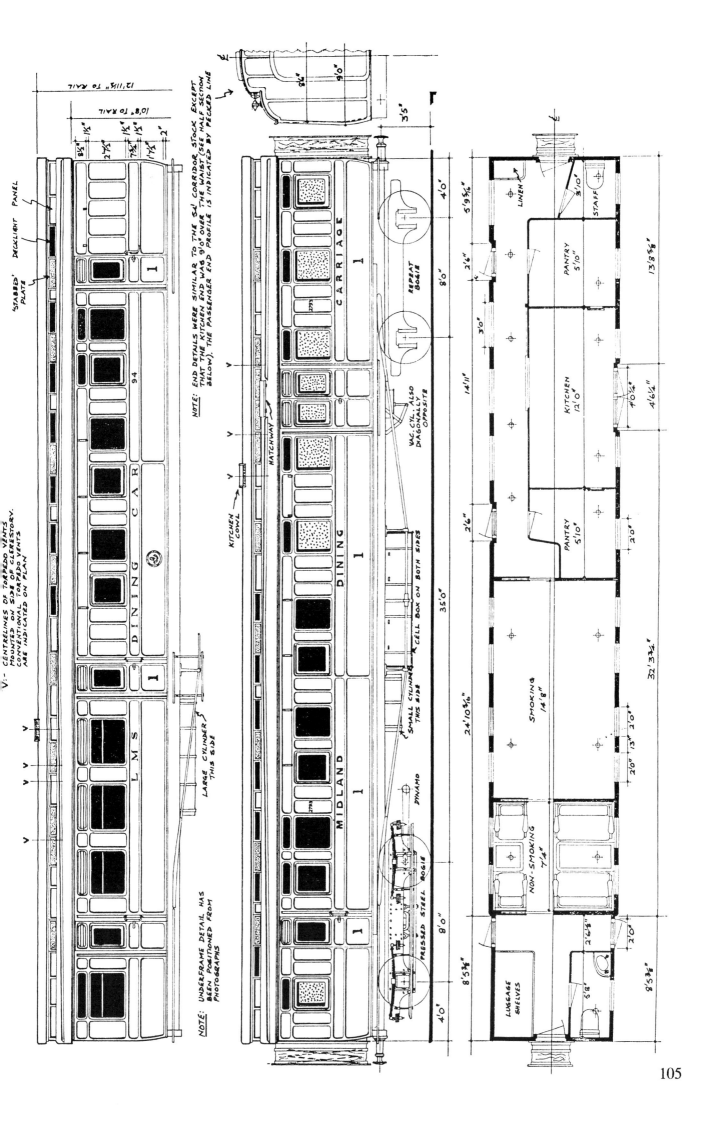

V:- CENTRELINES OF TORPEDO VENTS MOUNTED ON SIDE OF CLERESTORY. CONVENTIONAL TORPEDO VENTS ARE INDICATED ON PLAN

'STABBED' DECKLIGHT PANEL PLATE

12'11½" TO RAIL
10'8" TO RAIL

NOTE: END DETAILS WERE SIMILAR TO THE S.L CORRIDOR STOCK EXCEPT THAT THE KITCHEN END WAS 9'0" OVER THE WAIST (SEE HALF SECTION BELOW). THE PASSENGER END PROFILE IS INDICATED BY PECKED LINE

NOTE: UNDERFRAME DETAIL HAS BEEN POSITIONED FROM PHOTOGRAPHS

LARGE CYLINDER THIS SIDE

L M S
DINING CAR
1
94
1

KITCHEN COWL
HATCHWAY

MIDLAND
DINING
CARRIAGE
1
1
1
1
2793
2793

VAC. CYL. ALSO DIAGONALLY OPPOSITE
SMALL CYLINDER THIS SIDE
CELL BOX ON BOTH SIDES
DYNAMO
PRESSED STEEL BOGIE
REPEAT BOGIE

3'5"
4'0"
8'0"
14'11"
2'6"
3'0"
2'6"
5'9⅝"

4'0"
8'0"
35'0"
32'3¾"
24'10¾₆"
8'5¾"
8'5⅜"
2'6"
20"13"20"

LINEN
STAFF
3'10"
PANTRY 5'10"
KITCHEN 12'0"
PANTRY 5'10"
SMOKING 14'8"
NON-SMOKING 7'4"
LUGGAGE SHELVES
13'8⅝"
4'0½"
4'6½"
2'0"
5'8"
2'6⅝"
2'0"

105

LYR Attock Stock

With the opening of new carriage and wagon works in 1877 and the appointment of F.Attock as superintendent, a new style of carriage was introduced to the LYR. It embodied a smooth side with an inward step of just under one inch below the waistline - an inherent part of the construction which remained a design feature of all flush-sided LYR carriage stock until the grouping. The arc roof 'Attock' stock was built in many different types for over thirty years and the hundreds of such vehicles passed to the LMS. The drawings on this page (by Barry Lane and the late Gordon Heywood) represent common 8ft wide bogie types, all of which received the various styles of LMS livery. Withdrawals were heavy in the late 1930s but several lasted into early BR years.

PROTOTYPE DETAILS *

Quantity	LYR Numbers	1st LMS	2nd LMS	Extinct
46ft LAVATORY COMPOSITE, BUILT 1894-5 (LYR D28)				
30	282; 614	1005/141-53	19821-19839	1936 #
49ft BRAKE THIRD, BUILT 1894-9 - MAIN DRAWING (LYR D30)				
256	310; 439; 582; 813; 1279; 2651	13260-1/431	23358-23449	1939
49ft BRAKE THIRD, BUILT 1894-5 - FIVE COMPARTMENT (LYR D33)				
50	Included 2418	13189-13217	23450-23493	1941§
49ft FULL THIRD, BUILT 1894-1902 (LYR D34)				
808	1089; 1119; 1190; 1843; 2635	13584-13619	14387-15088	1951
54ft COMPOSITE, BUILT 1898-1903 (LYR D45)				
175	682-97; 705-54/65-819; 845-64	11242-80/353	17495-17652	1938
49ft FULL BRAKE (LYR D71)				
2	291; 292	5493/5495	33641-33642	1952 @

* Only sample running numbers are given in most cases
# First LMS numbers cyphered (ie '0' prefix) pre-1933
§ Except LMS 23482 which lasted until 1951!
@ Renumbered again in LMS standard series as 31950-1 in reverse order after the war!

Diagram 29 five-compartment Third Brake of 1893 at Halifax soon after the grouping. This was a slightly earlier type than the D33 version covered opposite, but displays all the typical Attock features. Like many others it has had the LYR letters replaced with a duplication of the LYR number (2226) and remains in pre-group livery. Many LYR carriages kept their old colours until withdrawal in the late 1930s, the last authenticated sighting being in 1943. (B.C.Lane Collection)

The first LMS livery gave pseudo 'panelling' to the otherwise smooth-sided LYR vehicles. Both these carriages are the same colour but the (unidentified) far example to D30 has been in service longer than the near one, a D45 54ft composite, which became 17597 in 1933 before withdrawal in 1938. (B.C.Lane Collection)

BASIC LYR CARRIAGE LIVERY

Sides: Lower panels carmine lake, upper panels tan
Ends: Dark Umber
Lining: Upper panels carried fine black lines round quarter and drop lights edged with pale orange lines. The waist had a pale orange line as did bottom mouldings. Ends were lined in tan
Insignia: Roman gold characters edged with very fine red and white lines (see also detail drawing on page 107)
Roof: White, degrading to grey
Remainder: All black

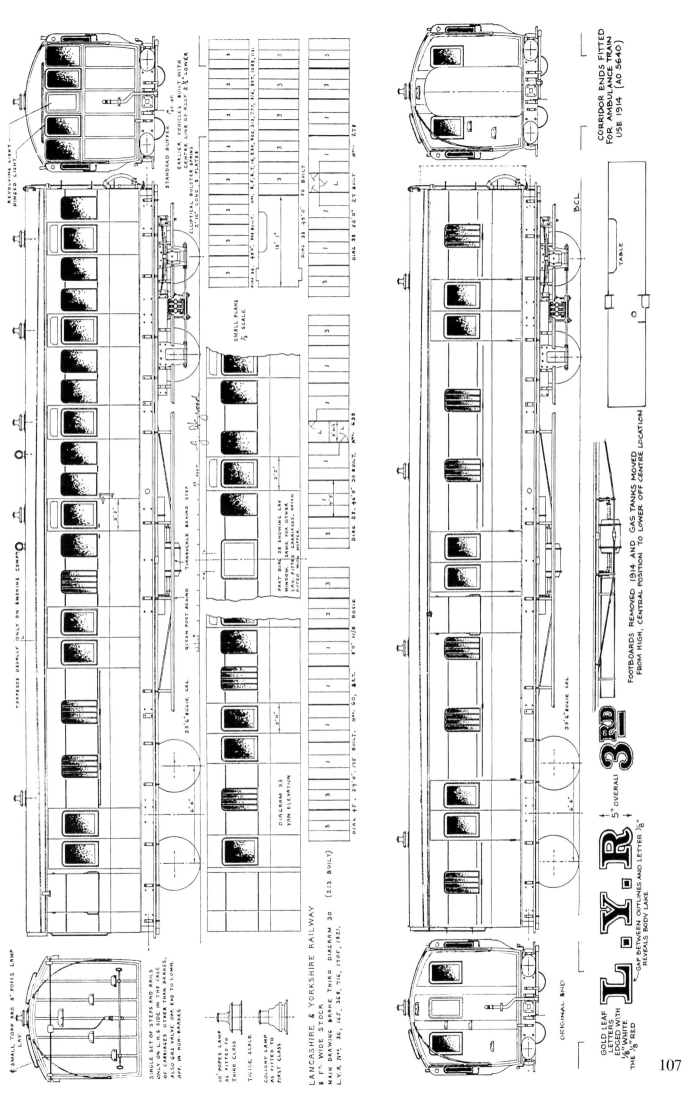

REVOLVING LIGHT
HINGED LIGHT

SMALL TORP: AND 8" POPE'S LAMP
LAV.

TORPEDOS USUALLY ONLY ON SMOKING COMP'T

STANDARD BUFFER

EARLIER VEHICLES BUILT WITH CENTRE LINE OF ROOF 2¼" LOWER

ELLIPTICAL BOLSTER SPRING 2'10" LONG, 8 PLATES

DIAG 24. 49'0" 500 BUILT. N°s. 3, F, 4, 7, 16, 830, 902, 313, 777, 816, 991, 1083, 1121

18' 1"

DIAG 33 45'0" 50 BUILT

SMALL PLANS ⅓ SCALE

QUEEN POST BEHIND   TURNBUCKLE BEHIND STEP

33'6" BOGIE CAS.

6'6"

2'2"

DIAGRAM 33 VAN ELEVATION

2'0"

DIAG 45. 54'0" 175 BUILT. N°s. 60, 827.

8'0" w/B BOGIE

N°. 278

10 FEET

PART DIAG 28 SHOWING LAV. WINDOW. SAME FOR OTHER LAV. FITTED CARRIAGES, OFTEN FITTED WITH HOPPER.

2'2"

1'3"

3'6½"

DIAG 28. 46'0" 30 BUILT. N°. 639

SINGLE SET OF STEPS AND RAILS ONLY ON L.H.S SIDE IN THE CASE OF CARRIAGES OTHER THAN BRAKES. ALSO GAS VALVE OPP. END TO COMM. APP. IN NON-BRAKES.

10" POPE'S LAMP AS FITTED TO THIRD CLASS

TWICE SCALE

COLIGNY LAMP AS FITTED TO FIRST CLASS

LANCASHIRE & YORKSHIRE RAILWAY
8 FT. WIDE STOCK
MAIN DRAWING BRAKE THIRD DIAGRAM 30   (213 BUILT)
L.Y.R N°s. 36, 165, 369, 716, 1705, 1921.

CORRIDOR ENDS FITTED FOR AMBULANCE TRAIN USE 1914 (AO 5640)

BCL

TABLE

FOOTBOARDS REMOVED 1914 AND GAS TANKS MOVED FROM HIGH, CENTRAL POSITION TO LOWER OFF CENTRE LOCATION

33'6" BOGIE CAS.

6'6"

ORIGINAL END

GOLD LEAF LETTERS EDGED WITH ⅛" WHITE THE ⅛" RED

L.Y.R 3RD
5" OVERALL

GAP BETWEEN OUTLINES AND LETTER ⅛" REVEALS BODY LAKE

107

LYR Attock Stock Developments

Corridor vehicles to the established pattern were built for the main Trans-Pennine services from 1904. The trains were composed of the usual thirds and composites with either a four or five compartment brake third at each end. Most types can be derived from the drawing of the brake composite and prototype details are given for all relevant types. The 16 brake composites were built for through running off the LYR and replaced similar non-corridor brake composites, the narrow body with arc roof being acceptable for clearance almost everywhere.

The final development of the arc roof carriage to this style came in 1904 for the Manchester and Oldham services and carried six per side in the thirds. Because of their width and the clearances on the Oldham line, door handles, grabs and 'bonnet' vents were recessed into the bodywork and there was no raised ducket in the guard's van. Later batches in 1908-9 had the van side tapered inwards to allow a sight line along the side of the train - more familiar on LYR corridor coaches of the time. They were amongst the first LYR stock to be electrically lit, though some later reverted to gas before 1914. They mostly ran in sets (BT+T+C+BT), approximately half the brake thirds and composites with second class seating before downgrading to third. Once again, prototype details are given of all varieties which can be derived from the brake third drawing. (Drawings by the late Gordon Heywood)

Corridor third No.990 to D63, still in LYR livery in the mid-1920s. The other side had quarterlights and looked very much like a normal compartment carriage. Built in 1905, it lasted until 1947 as LMS No.3253. (B.C.Lane Collection)

One of the 1908 batch of wide-bodied 'Oldham' brake thirds, No.24084 in the late 1940s. Twenty were built as the drawing with the final ten having tapered body sides - see text. The droplights were fixed to open half way as shown, most of them also having a bar across the opening to prevent passengers leaning out. (B.C.Lane Collection)

PROTOTYPE DETAILS *

Quantity	LYR Numbers	1st LMS	2nd LMS	Extinct
56ft CORRIDOR COMPOSITE BRAKE, BUILT 1904-6 (LYR D64)				
16	920-5; 929-34; 939-42	11455-9/62-4	7318-7333	1952
56ft CORRIDOR THIRD, BUILT 1904-7 (LYR D63)				
37	610; 990; 1312-5; 2694-8	13471-13482	3251-3274	1953
54ft CORRIDOR COMPOSITE, BUILT 1904 (LYR D62)				
10	910-919	11445-11454	4919-1928	1952
56ft CORRIDOR THIRD BRAKE (4-COMPARTMENT), BUILT 1905 (LYR D75)				
6	2941-2946	13713-13718	6501-6506	1951
54ft 'OLDHAM' BRAKE THIRD, BUILT 1904-9 (LYR D65)				
30	Included 1025	12502/385-99	24063-24092	1953
54ft 'OLDHAM' FULL THIRD, BUILT 1904-9 (LYR D66)				
32	634; 1388-9; 1399-1401	12186/815-7	15097-15121	1953
54ft 'OLDHAM' COMPOSITE (3/3/1/1/1/3/3), BUILT 1904-9 (LYR D67)				
23	521; 530; 555-6; 645	1106/184-6	17653-64/737	1953

* Sample running numbers only, save for final LMS series where, in all save the last two types listed, the full sequence can be given. Some of the 'Oldham' stock LMS numbers were intermixed with similar elliptical roof stock being built at the same time

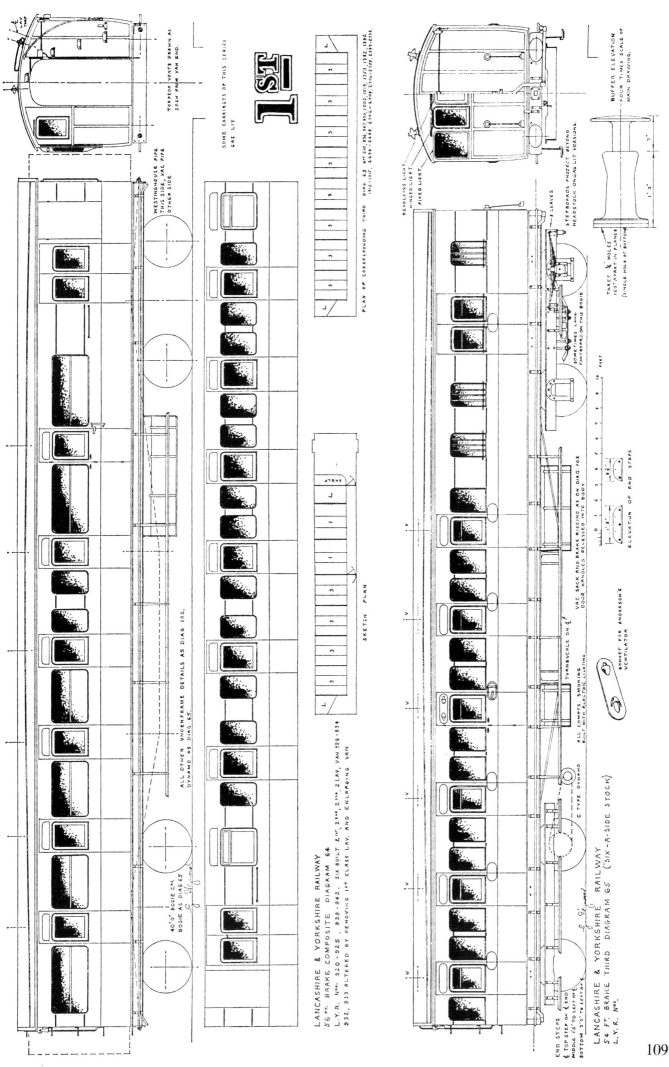

TORPEDO VENTS DRAWN AS
SEEN FROM VAN END.

SOME CARRIAGES OF THIS SERIES
GAS LIT

WESTINGHOUSE PIPE
THIS SIDE, VAC PIPE
OTHER SIDE

ALL OTHER UNDERFRAME DETAILS AS DIAG 102.
DYNAMO AS DIAG 65.

40'0" BOGIE C^RS.
BOGIE AS DIAG 65

1ST

PLAN OF CORRESPONDING THIRD DIAG 63 N°s 610, 936, 947, 990, 1002, 1015, 1313, 1382, 1392
1512–1315, 2624–2639, 2702–2709, 2706–2709, 2599–2591.

SKETCH PLAN

SHELF

LANCASHIRE & YORKSHIRE RAILWAY
56 FT. BRAKE COMPOSITE DIAGRAM 64
L.Y.R. N°s 920–925, 939–942. SIX BUILT 2^1st, 2^3rd, 2^3rd, 2 LAV, VAN 929–934
932, 933 ALTERED BY REMOVING 1st CLASS LAV. AND ENLARGING VAN

REVOLVING LIGHT
HINGED LIGHT
FIXED LIGHT

STEPBOARDS PROJECT BEYOND
HEADSTOCK ON GAS LIT VERSIONS.
SOMETIMES LAMP
FOOTBOARD ON THIS BOGIE

4 LEAVES

VAC SACK AND BRAKE RIGGING AS ON DIAG 102
DOOR HANDLES RECESSED INTO BODY

TURNBUCKLE ON ℄

ALL COMPTS. SMOKING.
BUILT WITH ELECTRIC LIGHTING.

C TYPE DYNAMO

BONNET FOR ANDERSON'S
VENTILATOR

ELEVATION OF END STEPS

BUFFER ELEVATION
—FOUR TIMES SCALE OF
MAIN DRAWING.

THREE ⅝ HOLES
120° APART IN FLANGE
(SINGLE HOLE AT BOTTOM)

7"

1'3"

END STEPS
℄ TOP STEP ON END
MIDDLE 7½" TO LEFT OF ℄
BOTTOM 23" TO LEFT OF ℄

LANCASHIRE & YORKSHIRE RAILWAY
54 FT. BRAKE THIRD DIAGRAM 65 (SIX-A-SIDE STOCK)
L.Y.R. N°s.

109

LYR Arc Roof Open Saloon Stock

LYR No.2509 to D44 (LMS 13325/958) when new. Gangways were added later and note the central lavatory, not repeated on the 56ft stock

Established LYR design changed in 1900 with the introduction of open saloons with centre aisle and gangways. The outer appearance was also novel in that the body was panelled and end doors recessed. This style continued on all later open carriages but panelling never appeared on conventional stock. The first new type, a picnic saloon, was shown to the GCR in August 1900, which was impressed by the "greatly superior riding and illumination", albeit the latter by incandescent gas lamps.

The LYR called them 'Centre Corridor' ('Vestibules' in LMS parlance) and several sets were built between 1900 and 1905 for the principal trains west of Manchester; but they were replaced with elliptical roof sets within the decade. The accompanying drawings by Barry Lane and the late Gordon Heywood allow four varieties to be featured (the full third by repeating the non-brake half of the brake third), most withdrawn by the late 1930s, but one or two coming to BR.

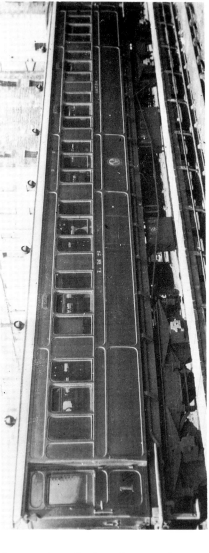

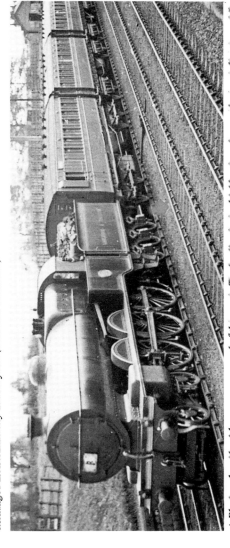

One of the 1905 batch to D51 which was built with Stones electric lighting. It is also riding on 8ft bogies but these were exchanged indiscriminately in later years (B.C.Lane Collection)

PROTOTYPE DETAILS *

Quantity	LYR Numbers	1st LMS	2nd LMS	Extinct
54ft THIRD CLASS PICNIC SALOON, BUILT 1900/1901 (LYR D44)				
3	185; 510; 2509;	11865;13325	956-958	pre-war
3	1858/72-3	13006/18-9	959-961	1953 #
56ft CENTRE CORRIDOR FIRST, BUILT 1901-5 (LYR D51)				
15	202-9/11/30-2; 129/31-2	10769-71/90-7	7563-7577	1951
54ft CENTRE CORRIDOR BRAKE THIRD, BUILT 1903-4 (LYR D58)				
7	2934-2940	13706-13712	9982-9988	1953
54ft CENTRE CORRIDOR FULL THIRD, BUILT 1900-02 (LYR D50)				
11	512; 600; 2721-6; 2930-3	13495-8/702-5	9630-9641	1943

* Sample numbers only in many cases within the LYR and 1st LMS series
# These three built in 1901 with 8ft bogies, the other three with 6ft 6in type

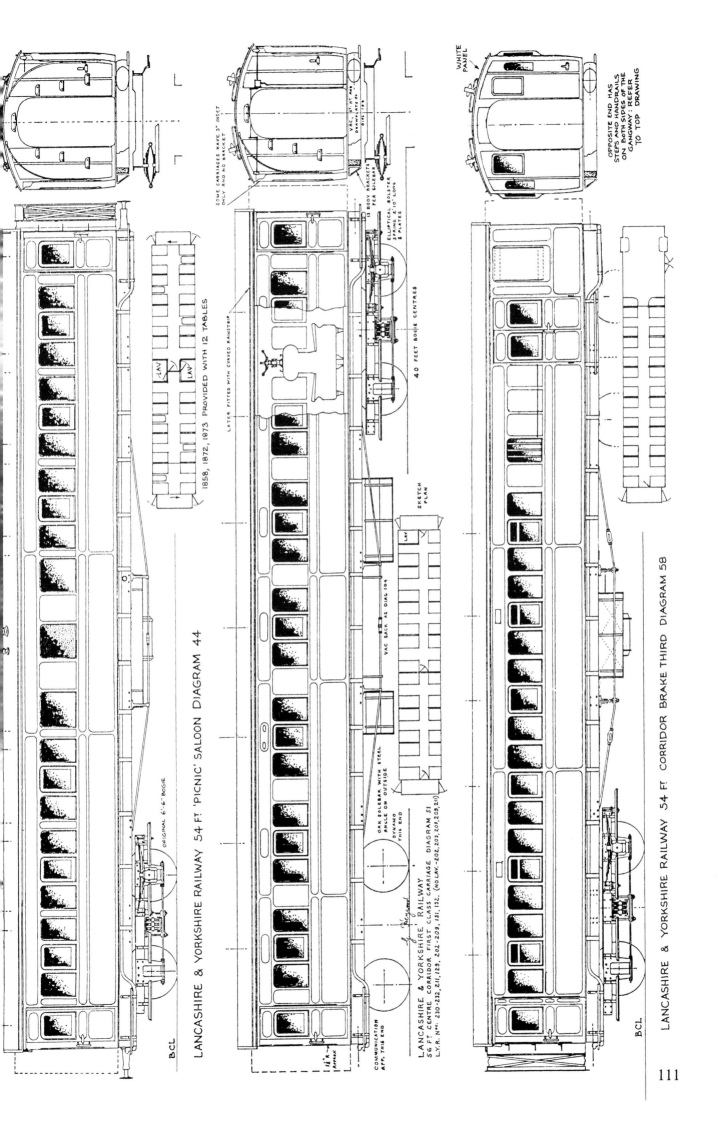

LANCASHIRE & YORKSHIRE RAILWAY 54 FT. 'PICNIC' SALOON DIAGRAM 44

1858, 1872, 1873 PROVIDED WITH 12 TABLES

LATER FITTED WITH CURVED RAINSTRIP

SOME CARRIAGES HAVE 3" INSET ONLY AND NO BRACKET

ORIGINAL 6'-6" BOGIE

BCL

VAC. AND HT. PIPE DRAWBAR AT AL SIDE 6'-6"

13 BODY BRACKETS PER BOLSTER

ELLIPTICAL BOLSTER SPRING 2'-10" LONG 8 PLATES

40 FEET BOGIE CENTRES

LANCASHIRE & YORKSHIRE RAILWAY
56 FT. CENTRE CORRIDOR FIRST CLASS CARRIAGE DIAGRAM 51
L.Y.R. Nos. 230-232, 211, 129, 202-209, 131, 132. (NO LAV.-202, 203, 207, 205, 210)

SKETCH PLAN

LAV

VAC. SACK AS DIAG 104

OAK SOLEBAR WITH STEEL ANGLE ON OUTSIDE

DYNAMO THIS END

COMMUNICATION APP. THIS END

WHITE PANEL

OPPOSITE END HAS STEPS AND HANDRAILS ON BOTH SIDES OF THE GANGWAY: REFER TO TOP DRAWING

BCL

LANCASHIRE & YORKSHIRE RAILWAY 54 FT. CORRIDOR BRAKE THIRD DIAGRAM 58

111

The first elliptical roof LBL sets with a first/second composite having a single lavatory. These vehicles were the earliest elliptical roof types to be built and were provided with standard large topedo vents which restricted their route availability, so all subsequent carriages had smaller vents along the roof centreline. Handrails on the ends were curved until 1910 when straight ones became standard, along with the not very obvious steel ends in place of panelled timber ends

LYR Elliptical Roof General Service Stock

The LYR adopted the elliptical roof (interestingly, to the limit of the Caledonian Railway loading gauge) in 1906, introducing compartment and corridor vehicles at the same time, both employing a developed form of the familiar 'Attock' styling - see page 106. These drawings by Barry Lane and the late Gordon Heywood feature some typical types.

The non-corridor carriages were supplied in formations of three, known as 'LBL' (Leeds/Bradford/Liverpool) sets, but also appeared in four-coach sets for many Manchester area workings, the extra carriage being a full third. The original sets had a composite with one central lavatory and 8ft wheelbase bogies, the later composites being as drawn.

The new 'Fleetwood' boat train and Liverpool-Newcastle services of 1908 received corridor coaches to exactly the same pattern but with a lavatory at each end of each vehicle - one lavatory only in the brake-ended types, of course.

The bogies were originally the 8ft standard type, but 'wide bearing' bogies appeared on subsequent batches and these were later extended to 10ft wheelbase. All brake-ended vehicles had the tapered-in van side on the luggage section, body width precluding any form of projecting lookout ducket within the loading gauge.

Diagram 105 corridor brake third No.6541 in simplified LMS livery. Built in 1910 it was amongst the last to receive wooden ends and curved handrails (on the far end), although it would have the wide bearing bogies from new. Electric lighting has been added, using the channel iron cradle to carry the battery boxes. This carriage lasted until 1953 (B.C.Lane Collection)

PROTOTYPE DETAILS *

Quantity	LYR Numbers	1st LMS	2nd LMS	Extinct
56ft NON-CORRIDOR LAVATORY COMPOSITE, BUILT 1906 (LYR D87)				
10	1070-1079	11551-11560	19883-19892	1953
54ft NON-CORRIDOR BRAKE THIRD, BUILT 1907-18 (LYR D94)				
211 #	1479-89; 1500-4	12884-12896	23856-24054	1959
56ft CORRIDOR BRAKE THIRD, BUILT 1908-18 (LYR D105)				
29 §	176; 635; 2454/550; 1648-50	12836/938-40	6524-6549	1954

* Sample numbers only in many cases within the LYR and 1st LMS series

Includes 14 vehicles (ex-Ambulance Train) returned to stock 1922/3 with slight detail differences

§ A somewhat confusing series: Only 21 of the original 1908 order for 24 went to the LMS, the three missing examples believed converted to ambulances in WWI. The later batches (three in 1916, two in 1918) were classed as three 'repairs' (brand new replacements for the original ambulances?) and two re-converted from ambulances. All that can safely be said is that 29 LYR numbers were allocated and that 26 carriages received second series LMS numbers!

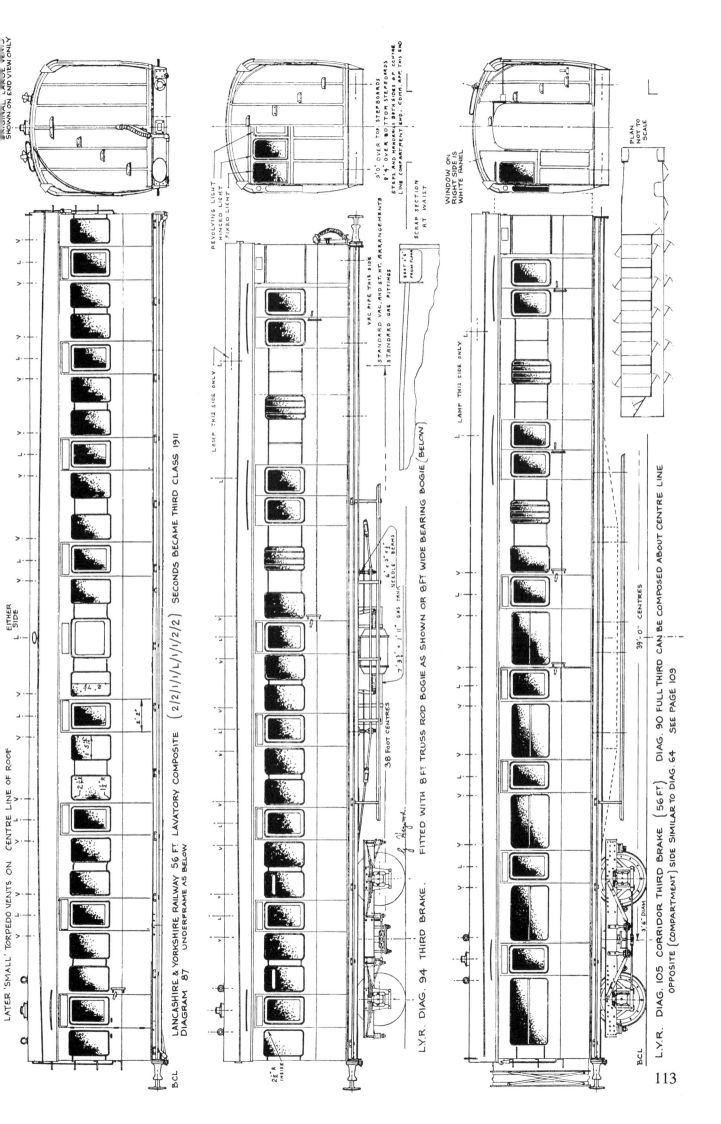

LATER 'SMALL' TORPEDO VENTS ON CENTRE LINE OF ROOF

ORIGINAL LARGE VENTS
SHOWN ON END VIEW ONLY

EITHER
L SIDE

$(2/2/1/1/L/1/1/2/2)$ SECONDS BECAME THIRD CLASS 1911

LANCASHIRE & YORKSHIRE RAILWAY 56 FT LAVATORY COMPOSITE
DIAGRAM 87 UNDERFRAME AS BELOW

BCL

REVOLVING LIGHT
HINGED LIGHT
FIXED LIGHT

9'0" OVER TOP STEPBOARDS
8'4" OVER BOTTOM STEPBOARDS
STEPS AND HANDRAILS BOTH SIDES OF CENTRE
LINE COMPARTMENT END. COMM. APE. THIS END

SCRAP SECTION
AT WAIST

LAMP THIS SIDE ONLY

VAC PIPE THIS SIDE

STANDARD VAC. AND ST. HT. ARRANGEMENTS
STANDARD GAS FITTINGS

SEAT 1'6
FROM FLOOR

38 FOOT CENTRES

6 x 3 x ⅝
NEEDLE BEAMS

7'9½" x 1'11" GAS TANK

L.Y.R. DIAG. 94 THIRD BRAKE. FITTED WITH 8 FT TRUSS ROD BOGIE AS SHOWN OR 8 FT WIDE BEARING BOGIE (BELOW)

WINDOW ON
RIGHT SIDE IS
WHITE PANEL

PLAN
NOT TO
SCALE

LAMP THIS SIDE ONLY

39'-0" CENTRES

3'6" DIAM

BCL

L.Y.R. DIAG. 105 CORRIDOR THIRD BRAKE (56 FT) DIAG. 90 FULL THIRD CAN BE COMPOSED ABOUT CENTRE LINE
OPPOSITE (COMPARTMENT) SIDE SIMILAR TO DIAG. 64 SEE PAGE 109

113

LYR Elliptical Roof Open Stock/Dining Car

Until 1907, the LYR possessed but two catering vehicles, both unique. One was a 12-wheel clerestory 'clone' of an award-winning LNWR design while the other (older) type was a 10-wheel oddity. For the Liverpool-Newcastle expresses and Fleetwood boat trains (see previous page), two first class dining cars were built with the new high roof and fully panelled style of the open stock - page 110. These luxurious cars were quite the equal of contemporary types on other railways.

At the kitchen end was a non-kitchen eight-wheeler for second and third class passengers (LYR D103 - all third from 1911). This too had the 'open' style of exterior panelling and similar repeats were built for Blackpool residential services and other expresses - see summary. All 14 shared near-identical outward styling with recessed, inward opening doors and gas lighting, although electric lighting was provided towards the end of the pre-group period. Most lasted until BR times, no doubt due to their 'modern' layout - the now well-nigh universal open saloon - and Barry Lane's drawings on this page feature this stock.

Several 56ft types were built with near-identical outer body shells (see summary table) and LMS No.9699 (LYR 3250/1st LMS 13774) was additionally interesting in having been ordered as a composite but delivered in 1911 as all third, second class by then having been abolished. This fact almost certainly explains its slightly out of sequence second LMS number in which it is seen here, now with electric lighting: note also that the figure '3' appeared on the body side and not the doors. The original D103 composite type differed from the later D95/101 carriages only in respect of interior partitions and the fact that it had a small pantry on the opposite side of the aisle to the lavatory - far end as seen here (B.C.Lane Collection)

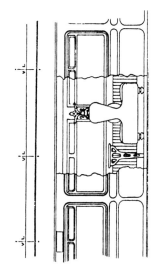

PROTOTYPE DETAILS

Quantity	LYR Numbers	1st LMS	2nd LMS	Extinct
56ft OPEN 2nd/3rd DINING COMPOSITE, BUILT 1908 (LYR D103)				
1	358; later 2699 (3rd class)	13476	9674	1951
56ft OPEN THIRD, BUILT 1908-9 (LYR D95)				
10	1362/75/9/90/4-5; 1412/5-6/8	12794/8/831-2	9649-52/4-9	1954 *
56ft OPEN 2nd/3rd DINING COMPOSITE, BUILT 1909/11 (LYR D101)				
3	3250-2	13774-13776	9672-3/9699#	1953
65ft 6in FIRST CLASS DINING CAR, BUILT 1907-8 (LYR D85)				
2	213; 214	10799; 10800	80; 81	1938

* Sample numbers only for this type within LYR and 1st LMS series
\# LMS No.9699 was third class from new (1911) - see appended view

NOTE: During LMS days, the ex-LYR kitchen/diners, like those of the Midland, G&SWR and LNWR (plus ex-Caledonian Pullman diners for that matter), found further useful employment in the Highlands after LMS standard types took over south of the border.

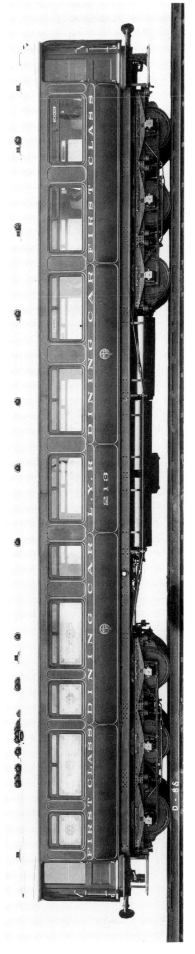

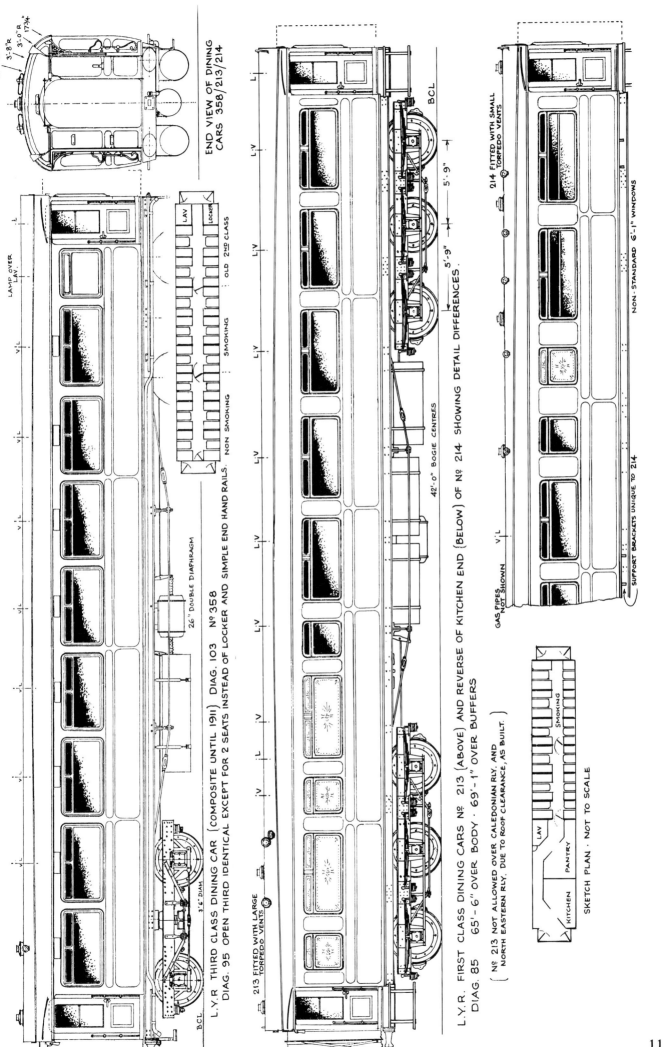

END VIEW OF DINING
CARS 358/213/214

3'-8"R
3'-0" R
17¾

LAMP OVER
LAV.

L.Y.R THIRD CLASS DINING CAR (COMPOSITE UNTIL 1911) DIAG. 103   No 358
DIAG. 95 OPEN THIRD IDENTICAL EXCEPT FOR 2 SEATS INSTEAD OF LOCKER AND SIMPLE END HAND RAILS.

LAV
LOCKER
OLD 2ND CLASS
SMOKING
NON SMOKING
26" DOUBLE DIAPHRAGM

3'-6" DIAM

213 FITTED WITH LARGE
TORPEDO VENTS

BCL

BCL

42'-0" BOGIE CENTRES

5'-9"

5'-9"

L.Y.R. FIRST CLASS DINING CARS No 213 (ABOVE) AND REVERSE OF KITCHEN END (BELOW) OF No 214 SHOWING DETAIL DIFFERENCES.
DIAG. 85   65'-6" OVER BODY · 69'-1" OVER BUFFERS

(No 213 NOT ALLOWED OVER CALEDONIAN RLY. AND
NORTH EASTERN RLY. DUE TO ROOF CLEARANCE, AS BUILT.)

214 FITTED WITH SMALL
TORPEDO VENTS

GAS PIPES
NOT SHOWN

NON-STANDARD 6'-1" WINDOWS

SUPPORT BRACKETS UNIQUE TO 214

KITCHEN
PANTRY
LAV
SMOKING

SKETCH PLAN · NOT TO SCALE

The upper view shows NSR arc roof third No.110 (believed to have become LMS 14869/15266), probably when new. The lower view shows elliptical roof brake third in full LMS livery with its first series LMS No.14970. It later became No.24129. The vehicle on the extreme right is unidentified but gives additional detail of the NSR style of panelling

North Staffordshire Railway Bogie Stock

The drawings on this page, specially prepared by the late Gordon Heywood for the 1968 version of this survey, represent typical NSR bogie stock, built to a 49ft 2in body length (52ft 6in over buffers) which lasted well into LMS days and even to BR. The top and centre drawings depict standard NSR elliptical roof types from 1909 (brake third and lavatory composite) while the arc roof full third is from a slightly earlier period. Features to be noted are the characteristic turn-under at the carriage end, panel styling reminiscent of both LNWR and SE&CR practice and the prominent guard's duckets on the brake third which brought the overall width to 9ft 4in. The lavatory composite was particularly well equipped, all compartments having access to toilets, something which LMS standard designs never offered - see page 64.

It has not been possible to verify total quantities built, full running number series or withdrawal dates, but the details offered are believed to be correct as far as they go - typical numbers only, not full lists. What is known is that the last of the elliptical roof vehicles ran on well into the 1950s and that one of the brake thirds (unidentified) found its way onto the Fenchurch Street-Southend services and duly received an 'E' prefix to its LMS number!

SAMPLE NUMBER DETAILS

Type	NSR Numbers	1st LMS	2nd LMS
Brake Third	18; 26; 33; 51	14967-70	24120-24129
Lavatory Composite	259; 279	14860; 14923	19919-19926 *
Arc roof Third	109;110	14859/69	15265-6 §

* LMS numbers somewhat conjectural but believed correct
§ Almost certainly far more than this but numbers unavailable

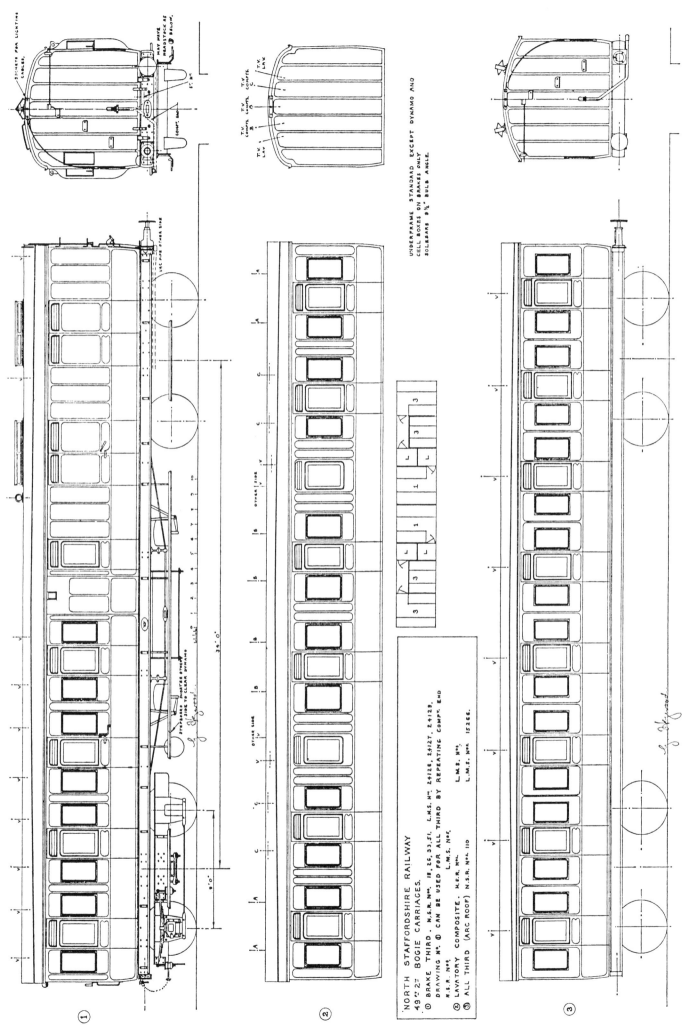

NORTH STAFFORDSHIRE RAILWAY
49' 2" BOGIE CARRIAGES.

① BRAKE THIRD. N.S.R. Nos. 18, 26, 33, 51. L.M.S. Nos. 24128, 24127, 24129.
DRAWING No. ① CAN BE USED FOR ALL THIRD BY REPEATING COMPT. END
N.S.R. Nos.   L.M.S. Nos.

② LAVATORY COMPOSITE. N.S.R. Nos.   L.M.S. Nos.

③ ALL THIRD (ARC ROOF) N.S.R. No. 110   L.M.S. No. 15266.

UNDERFRAME STANDARD EXCEPT DYNAMO AND
CELL BOXES ON BRAKES ONLY
SOLEBARS 9½" BULB ANGLE.

A fine official view of Furness Railway six-wheel brake third No.13 (LMS 15063/2792) whose bodywork and livery details conserve to give a definitive impression of the general styling of all the Furness stock featured in these pages

Maryport and Carlisle Stock

The late Ross Pochin's drawings illustrate two typical M&C types, though it has not been possible to obtain supporting photographs of either of them.

PROTOTYPE DETAILS

Five compartment Third Class: One of three built by Metropolitan C&W in 1897. Two scrapped before grouping but the survivor became LMS 19044, renumbered 26703 in 1933 and scrapped in 1934.

Eight compartment Bogie Third Class: One of three built in 1907-8 by Hurst Nelson (one) and R.Y.Pickering (two). They became LMS 19045-7 in 1923 (15338-40 in 1933) and although scrapping dates are not known, No.15340 is known to have lasted until 1938.

Furness Railway Stock

In the original version of this review the late Ross Pochin's drawings were used to illustrate two typical Furness types and some of these are repeated here together with further Furness carriage drawings by Mike Peascod, who is also responsible for drafting the additional notes now offered. On this page are featured typical Furness six-wheel types by Mike Peascod along with Ross Pochin's end view of the same type and his half elevation of an eight compartment cove roof bogie non-corridor third class. The end elevation of this carriage, together with Mike Peascod's drawing of the equivalent third brake will be found on the next page, along with the prototype details for these types.

The typical six-wheel carriages shown on this page were built during 1893-8 by Metropolitan C&W and Ashbury, at least 82 thirds and four (out of an original six) brake thirds reaching the LMS. The full thirds were the most numerous of all Furness carriage types and their scrapping was slow, M15311M - presumably renumbered (by BR?) for some reason - being recorded at Cleator Moor in 1955!

PROTOTYPE DETAILS

Quantity	Sample FR Numbers	1st LMS	2nd LMS	Extinct
FULL THIRD				
82	10; 17; 45; 49	15187-15274*	26653-26701	c.1955
BRAKE THIRD				
6	13-18	15063-15066	27792-27795	1938

* This series was exclusively this type, but totals 87 vehicles. The gaps (if any) cannot be identified and it is therefore just possible that 87 carriages were inherited by the LMS

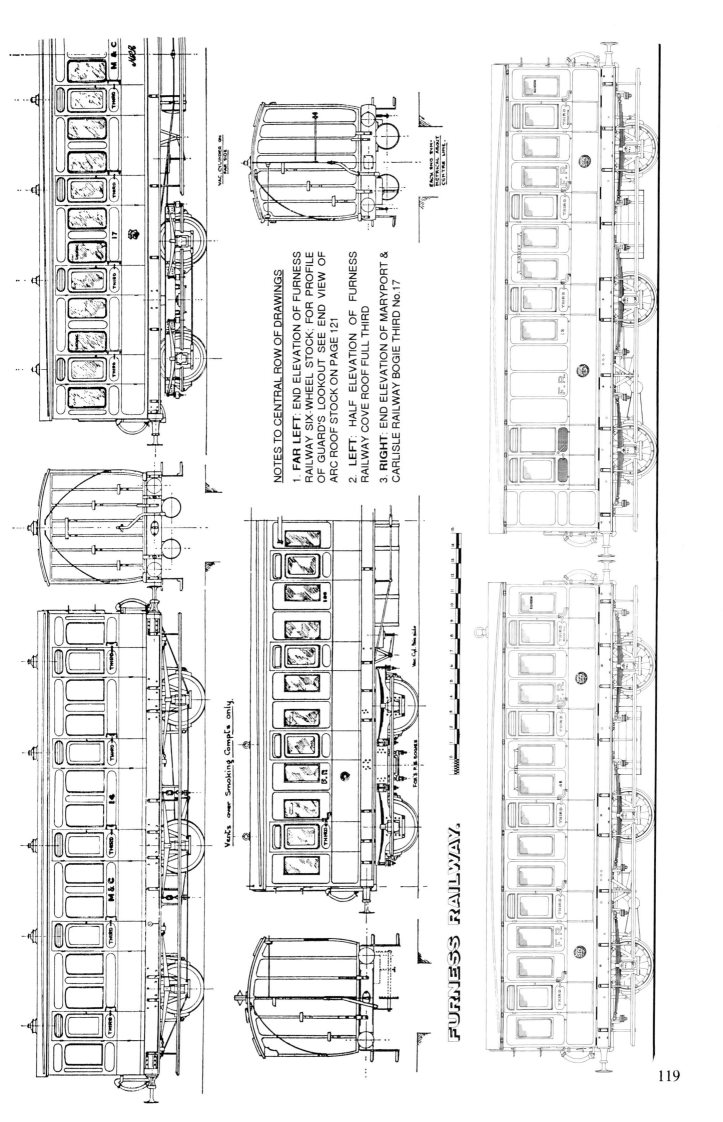

VAC. CYLINDER ON FAR SIDE

EACH END SYM-METRICAL ABOUT CENTRE LINE.

NOTES TO CENTRAL ROW OF DRAWINGS

1. **FAR LEFT**: END ELEVATION OF FURNESS RAILWAY SIX-WHEEL STOCK; FOR PROFILE OF GUARD'S LOOKOUT SEE END VIEW OF ARC ROOF STOCK ON PAGE 121

2. **LEFT**: HALF ELEVATION OF FURNESS RAILWAY COVE ROOF FULL THIRD

3. **RIGHT**: END ELEVATION OF MARYPORT & CARLISLE RAILWAY BOGIE THIRD No.17

Vents over Smoking Compts only.

FURNESS RAILWAY.

Furness Railway Bogie Stock

Mike Peascod's drawings on this page show the 49ft cove roof brake third which matches the full third on the previous page, together with two typical semi-corridor 47ft composite types from a decade earlier.

The cove roof stock was built during the 1906-15 period, the full thirds appearing during 1912-15, the brakes slightly earlier. They were long-lasting carriages, withdrawal not beginning until 1942, and many lasted into the BR period - see appended picture. The end elevation (by Ross Pochin) shows the non-brake version, but the brake end can be derived by combining the cove roof profile with lookout dimensions and step arrangements given for the 47ft arc roof semi-corridor stock.

The latter (six of each type) were built by Metropolitan C&W in 1897 for through trains onto the Midland Railway for the Leeds and Bradford services to Barrow Docks and the Isle of Man boats. They were the first bogie carriages used by the FR and also the first to have lavatories, access to which (unlike that of much contemporary stock from other companies) was available from all compartments. The FR diagram book at the grouping shows the internal layout as a mirror image of the works drawings from which these versions have been prepared, suggesting that some may have been built to each layout; the external elevations were not affected.

Furness Railway cove roof 49ft full third No.M15311 (ex-1st LMS 15132 and, probably, FR No.101) of the 1912 batch at Moor Row, September 1954, some eight months before its withdrawal. (Mike Peascod Collection)

PROTOTYPE DETAILS

Quantity	Sample FR Numbers	1st LMS	2nd LMS	Extinct
49ft COVE ROOF FULL THIRD, BUILT 1912-15				
17	98-109	15106/130-45	15309-15325	1956
49ft COVE ROOF BRAKE THIRD, BUILT 1906-7				
4	6-9	15055-15058	24146-24149	1946
47ft SEMI-CORRIDOR BRAKE COMPOSITE, BUILT 1897				
6	69-74	15030-15035	19930-19935	1937
47ft SEMI-CORRIDOR LUGGAGE COMPOSITE, BUILT 1897				
6	75-80	15009-13/54	25946-25951	1939

A detailed close-up of the luggage doors and first class compartments of an unidentified Furness Railway 47ft semi-corridor luggage composite. Though obviously posing for the camera, the young men featured are not unlikely to have been travelling in this degree of comfort, their clothes suggesting either the uniform of some form of rather expensive Public School or other similar well-to-do origins.... (Mike Peascod Collection)

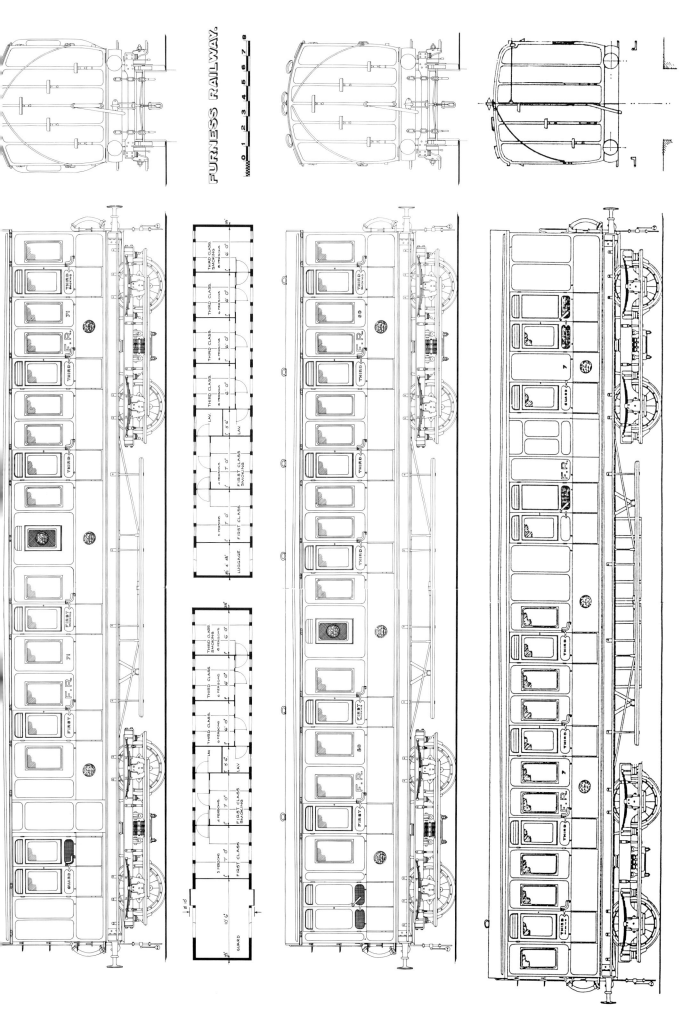

FURNESS RAILWAY.

0 1 2 3 4 5 6 7 8

Caledonian Railway 'Grampian' Corridor Stock

The celebrated 'Grampian' stock was introduced in 1903 mainly for the Aberdeen services from Glasgow and Edinburgh and fully reflected the then current trend towards maximum permissible height and length. Seven types were built and the two appended drawings by the late Iain R.Smith (made from field measurements of actual vehicles) are typical.

The stock was built in modest quantities until 1909, internal appointments were of a high order and the thirds had armrests. Apart from the Aberdeen line, they saw limited employment on Clyde Coast expresses and were not unknown on Anglo-Scottish duty - eg Glasgow to the West of England where the featured brake composites would no doubt come into their own. No doubt because of the high quality of their internal appointments, they lasted for a long time.

PROTOTYPE DETAILS

Quantity	CR Numbers*	1st LMS*	2nd LMS	Extinct
CORRIDOR BRAKE THIRD BUILT 1906-1909				
14	1329-31; 1345-8	17385-7/401-4	6579-6592	1955
CORRIDOR BRAKE COMPOSITE, BUILT 1905-1908				
14 #	57; 76; 132/8; 293; 369/70	15736/8; 15955/6	7377-7390	1955

* Sample numbers only for CR and 1st LMS series
\# Some sources give eleven only built to this type but the second LMS numbers and the appended picture clearly indicate this quantity (at least)

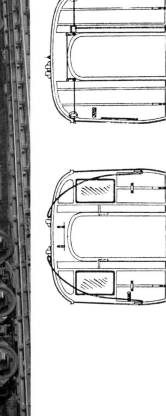

Like their near contemporary '2pm' West Coast 12-wheelers (see page 90), the 'Grampians' also lasted for the best part of 45-50 years as witnessed by the two examples shown here which feature both types covered by the drawings, one each from the compartment and corridor side. The compartment side view shows brake composite No.SC7390M in BR red and cream livery c.1953, still bearing most of its original panelling save for a little matchboard replacement at the far end. The corridor side view shows a third brake (believed to be either 6590/2) in plain dark red livery (LMS?) in 1949. Although notionally built to the limit of the structure gauge, these carriages actually displayed a slightly flattened roof centre compared with the full elliptical profile of the carriages on the next two pages, which difference can just be appreciated in these views (Author's Collection - 2)

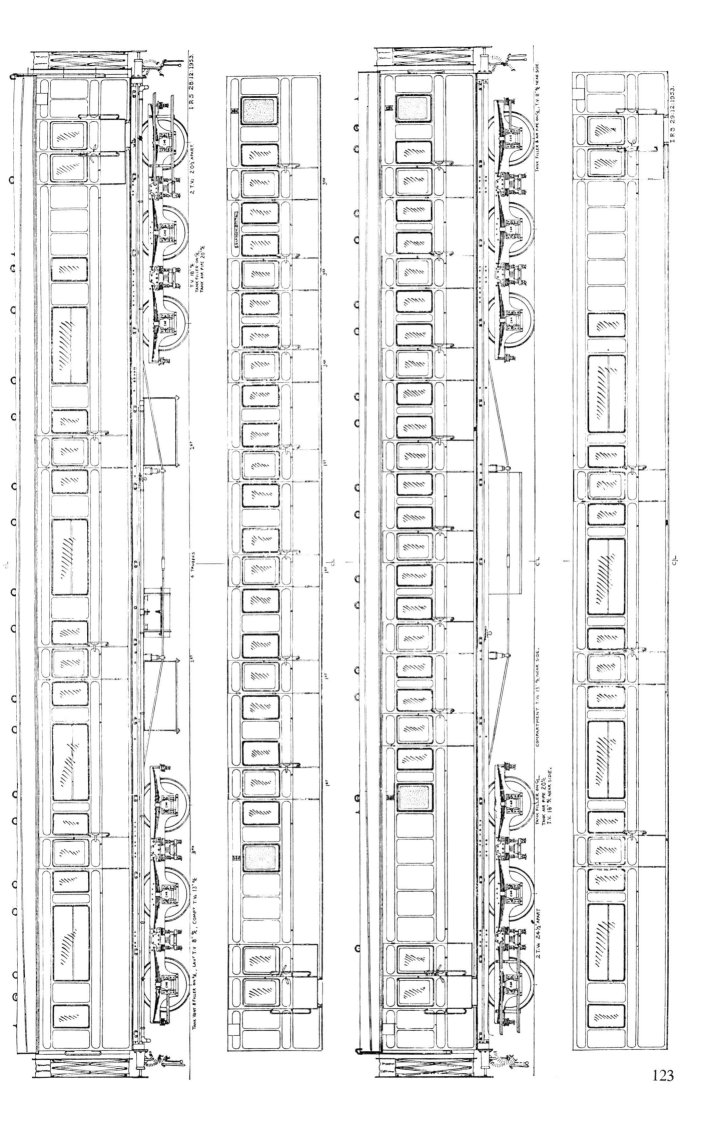

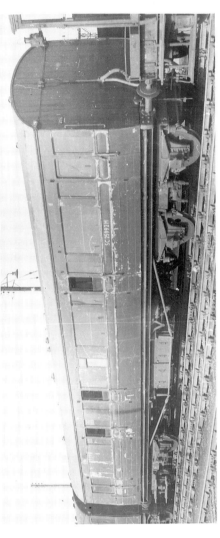

An official view of CR No.468 (LMS 16054/25995), the first of the semi-corridor lavatory brake composites to be given the angle-trussed type of underframe. Note also the faithfully rendered panelling effect - mostly in paint (see text)

The earlier round bar and queenpost underframe is seen on an opposite side view of brake composite No.SC25992M at Keith, late in its life on 15th September 1956. The plain red livery serves to reveal the actual simplicity of the panelling itself compared with the earlier liveries adopted by the CR and LMS (The late A.G.Ellis, courtesy Jim Smellie)

PROTOTYPE DETAILS

Quantity	CR Numbers*	1st LMS Numbers*	2nd LMS	Extinct
SEMI-CORRIDOR LAVATORY BRAKE COMPOSITE, BUILT 1920/1922				
7#	61; 131; 159; 445-6	15721/49/76/8	25988-25994	1957
5	468-472	16054-16058	25995-25999	1957
NON-CORRIDOR COMPOSITE, BUILT 1922-3				
13	452-9; 473-7	16038-45/59-63	17822-17834	1957
NON-CORRIDOR BRAKE THIRD, BUILT 1920-2				
18	1287; 1420/9/38-43	17343;19089-98/106-11	24263-74/80-5	1958

* Sample numbers only in some cases for CR and 1st LMS series
\# Round bar and queenpost underframes, remainder (all types) angle-trussed

Caledonian Railway 57ft Non-Corridor Stock

The Caledonian adopted 57ft as a standard length in 1912, the carriages depicted on this page (all drawn by the late Iain R.Smith) representing the final types being built by the company, some appearing in 1923. A variety of detail changes had been seen between 1912 and 1922 but by the time of the carriages shown here, design had settled down to the use of 8ft bogies with simplified 'above waist' panelling (half-round beading being considered adequate), with 'proper' panelling only along the waist level. The absent 'panelling' was faithfully reproduced in paint, both in CR days and for the first ten years of the LMS.

Two varieties of underframe are shown, the semi-corridor lavatory brake composite (upper elevations) shows the earlier 'round bar and queenpost' type, while the non-lavatory composites (3F+5T) and brake thirds (lower elevations) had the final angle trussed type. The numbers quoted are with underframes as drawn, save for some brake composites built in 1922, which also had angle-trussed frames: 2nd LMS 25995-9 - see table. It should be noted that the vertical tongue/groove boarding on the compartment side of the brake composite is a latter day repair and is typical of the meticulous attention to detail shown by the original draughtsman who always used field measurements of actual surviving carriages; the vehicle is otherwise shown in 'as built' condition.

The semi-corridor stock was built for long distance stopping trains and (especially the brake composites) for through workings. The non-lavatory stock was widely used for local services, particularly around Glasgow, often formed into three coach sets BT+C+BT. Matching nine compartment thirds and eight compartment firsts were also built, which could readily be derived from these drawings, and they all ended their lives on the Glasgow Central Low Level line.

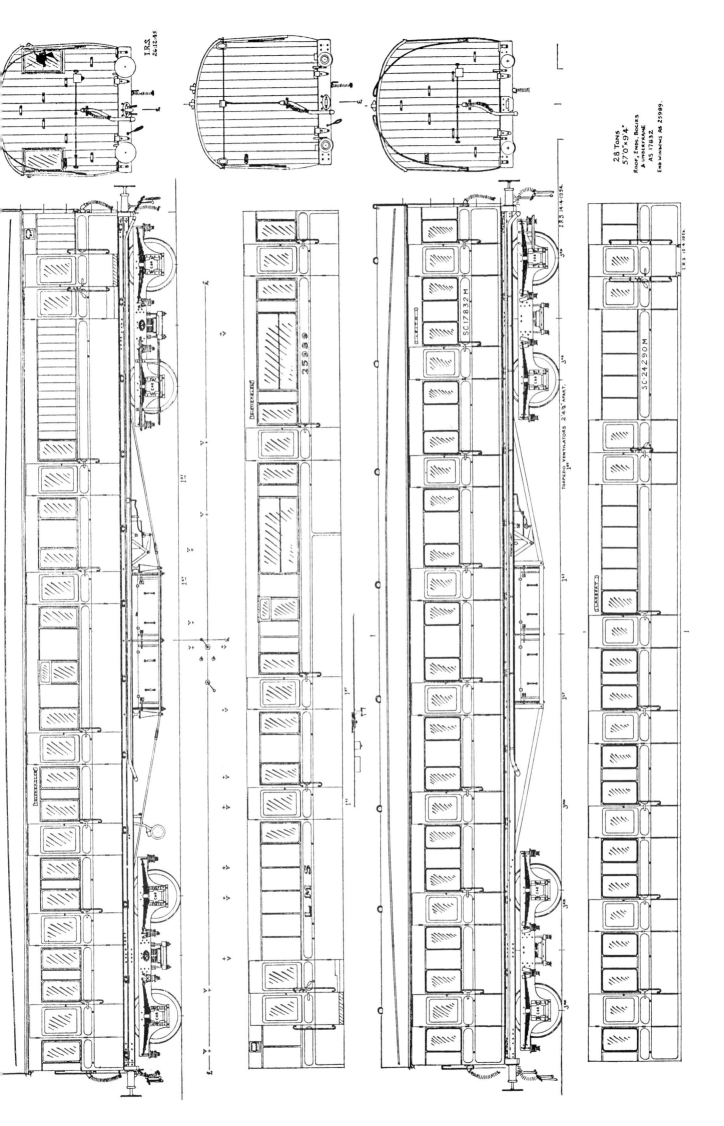

I.R.S.
24-12-45

I.R.S. 14-4-1954.

I.R.S. 15-4-1954.

28 TONS
57'0"x9'4"
ROOF, ENDS, BOGIES,
& UNDERFRAME
AS 17832
END WINDOWS AS 25989.

25989

L M S

SC 17832 M

SC 24290 M

TORPEDO VENTILATORS 2'4½" APART.

Caledonian Railway Corridor Stock

The first drawing, courtesy Jim Smellie, shows a neat 50ft full brake, six being built in 1914 at St Rollox. In appearance, they matched the contemporary corridor stock and ran on the (unique to the Caledonian) 10ft Fox pattern bogies which came between two periods of using 8ft Fox types. Dual fitted when new (to allow through running), they had the Westinghouse brake removed by the LMS in the 1930s.

Iain Smith's drawing of the 57ft corridor composite represents the final Caledonian development of the 57ft corridor type which had first appeared in 1912 with full panelling, 8ft 8in wide body and a different bogie design. Like those described on the previous page, their building straddled the grouping and, again like the contemporary non-corridor types, the adoption of both a 57ft length and angle-trussed underframe, together with matchboard ends and high roof, produced carriages very similar in character to those built to LMS standard design from 1923, though it is perhaps worth mentioning that the 4F+3T layout of the CR corridor composites was eventually 'reversed' by the LMS. *En passant*, it is probably also worth re-iterating that the LNWR, LYR, Midland and G&SWR had all come to much the same conclusion in terms of overall structural envelope and carriage length.

As with the contemporary non-corridor designs, the livery of these vehicles faithfully reproduced 'panelling' on the plain surfaces above the waist until the adoption of the LMS simple livery in 1934. They lasted until the mid-1950s, by which time their bodywork had often been sadly marred by makeshift repairs.

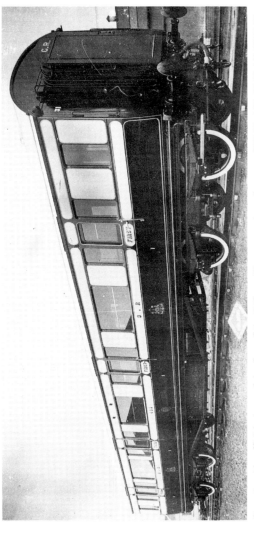

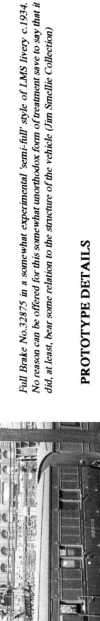

Opposite side official views of the first of the 57ft corridor composites when new (CR No.460, LMS 16046/4962). Again, see previous page, note the elaborate painted panelling above the waist. The upper view also shows the final full height semi-elliptical roof - c.f the Grampian Stock, page 122

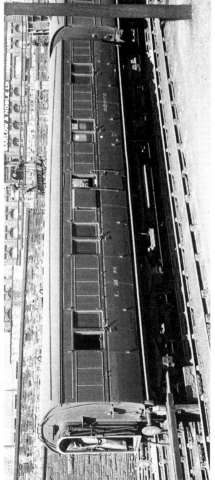

Full Brake No.32875 in a somewhat experimental 'semi-full' style of LMS livery c.1934. No reason can be offered for this somewhat unorthodox form of treatment save to say that it did, at least, bear some relation to the structure of the vehicle (Jim Smellie Collection)

PROTOTYPE DETAILS

Quantity	CR Numbers	1st LMS Numbers	2nd LMS	Extinct
50ft CORRIDOR FULL BRAKE, BUILT 1914				
6	4;44;84;104;195;142	6304/33/67/80/452/91	32870-32875	1958 *
57ft CORRIDOR COMPOSITE, BUILT 1923				
4	460-463	16046-16049	4962-4965	1956

* CR No.44 (LMS 6333-32871) was put into departmental stock as DM395039 in 1952 and not finally withdrawn until 1959

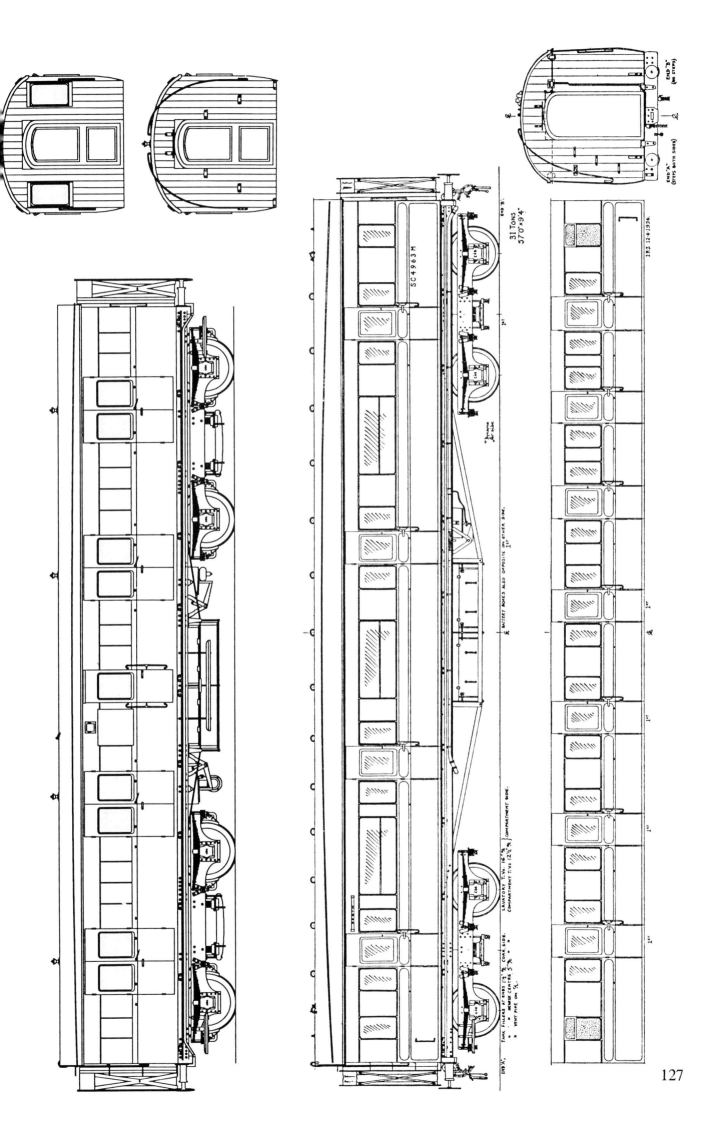

SC4963M

31 TONS
57'0"×9'4"

END "B".

END "B"
(NO STEPS)

END "A"
(STEPS BOTH SIDES)

TANK FILLERS AT ENDS 1¼"⌀ CORR. SIDE.
" " " " " MEMBR CENTRE 5"⌀ " " "
" " " " VENT PIPE ON 9L.
LAVATORY T.Vs 16"⌀
COMPARTMENT T.Vs 12½"⌀ COMPARTMENT SIDE.
BATTERY BOXES ALSO OPPOSITE ON OTHER SIDE.

I.R.J. 12·4·1934.

G&SWR 43ft General Service Non-Corridor Stock

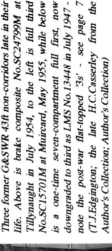

Three former G&SWR 43ft non-corridors late in their life. Above is brake composite No.SC24799M at Tillynaught in July 1954, to the left is full third No.SC15701M at Muircard, May 1955, while below is a one-time seven-compartment full first, now downgraded to third as LMS No.13448 in July 1947 - note the post-war flat-topped 3s' - see page 7 (T.J.Edgington; the late H.C.Casserley from the Author's Collection; Author's Collection)

These characteristically neat and well finished G&SWR carriages were built over a period of about 20 years from the early 1890s onwards and because of the extra space available compared with the 1968 edition, it is possible to augment Iain Smith's typically thorough field surveys of two varieties (brake third and brake composite) with the full third and full first equivalents from the drawing board of Alistair Wright, to whom additional thanks are also due for supplementary information.

The panel style depicted was more or less the G&SWR standard from 1893 until grouping and somewhat reminiscent of early Clayton Midland stock - page 94. The slightly changed arrangement of door and panel detail on the opposite side of the brake third should be noted (top elevation) and it should be mentioned that the brake composite (second elevation from the top) was a relatively late addition to the series (1911), intended to replace older six-wheel types on services requiring only limited seating capacity.

Originally gas-lit, most of these carriages were later converted to electric lighting (exact dates not known). After grouping they migrated somewhat from the G&SWR area, in particular to the Glasgow Low Level lines and for football specials. First class compartments were eventually downgraded to third during LMS days (when scrapping also began) but quite a few survived into BR times.

PROTOTYPE DETAILS

Quantity	G&SWR Numbers#	1st LMS#	2nd LMS#	Extinct
BRAKE THIRD				
*19	355-60; 556-68	18430-18447	24352-24362	c.1955-6
BRAKE COMPOSITE, BUILT 1911				
5	69-73	18565-18569	24795-24799	c.1955-6
THIRD CLASS				
c.127	318-24; 450-89; 569-632	17876-80;18175-84	15701-15716	c.1955-6
FIRST CLASS				
c.100	20-30; 41-9; 80-9; 92-160	see note §	13441-13559 §	c.1955-6

Sample numbers only in most cases

* Quantities built apply to the G&SWR number series quoted; there may well have been additional examples not listed here

§ Second LMS numbers are as downgraded to third. In 1933, all residual G&SW full first (of all types) were allocated 10651-99, their 1923 LMS numbers having been mostly if not entirely in the 17452-607 series. Unfortunately, it has not been possible to identify the type depicted from the full 1923/33 number series

128

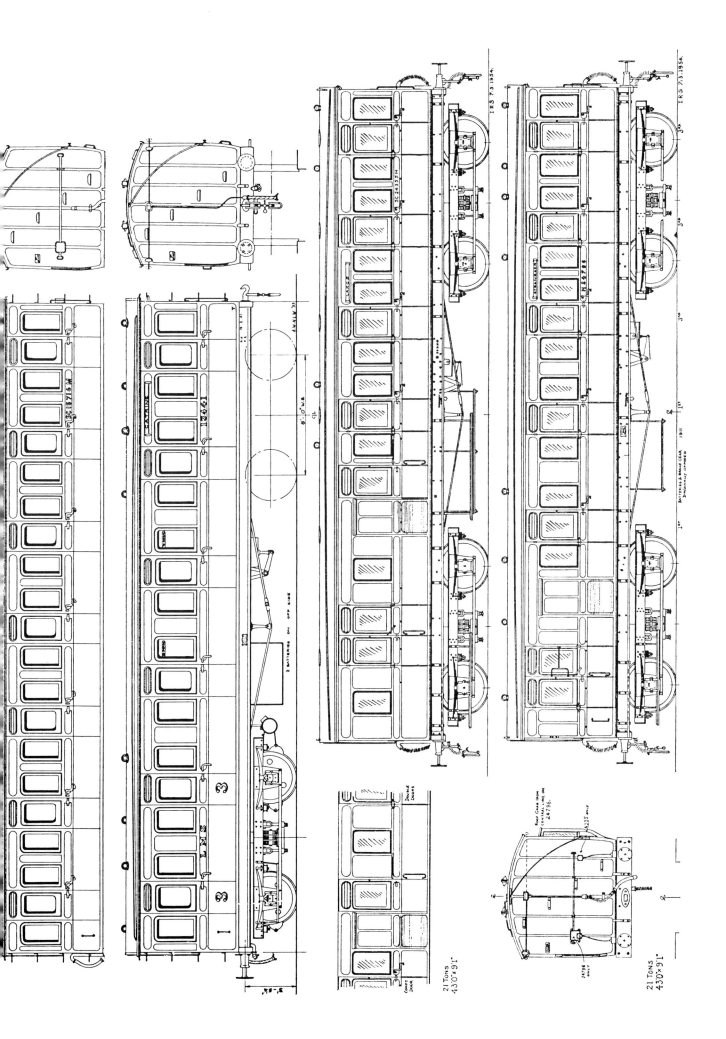

G&SWR Gangwayed Stock

Because of its regionally compact nature, the G&SWR did not have much need for gangwayed stock, the bulk of its long distance services being cross-border in nature (in conjunction with the Midland) and therefore catered for by Joint Stock carriages such as those offered on pages 100-103. However, when corridor stock was needed for its own use, the railway could offer carriages comparable with the best in the land, these two typical examples from the pen of the late Iain R.Smith serving as excellent evidence.

The first drawing shows a 57ft corridor composite from the Peter Drummond period, dating from 1921, typifying final G&SWR practice and displaying the minor detail changes introduced during his time. Apart from the larger overall size - much the same as most other railways had moved to at the time - most noticeable were the change in commode handles and the rounded corners to all panelling. There were matching thirds and brake thirds and the carriages mostly found use on the non-Joint Stock Glasgow-Carlisle operations, becoming rather more scattered after the grouping and lasting until the mid-1950s.

The second drawing depicts the only Scottish-built dining car to feature in this book. This very elegant vehicle emerged in 1921 during the brief term of office of R.H.Whitelegg and shows evidence of this in the reversion to square cornered lower panel corners above the waist. It had stained glass toplights flanking the glass vane ventilators above the main windows and the doors were slightly recessed. Unfortunately the riding of its original 10ft 6in four-wheel bogies was not good and in 1926, the LMS fitted the Caledonian six-wheel type shown here.

One of but three G&SWR dining carriages, the other two being of ex-M&GSW and Drummond G&SWR origin respectively (there being little call on G&SW metals for dining services other than through workings south of the border), this fine car served out its time on the the Highland section, being withdrawn in the mid-1950s.

It has not been possible to illustrate the featured G&SWR composite, but this unidentified brake composite from the same series in BR red and cream livery gives ample supporting details of the general style (Author's Collection)

This view of former G&SWR Restaurant Car No.SC299M in BR red and cream livery c.1955 clearly shows the Pullman-like styling of this handsome vehicle. In spite of its generally sound looking condition, the carriage is thought to have been waiting to be broken up at the time the picture was taken (Author's Collection)

PROTOTYPE DETAILS

CORRIDOR COMPOSITE, BUILT 1921
Six built: G&SWR 1,2,107-9,118; 1st LMS 18491/2/537-9/45, 2nd LMS 4978-83

COMPOSITE DINING CAR, BUILT 1921
G&SWR No.3, 1st LMS No.15888, 2nd LMS No.299

BASIC G&SWR CARRIAGE LIVERY IN 1922

The final carriage livery adopted by the Glasgow and South Western Railway was identical to that of the Midland Railway in all basic essentials. There is, however, reasonable evidence to suppose that latterly, at least, some G&SWR carriages were emerging from shops with pinkish buff shade of roof paint

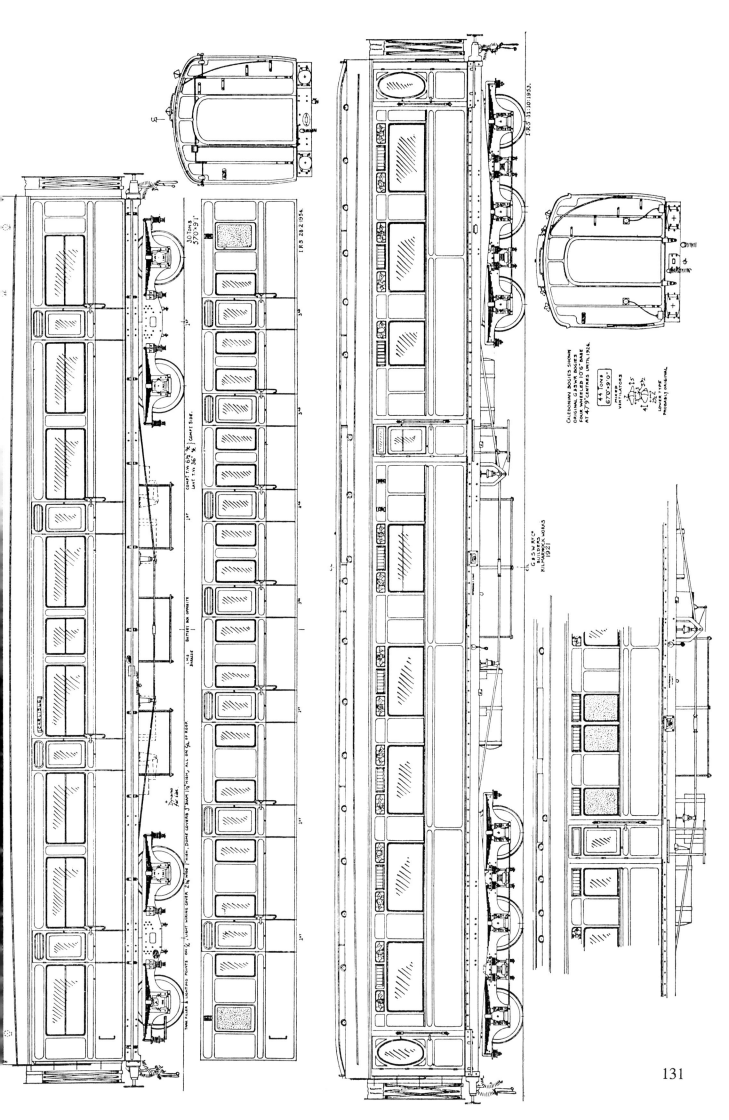

CALEDONIAN BOGIES SHOWN
ORIGINAL G&SWR BOGIES
FOUR WHEELED 10'6" BASE
AT 47'9" CENTRES UNTIL 1926.

44 TONS
67'0"·9'0"

FIXED
VENTILATORS

LOWER TYPE
PROBABLY ORIGINAL

I.R.S. 11:10:1953.

G&SWR C°
BUILDERS
KILMARNOCK WORKS
1921

30 TONS
57'0"·9'1"

COMPT T.W. 6½ %
LAVT T.W. 36 %

COMPT SIDE.

1ST

I.R.S. 28·2·1954.

131

Colour Panels

The appended panels (not to scale but see dimensional details on pp 6/7) show mounted LMS transfers from the author's collection, the colours being only as accurate as photography permits; in particular, the difference between the gold and 'straw' emblems may not be as apparent as in reality. The gold emblem has gilt/vermilion lining with rounded corners and the straw version has a rectangular straw surround. The pseudo door panel shows the chrome yellow shaded transfers of the 1934-40 period along with the yellow/vermilion lining used for non-corridor stock until c.1934. (Photography: B.C.Lane)

Bibliography

(An Illustrated History of) LMS Standard Coaching Stock Vols I/II (Jenkinson/Essery): OPC 1991/1994 *
(A Register of) West Coast Joint Stock (Casserley & Millard): HMRS 1980
LNWR Carriages - A Concise History, including West Coast Joint Stock (Jenkinson): Pendragon 1995
Midland Carriages - An Illustrated Review (Jenkinson/Essery): OPC 1984
Midland Railway Carriages Vols I/II (Lacy & Dow): Wild Swan 1984/1986
Carriages & Wagons of the Highland Railway (Hunter): Turntable Enterprises 1971
Highland Railway Liveries (Geddes & Bellass): Pendragon/HMRS 1995
Preserved Railway Carriages (Lloyd & Brown): Silver Link 1992
(The History of) British Railway Carriages 1900-1953 (Jenkinson): Pendragon 1996

* Vol.3 expected in the year 2000